AN ARTIST'S LIFE

AN ARTIST'S LIFE

50 Years of Self-Portraits

CARLTON DAVIS

with co-author PETER LOWNDS

An Artist's Life

Copyright © 2024, Carlton Davis

Published in the United States by Art Dock
Los Angeles, California

First Edition

ISBNs: Paperback: 979-8-9911748-0-0
Ebook: 979-8-9911748-1-7
Hardcover: 979-8-9911748-2-4

Printed in the United States of America.

Cover and book design: Patricia Bacall Garver

CONTENTS

- **Co-author**

  Peter Lownds

- **Book Design**

  Patricia Bacall Garver, BacallCreative.com

- **Manuscript Editors**

  Gillian MacDonald

  Virginia Tanzmann

- **Photographer**

  Ed Glendinning

  Digital Capture LA

- **Special Thanks**

  Diana Edkins, Art Resource (AR), NY

  Daniel Trujillo, Artist's Rights Society (ARS), NY

  The Andy Warhol Foundation, NY

  Arp Museum, Remagen, Germany

  Birmingham Museum of Art, Birmingham, Alabama

  Frank Gehry

  Getty Research Institute

  The Phillips Collection, Washington, D.C.

  Pollock Krasner Foundation

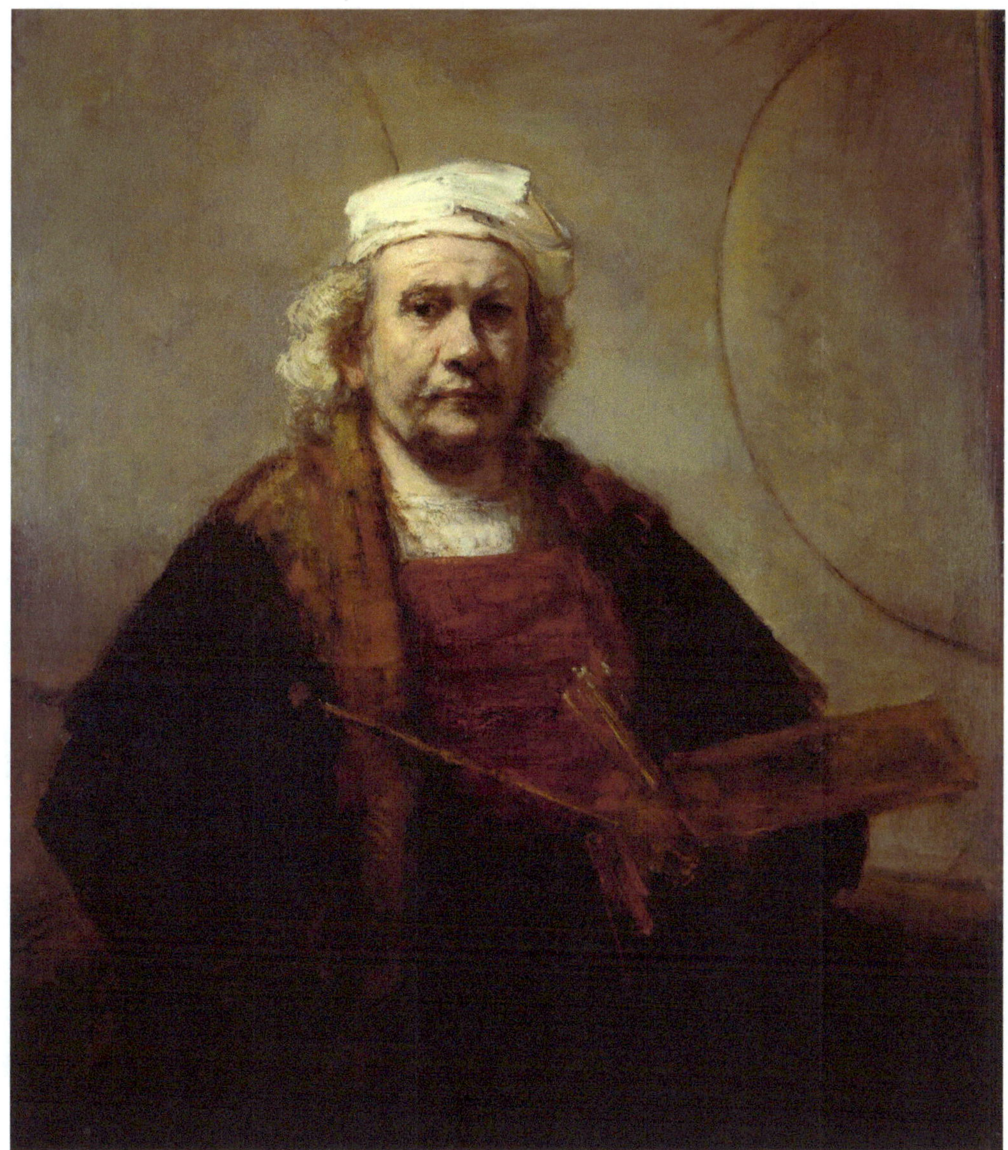

Self-Portrait with Two Circles, 1665-1669, Rembrandt van Rijn, oil on canvas,
45" × 37" (114 cm × 94 cm), Kenwood House, London

1970
CONTEMPLATING REMBRANDT

ondon, 1970. Screaming "Smash capitalism!" and "Ho! Ho! Ho Chi Min!", I rushed toward the American Embassy on Grosvenor Square as one of a youngish mob of malcontents. A protective phalanx of mounted police readied their steeds to confront our onslaught. When they charged forward, brandishing bully clubs and knockin' noggins, we streamed across the square, dispersing into a maze of side streets and taking refuge in London Underground stations. I retreated to Kenwood House on Hampstead Heath to commune with my master, Rembrandt van Rijn, whose *Self-Portrait with Two Circles* awaited me.

My long-suffering sixty-year-old mentor observed me with weary self-assurance. He flaunted his pockmarked skin, jowls, wrinkles, unpretentious black cape with scruffy fur collar, red vest, mottled

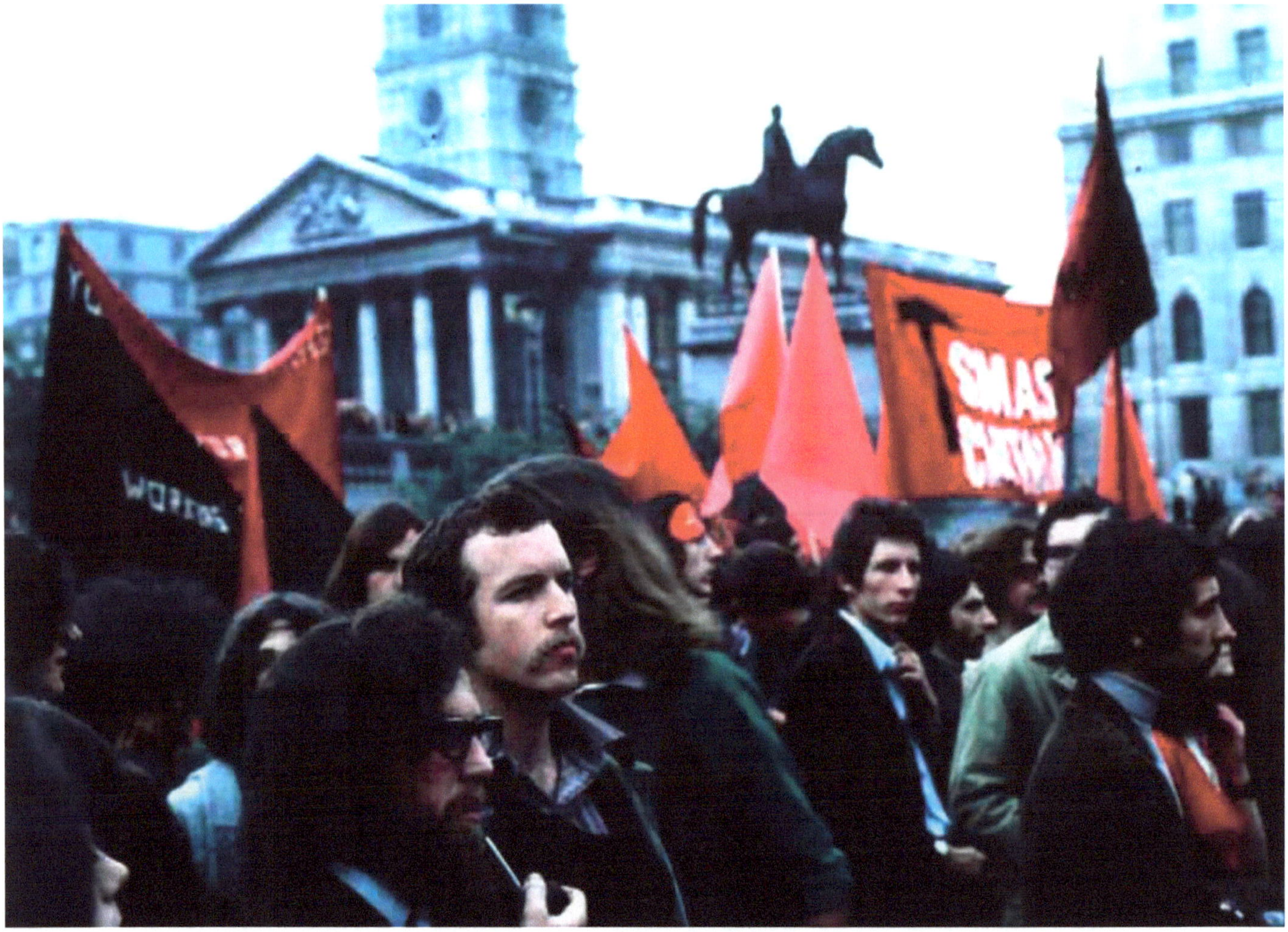

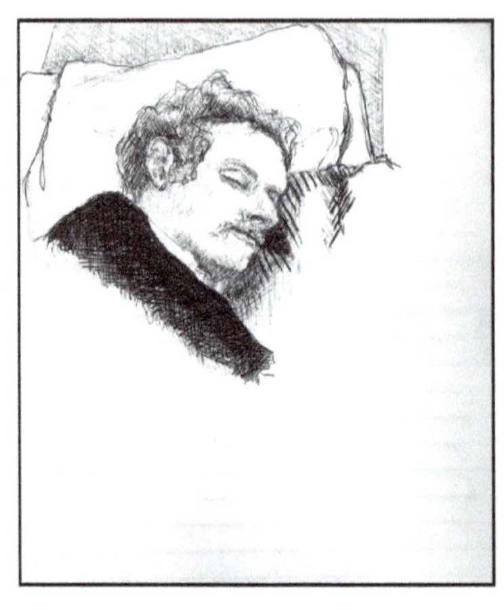

Students at the anti-Vietnam war protest, Grosvenor Square, London, UK, 1970

white shirt, and cap atop unshorn hair. In his left hand were a maulstick, brushes, and a palette. The tannish-bluish background was effused with velvety light that flowed across the surface of his head from the upper left, illuminating a little more than half his face. The somber tones and shadows focused my gaze on a bright spot at the tip of his bulbous beacon of a nose. The portrait's tranquility balanced and belied its subject's grief. A private niche in mid-17th century Holland opened before me and invited me in. Absorbing his masterful calm consoled me. "This is the way the world works; get used to it," he murmured, and I listened.

My girlfriend at the time was an art student. I brought her to Kenwood House and Rembrandt, and then she created a portrait of me that furthered my desire to be an artist.

I stared at Rembrandt's 1660s self-portrait often over the years. Every time I traveled to London, I'd visit Kenwood House. In 1970, about to leave England for the US, I noted what my contemplation had revealed, "When you get very close, it dissolves into a set of deliberate brush strokes and subtle color

Carlton Davis by Reiko Sunami, 1970, ink on page of composition book, 4½" × 5½" (11.4 cm × 12.7 cm)

relationships. The paint, applied in impasto, smears, scumbles, smudges, and with the lines drawn with brushes and brush stick ends, creates an impression of extraordinary realism. Rembrandt is there, an enduring presence, his creative method forever a fresh exploration in which the maker is aware of who he is and how he makes art." The master demanded I find a way to become an artist, too.

Self-portraits are a means of understanding the nature of the changing self and its connection to all human experience and the world it inhabits. I studied celebrated examples of the *genre* to deepen my understanding of the nature of self-portraiture. Focusing on Rembrandt, growing familiar with his *oeuvre* and trying to contextualize it, I examined self-portraits made when the cocksure young man first traveled to Amsterdam, in midlife when he costumed himself in the exotic robes of Turkish and French nobility and became the darling of the Dutch *nouveau riche*, and in his declining years when he fell out of favor amid scandal and excess. Rembrandt rendered

his likeness for 39 years. His look transformed over time. His nose changed, his face widened, and his eyes separated a little more. This is also true of the self-portraits I have been making with increasing ease and joy for almost half a century. The recorded image sometimes varies from what I really looked like, but they all bear an uncanny resemblance to what and how I was feeling amid my life's ever-mutable circumstances.

I got off to a late start, but I have lived longer than my favorite Hollander. When I began, I had no idea what I was doing. My first self-portrait came about because I was compelled to draw something other than a design or an interpretation of some place I had visited. Rembrandt's self-portrait came to mind, and the subject matter was close at hand. Making an image of myself became a habit undertaken in successive years, abandoned for a time, and then begun again. The more I drew them, the more I became interested in what other artists had done; and the more I saw, the more I tried to discover

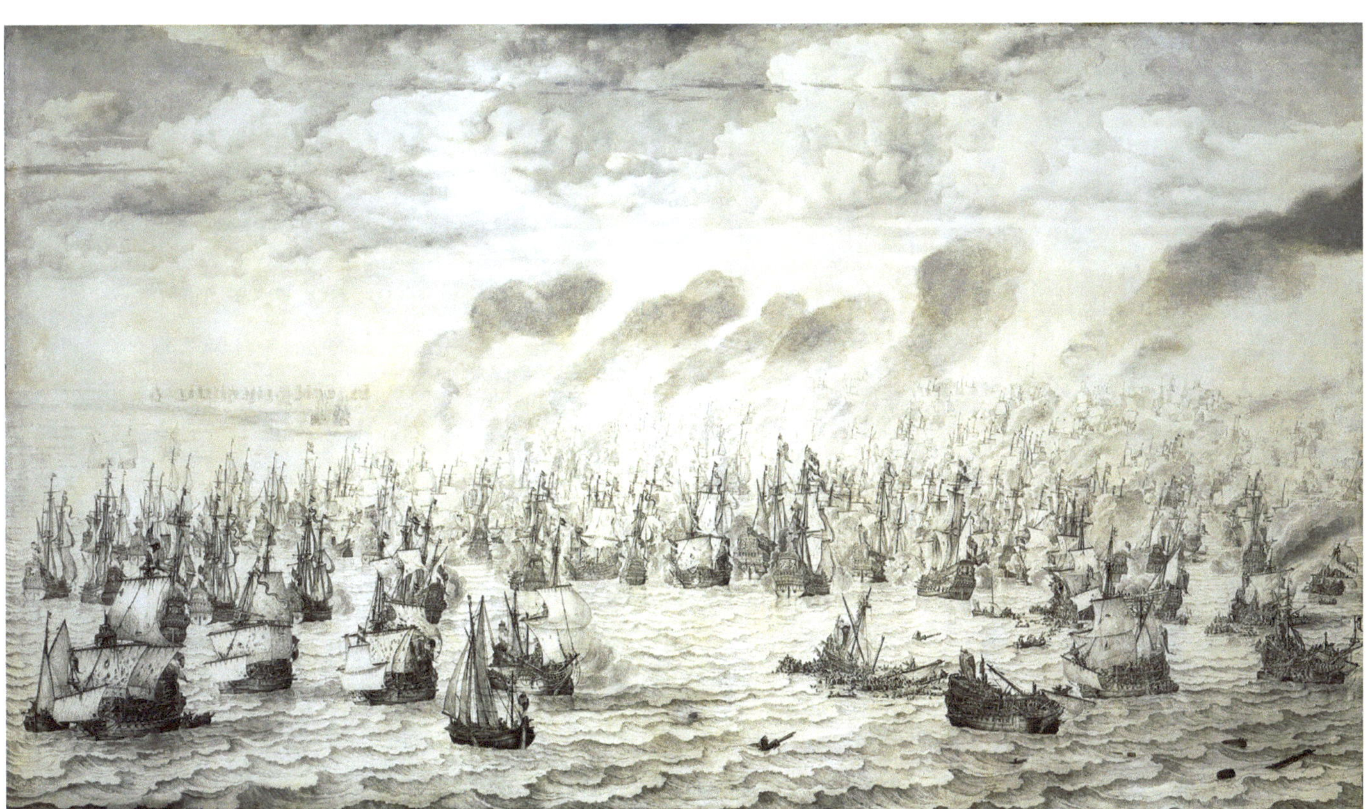

The Battle of Scheveningen, August 10, 1653, Willem van de Velde the Elder, 1657, ink and oil on canvas, 66.9" × 113.7" (170 cm × 289 cm), Rijksmuseum, Amsterdam

what I could do with different means. No matter what I drew with – pencils, watercolors, pastels, or oil sticks – I recognized that my self-portraits bore emotional baggage that, for lovers of and thinkers about modern art, might make self-portraiture seem passé. I decided not to let that deter me.

Nine years after making his 1660s self-portrait, Rembrandt died a pauper. He often returned to his unpretentious roots as a tradesman from Leiden where his father had been a miller and his brother a shoemaker. The once-renowned artist was humbled but unbowed. His reputation with his clients and contemporaries had been tarnished because he took his housekeeper as a lover after the untimely death of his beloved wife, Saskia. Rembrandt created his 1665-1669 self-portrait while he managed his increasing isolation and commercial rejection. It is a powerful portrayal of a declining man in a declining society.

When Rembrandt started the painting in 1665, he had a view of the Amsterdam docks from the studio on the top floor of his residence. The Netherlands and its greatest artist were in turmoil. I imagine the elderly Rembrandt, consumed with worry about his declining circumstances, peering out of the window at the Dutch navy's war-torn ships returning from maritime skirmishes with the British. The Battle of Scheveningen in the first Anglo-Dutch war was the beginning of the decline of the Netherlands' world power. In 1665, New Amsterdam fell to the victorious Britons and became New York City. Rembrandt might have considered the remnants of the fleet a visual metaphor for his mounting problems. Four years later, when Rembrandt finished his final self-portrait in 1669, he went bankrupt. He lost his home and his studio, and his possessions were sold to his debtors. Despite his artistic legacy and late 17th-century Holland both waning at the time, for me, Rembrandt's self-portraits of his aging body represent the greatest artist I have ever known.

In the mid-17th century, the Netherlands was described as "a counting house with a navy." The United States I have inhabited for over three-quarters of a century has an analogous culture. It is still the mecca of capitalism, and in many respects, we are the 21st-century heirs to the Dutch of Rembrandt's time. Powerful but flawed, we face inevitable decline.

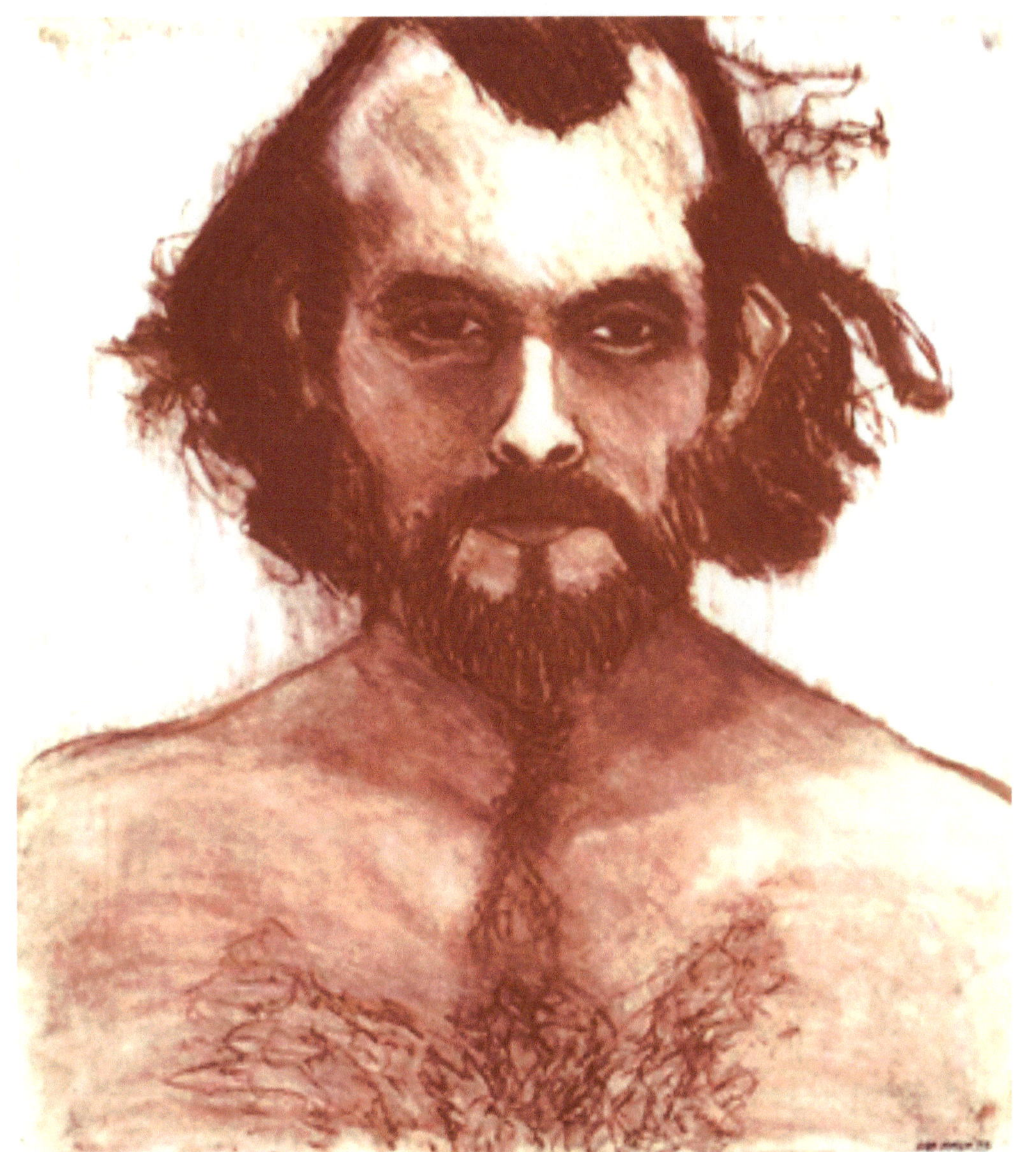

Self–portrait #1, 1973, Carlton Davis, red conté crayon on paper, 15.75" × 13" (40 cm × 33 cm)

CHAPTER 1

1973
MELTING THE ICE

n 1973, Picasso died at his villa in the sun-soaked south of France. Also in 1973, in wind-whipped Illinois near Lake Michigan from the enclosed, weather-proofed patio of an Italian restaurant on Broadway, my friends and I watched as a battalion of fire trucks roared up the street. "I hope it's not my place that's on fire," I remarked. "Probably not, Carlos," my friend replied, referring to the militant Venezuelan terrorist Carlos the Jackal who was on Interpol's most wanted list. My friends called me Carlos because of my radical and artistic pretensions. "You terrorist jackals aren't burning this far north yet!" he continued. We returned to our pasta. I spent that night at my girl-friend's place. The next morning, I discovered my pad had been torched, my possessions were a total loss, and most of my books were beyond repair.

I encountered thin sheets of ice coating the apartment block's facade below the fourth-story's shattered windows. The security guard helped me rip off the warped plywood barring the entryway, and we entered the lobby sloppy with half-frozen water mixing with the debris and broken glass. "What happened?" I asked. "Friday night. The cops say a hoodlum gang firebombed the back stairs." The guard leaned forward, almost whispering, and added, "If you ask me, it was the owner. Arson. The landlords are burning up the old apartment buildings all around here close to the lakeshore to build big towers." Nodding, I muttered, "Fires define Chicago, and the crooks are everywhere in our land. Didn't our president, Tricky Dick, declare, while dramatically waving an arm over his head, 'I am not a crook?' He lied."

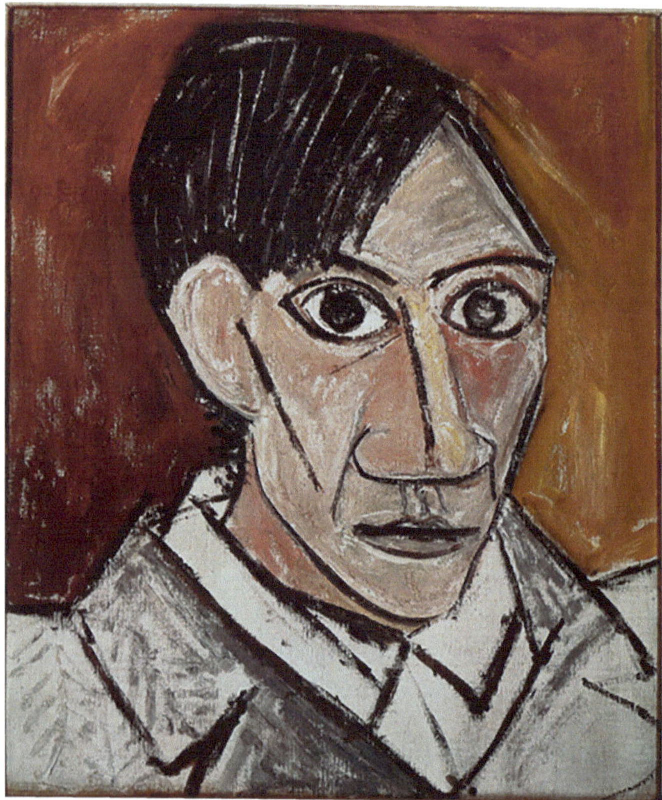

Pablo Picasso self-portrait, 1907, oil on canvas, (50 cm x 46 cm). National Gallery, Prague, Czech Republic

With slush seeping into my shoes, I climbed the stairs and passed through my fire-axed door into apartment 404. Soggy and ice-encrusted books lay scattered over the living room floor. A book of Picasso's art was flipped open to a crinkled page showing his 1907 self-portrait. This book was the only one that wasn't destroyed. The other art books had pages wrinkled into wavy corrugated slabs that spoke volumes to my current dilemma. I was incensed that my precious collection of monographs on famous artists, my tenuous connection to the domain of visual art, was damaged beyond salvage. Frozen, waterlogged pages of type could be peeled one from the other, but most wet pages of art reproductions were stuck together. The kitchen had melted and turned black; walls, floor, cabinets, dining table, and chairs were all charred. The plastic laminate counter was bubbled and warped. Plastic dishes and glasses were welded to the surface in sculptured shapes. The sodden bed was covered in fallen plaster fragments. Only the clothes closet was spared. The shelf above the hung garments was undamaged, and this had preserved the portfolio of my first art drawings. I pulled my *Giant Jacks* and first self-portrait out of the cardboard sleeve and stared at my glowering 1970s rock star image crowned by a glorious, disheveled mop of hair, which would not last long. The eyes were as penetrating as Picasso's in 1907. The conté crayon drawing preserved my Jackal's viperous resentment for posterity.

The printed rubbish reminded me that the clock was ticking. God only knew how much time I had left to respond to Rembrandt's demand. I needed to stop vacillating and choose a career: would it be art or architecture?

I had come to Chicago to learn how to build a building and see if I could stand being an architect. I had returned to America from the UK because, at 29, I was unlikely to be drafted and sent to Vietnam. I only had one semester to go to complete my master's degree in architecture. I believed that, after finishing my degree, I would know how to design, but know little about how buildings, especially big ones, were put together. Chicago was considered the best place to train in the art of building construction. I didn't like the training very much; a junior architect's work consisted mainly of drafting wall sections, stairs, and bathrooms. However, I was delighted to attend drawing class at the Art Institute of Chicago, where my drawing skills improved.

I made my first large drawing on Arches paper with colored pencils. I called the drawing *Giant Jacks*. Jacks, six-stemmed, three-dimensional metal stars, are the modern version of an ancient game of dexterity called *knucklebones*. Homer referred to the game in *The Iliad* and *The Odyssey*. A sheep's hock bones were tossed in the air, and the player attempted to catch all the bones on the back of one hand. The game had many variants. I liked not only the reference of the game's elements to cultural history but also the skills of the contemporary game alluded to in my drawing. Modern American jacks is played by bouncing a small red rubber ball in the air while the player tries to pick up the jacks, which can be as many as twelve, before the ball hits the ground. I was good at the game when I was a child.

My drawing rendered a jack and the red rubber ball much larger than reality. They were huge elements placed on the floor by the base of a wall with tall baseboard trim. This was a child's eye view. I liked to draw as a child, and I grew up to be pretty good at it. I was also a man involved in a game of skill. Could I pick up many jacks, only a few, or none? Would I become accomplished as an artist *and* an architect? Would it be one or the other or would I be a washout at both? In jacks, if you hesitate or vacillate, you will inevitably lose by acquiring none of the jacks or dropping those you hold.

I tossed my wet, burned belongings into the alley. A telephone lineman, a fat swarthy fellow on a nearby pole, laughed and yelled, "Hey, you long-haired hippie un-American freak, you got what you deserved, and I'm glad." I gave him the finger, gathered my salvageable clothes, books, and portfolio, and went back to my girlfriend Johanna's place. I pinned my salvaged rock star image and a reproduction of Picasso's 1907 wide-eyed Cubist djinni on the wall next to a window that looked out on the distant, recently constructed Sears Tower. My 1973 portrait embodied the zeitgeist, "Don't trust anyone over thirty!" At twenty-nine, I had already succumbed to the middle-class philosophy represented by America's giant capitalist fortress on the Lake. I was a junior architect for the firm that had designed the Sears Tower.

Picasso created his self-portrait the same year as *Les Demoiselles d'Avignon* when he was twenty-six. His style was radically new, expressionistic, and confrontational. One eye stared straight ahead, while

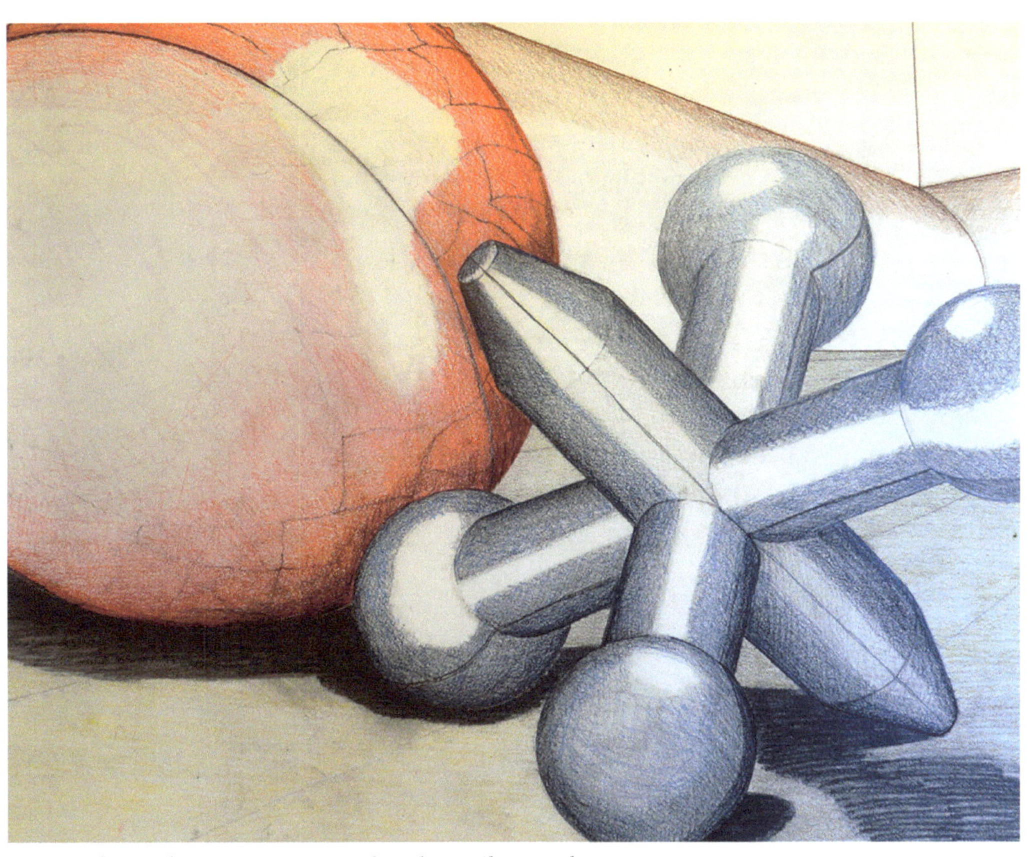

Giant Jacks, Carlton Davis, 1973, colored pencil on Arches paper, 23" × 29" (58.42 cm × 73.66 cm)

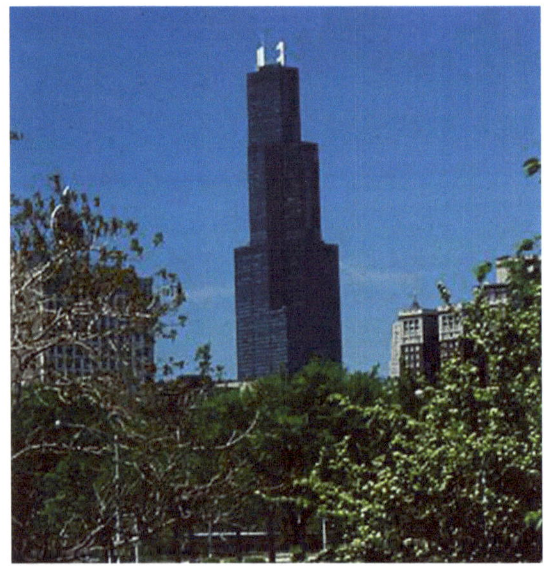

Sears Tower, Chicago, USA, 1973,
architects Skidmore Owings and Merrill (SOM)

On a bitterly cold day in the Windy City, I gazed at the Sears Tower, then the world's tallest building, looming in the distance alongside my self-portrait pinned to one side of the window. The two antennae crowning the slick black tower penetrated the sky like a satyr's horns, confidently and arrogantly asserting the supremacy of the city's architecture. Picasso's self-portrait proclaimed art's ability to change human perception. The Sears Tower boasted the state of technology, of building 108 stories above the ground. My draftsman's assignments bored me. My heart wasn't in it. My heart was in art.

Art called, and I had to heed it. The journey would be long, and I could fail. I desired the freedom, authenticity, and joy that Picasso possessed. At ninety, confronting his fate, he drew a pencil-and-crayon specter. He was both a child and a master, incapable of hiding his terror at the end of the road. My caged soul glared back at me from my first self-portrait, demanding I do everything within my power to care for it so that, one day, it would be set free.

the other dissolved. The brows flattened the surface, prefiguring the fragmentation of his later work. The ear smashed against the plane of the canvas, its geometry aligned with a black streak across the cheek, while other black strokes became the face and clothes. The hair was a bent flat plane of black streaks. The mask served as an individual likeness and a figurehead of avant-garde art. My drawing had none of Picasso's revolutionary aesthetic, yet it shared a couple of his virtues. One eye looked fiercely at the observer while the other drifted away. One ear was fully there, while the other almost disappeared in the field of hair. The background looked as if a thin veil of ice had been splashed across the forehead and wetted and had frozen the nose. My drawing was not a tribal mask but a vaporous ghost, haunted by his artistic pretensions. 'Carlos the Jackal' was a soul on ice.

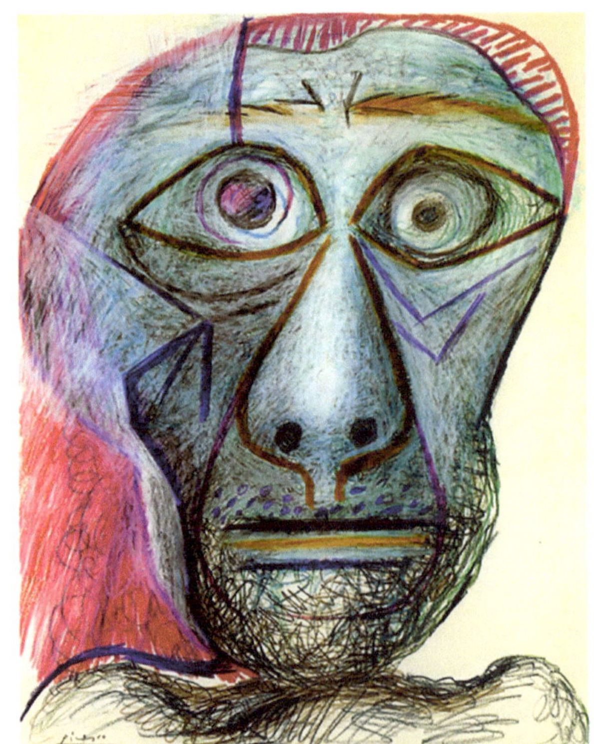

Self-Portrait Facing Death, 1972, Pablo Picasso, pencil and crayon on paper, 25¾" × 19¾" (65.4 cm × 50.16 cm), Private collection.

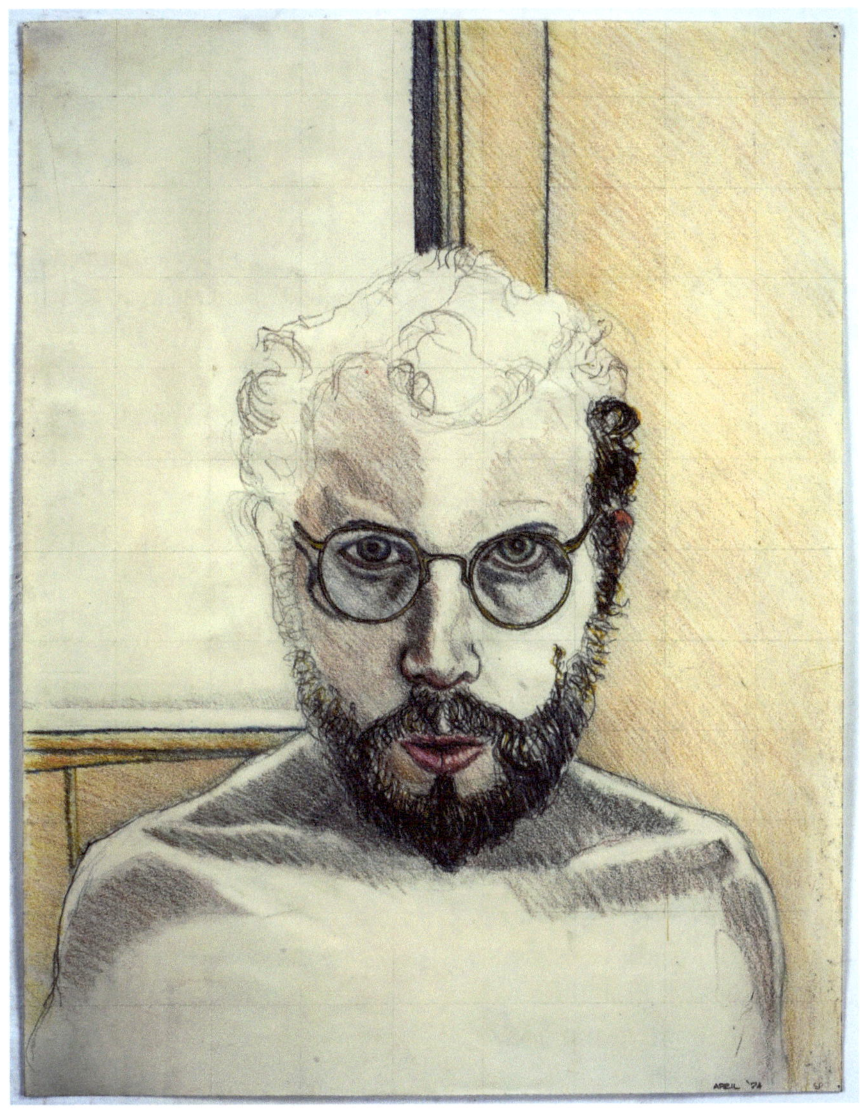

Self-portrait, 1974, Carlton Davis, colored pencil on paper,
17.75" × 23.5" (45.08 cm × 59.69 cm)

CHAPTER 2

1974
THROUGH THE WINDOW SHADE

imagined Claes Oldenburg, one of my art idols, visiting me in Chicago. We stood at the window looking at the Sears Tower in the distance. My second self-portrait was pinned to the wall, next to a sexy photograph of Johanna, my fiancée.

'Too bad," he remarked. "You missed an opportunity."

"What do you mean?" I inquired.

He cleared his throat and recited from memory:

"Call the roller of big cigars,
The muscular one, and bid him whip
In kitchen cups concupiscent curds.
Let the wenches dawdle in such dress
As they are used to wear, and let the boys
Bring flowers in last month's newspapers.
Let be be finale of seem.
The only emperor is the emperor of ice cream."

"Who wrote that?" I wanted to know.

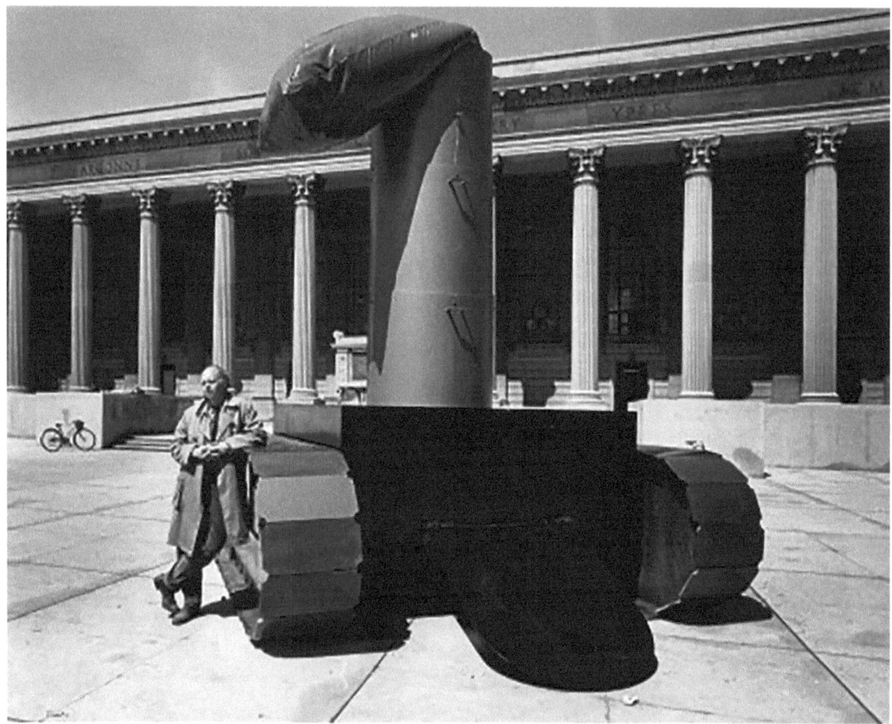

Claes Oldenburg, "*Lipstick Ascending on Caterpillar Tracks*," 1969, Harry Shunk and Shunk-Kender Photographs

We shared a mournful moment. Then, my mentor rested his hand on my shoulder.

"What kind of art do *you* make, Carlton?"

"Call me Carl. I like to draw. I was trained as an architect. I draw art signs for museums and monuments, and do self-portraits, like this one here."

"Call me Claes. May I ask your age?"

"I just turned 30."

"Dedicate yourself to a specific field. Art biz is show biz. You'll be type-cast. You mentioned 'art signs.' What are they?"

"The one I've been working on recently is big and round and perched on the end of a long stick,

"Wallace Stevens, a Hartford insurance executive who wrote poetry on the side until he hit the big time in 1954. 'Let be be finale of seem,' is the finest epigram I know for the art-making process."

I took Oldenburg's laughter as my cue. "When your first public sculpture, *Lipstick Ascending on Caterpillar Tracks,* was commissioned by The Colossal Keepsake Corporation, a group of Yale faculty, art, and architecture students who tapped into a university fund for campus beautification, I was one of the students who helped mount it. I remember filling the giant airbag on top with plastic pellets, so it had enough heft to stand straight."

Claes clapped my back in jubilant recall. "I wanted the end of the lipstick to be able to deflate like guys do after sex. Less than a year later, the commissioners of the bequest decided, without consulting me, to make what we could call the *glans* from the same metal as the shaft and paint it red. What Stevens referred to as 'be,' the life force, vanished. The piece morphed from what Janis Joplin called 'a hunk of burnin' love' to a hunk of junk. When what you make is purchased, do as Dante recommended and 'abandon all hope.'"

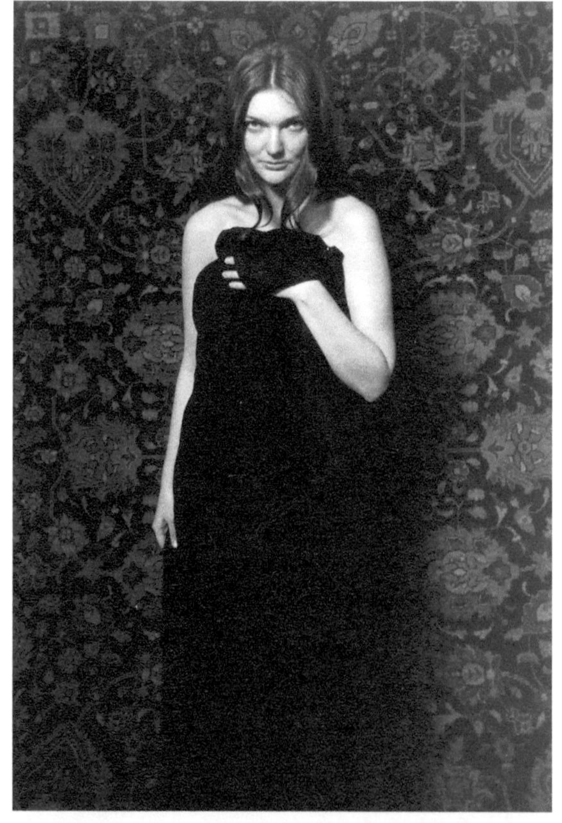

Johanna in a photographer's studio, 1973, photographer unknown

like a lollipop a chick might twiddle in her hand then lick with her tongue to turn someone on. They're erotic, like a lot of *your* stuff. People want to touch them, play with them, take them home."

I opened my portfolio to show Claes a sign I'd created for the Contemporary Art Museum in Chicago.

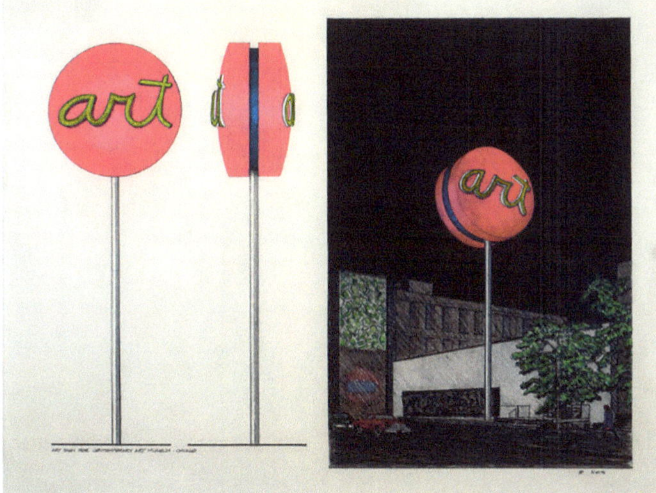

Art sign for the Museum of Contemporary Art, Chicago, 1974, 18" × 24" (45.7 cm × 60.9 cm), colored pencil and graphite

"That's great!"

"My self-portraits are emotional. This one's about the hunger to be someone. I'm selfish, obsessive, impatient. I want to be unique, a force to be reckoned with, like you!"

We were living in interesting times. *Deep Throat* was doing landslide business at the X-rated cinemas. *The Chicago Tribune* was replete with articles about sexual freedom, bra-burning, and 'the feminine mystique.' Bette Midler, spouting *double entendre* innuendos like Mae West, was packing the 3,800-seat Auditorium Theater. In my imagined conversation, Claes had claimed that art biz was synonymous with show biz. I didn't want to languish in the wings. My story would propel my art. Claes Oldenburg was my mentor and, at least for the moment and in my mind, I had his ear.

"I cut my hair short because liberated women don't dig hippies. I trimmed and shaped my beard because

I wanted to look like a sexy professional posing naked in front of a mirror."

"I think it's risky to mess around with sexual content."

"Wait a minute! What about *Symbolic Self-portrait with Equals*? I think it drips with sexual energy, or at least with postal-coital feeling. You represent yourself as an artist with his tongue hanging out after a night of heavy drinking. The electric energy of sex is presented by the wall plug and light switch."

I saw this lithograph in one of Chicago's galleries. I couldn't afford to buy one, but I did make a napkin sketch from memory while sitting in a café lusting after Johanna and explaining to her why I saw this lithograph as representing the artist recovering from a night of debauchery.

"The electrical devices and the Mickey Mouse projector with unwound film gave your intent away," I said in my daydream. In my mind's eye I could see Johanna scoffing at my intellectual musings.

"What about the ice cream bar?

"You read too much into the piece—it's merely a play with the kinds of common things I might have made as soft kapok objects for my store and a visual puzzle for the viewer to solve," my imagined Oldenburg chortled.

"To me, your print hums with sexual electricity. The ice cream bar merely ties the work back to similar pieces in your *oeuvre*. The slight bite from a lover's teeth. The feminist rebellion has created a libertine mood that you ride like a genie. Meanwhile, in the mid-west, where I reside and you once did, conservatism, mania, multiple addictions, like an oil slick of shame on Lake Michigan, have stopped me cold."

This kind of talk was anathema to Johanna, who treasured her privacy and, by conjugal rights, mine. I had to remember not to let loose like this when she was around, but I loved the high. Claes wandered back to the window, raised the shade, and stood staring out at the world. He hadn't heard a word.

The last time I saw Paris, I encountered Auguste Rodin's drawing of Salammbô at his eponymous museum. Loose, free, and daring, the sketch evinced the artist's confidence and control. Engrossed, I peered at it for as long a time as I had Rembrandt's painted self-portrait. I savored each swipe, smudge, and altered line of Rodin's pencil. I was in awe of how intimate he was with womanly sensuality. It was not until we traveled to the Greek island of Mykonos that I could begin to understand the freedom with which artistic masters worked. What I experienced there had nothing to do with making art; it was an unexpected lesson in the art of living.

Back to my imagined conversation. I shared a visual sequence with Claes that I had run, frame by frame, in the editing bay of my head. Johanna and I had stripped naked in an isolated cove and plunged into a pool so translucent that the submarine landscape resembled a tapestry of bold colors striated with iridescent fish. Johanna's skin was alabaster, her waist a luscious curve, her breasts buoyant. Aroused, we made love.

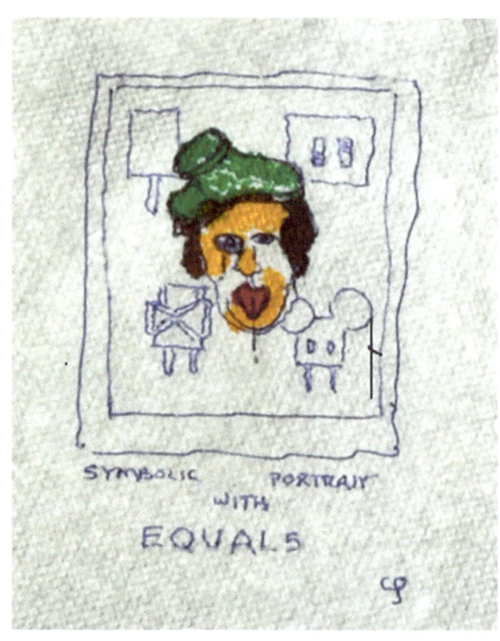

Symbolic Portrait with Equals, paper napkin sketch after Claes Oldenburg, 2024, Carlton Davis, no scale

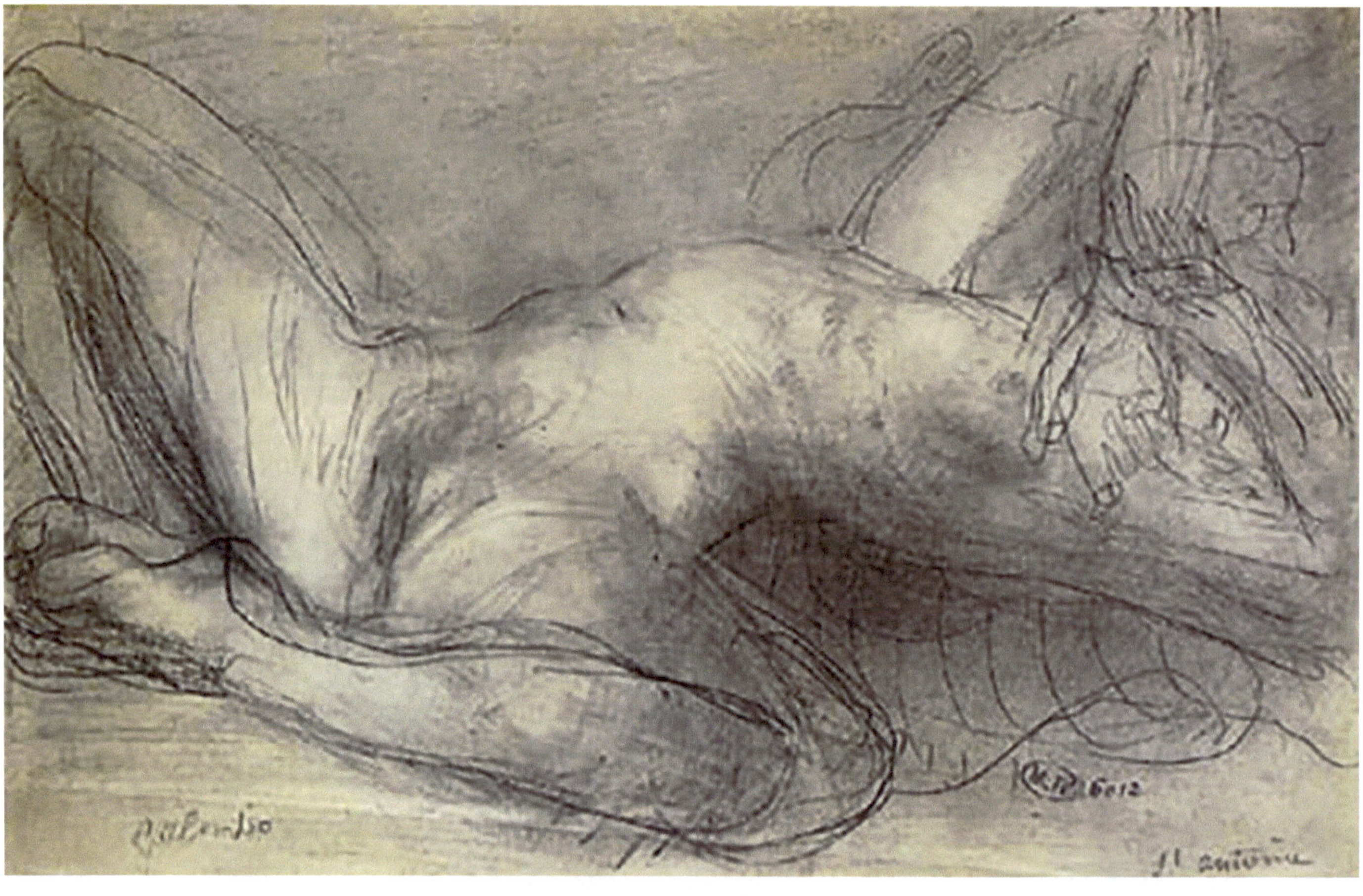

Salammbô drawing, paper with pencil and paper stump used for smudging, Auguste Rodin, 1900, 8.25" × 12.25" (20.4 cm × 31 cm), Musée Rodin, Paris

Sometime after the aqueous climax, I noticed a man and a dog standing on the bluff above the beach, waving and barking, respectively. Paradise lost.

On Mykonos, the ice formed inside me by decades of trauma and inhibition began to melt. I luxuriated in sensual surroundings, and the desire I felt for my soon-to-be wife was a source of delight. For the first time, I felt what I imagined liberated artists took for granted: that I was at play in a boundless creative field. Rodin's loose, gestural drawing of Salammbô exemplified the freedom I would one day express in my work. Simultaneously, my anxiety was triggered by the mere thought of returning to my homeland. I worried that I was still a long way from becoming an artist with something new to add to a visual world where drawing from life was denigrated as 'realism.' Otherwise, I felt fortunate to have made it to 30 more or less in one piece.

At the end of August, we boarded TWA Flight 841, which originated in Tel Aviv, stopped briefly in Athens, and terminated in New York. A week later, the same flight exploded over the Ionian Sea after taking off from Athens, where we had boarded. There were no survivors. A Palestinian liberation group claimed responsibility for a bomb placed in the airplane's cargo hold. The tragedy was the first 'terrorist attack' on a commercial airliner.

I would say, looking back, that we were involved with our own lives most of the time, and came together often to celebrate our mutual physical

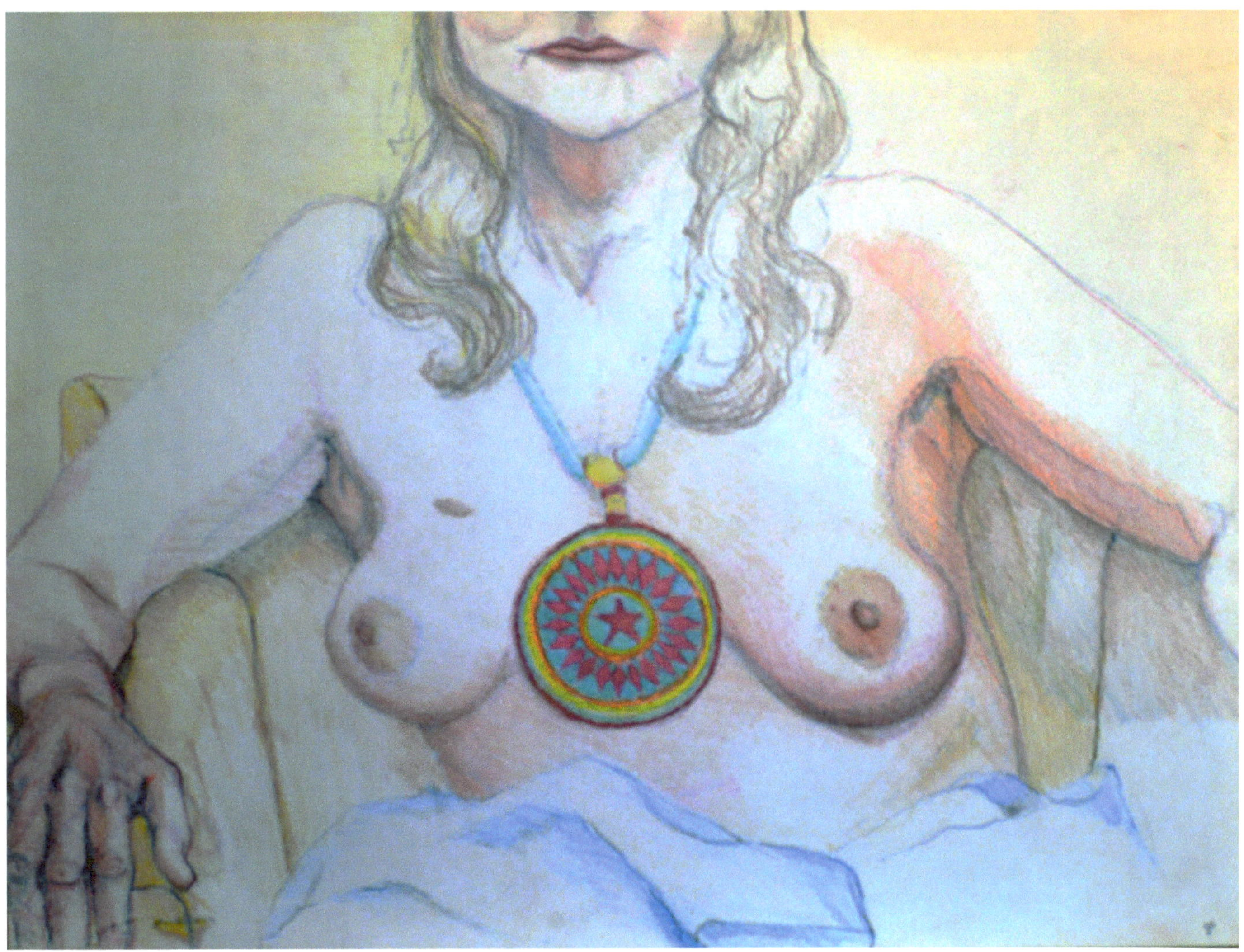

Johanna, 1974, Carlton Davis, colored pencil on paper, 18" × 24" (45.72 cm × 60.96 cm)

delight. However we conduct it, life continues. Johanna's tranquil exterior belied her sexual intensity, which provided a welcome respite from my jagged and care-laden life. The TWA 841 flight we booked could have had a bomb in the hold. Stevens's 'Let be be finale of seem' is a cryptic catchphrase that our idyll on Mykonos did not disprove.

My goal was always to follow my weird ways as an artist. The intimate portrait I drew of my fiancée was a preliminary validation that I could organize, render, and appreciate the relationship between what is and what is not art. I made it soon after the explosion of Flight 841. She would come home from her job as a writer and editor of the weekly newsletter of a large urban hospital and spend long periods sitting quietly. I never heard her use the word 'meditation,' but it was clear that she was comfortable with herself. Sitting for her portrait was something we both savored. I focused on her torso and breasts with a large, beaded pendant, acquired in Greece, resting between them. She had a slight smile and sat confidently with her hands on the arms of the chair. The pale blue fabric on her lap is a bedsheet, perhaps a reminder of all the good times we spent between them. Her tranquility was a gift. I drew nothing from her cheekbones up. Perhaps it was my way of avoiding her penetrating gaze so I could focus on her beautiful breasts and bountiful heart.

In retrospect, my rendering of Johanna and my self-portrait were both unfinished, transitional images. Although drawing was my chosen portal, I had yet to find a unique and recognizable style. Perhaps I should have raised the shade on the skyscraper cock of the Sears Tower and crowned it with a satyr's horns, as Claes had suggested. "Follow Rodin's lead, find your own way, and enjoy yourself," was a vital communiqué I derived from his work.

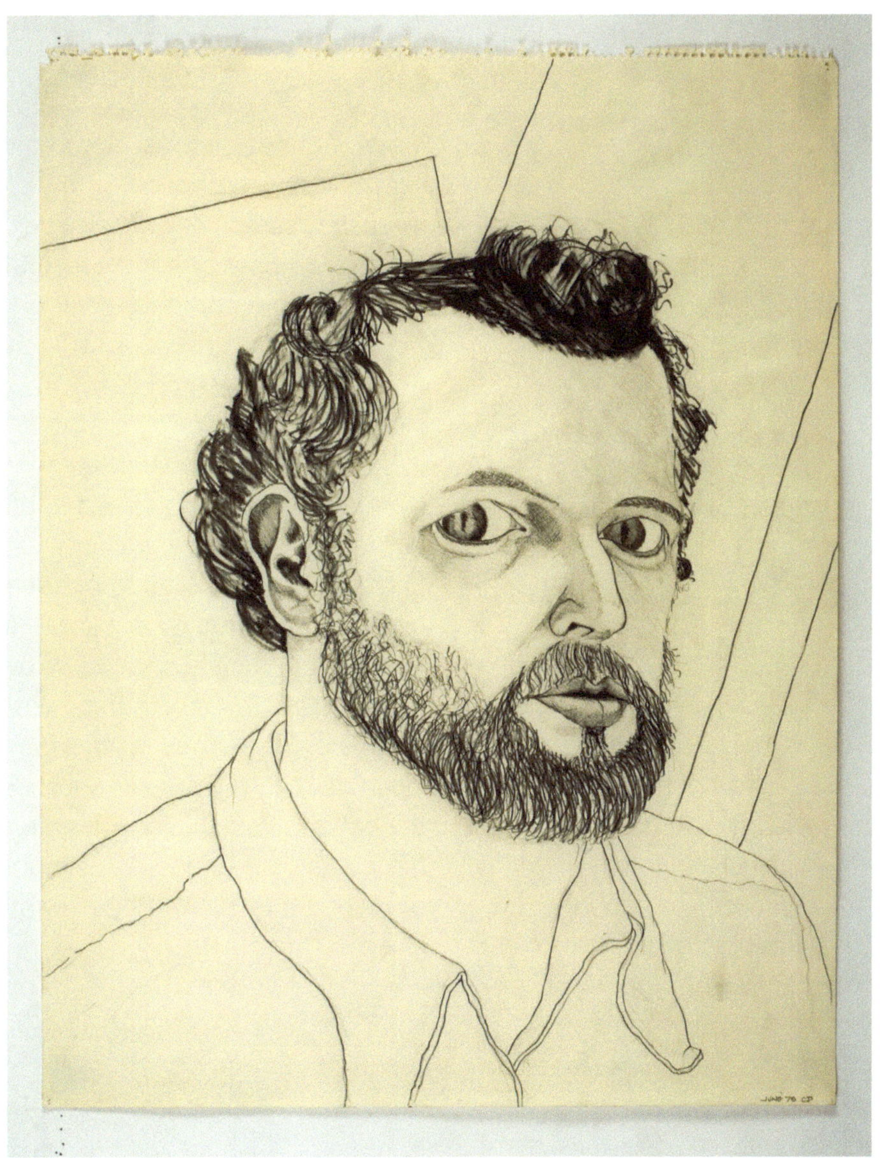

Self-portrait, 1976, Carlton Davis, graphite pencil on paper, 18" × 24" (42.72 cm × 60.96 cm)

CHAPTER 3

1976
THE JUDGING EYES TURN WEST

The darkness deepens. Shrieking voices cry.
Below these fantasies of glass that crowd our sky
and hatred like a whirling paper in a street
tears at itself where shame and hatred meet.
Show me, old friends, where in the darkness still
stands the great republic on its hill!

From *Night Watch in the City of Boston*
by Archibald MacLeish

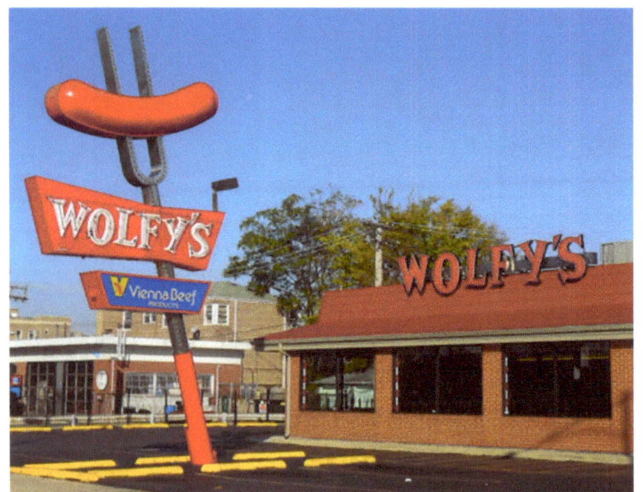

Wolfy's Hot Dog Stand, 1976. Chicago, Illinois

In the Bicentennial year of 1976, MacLeish's words were for Boston, but the anguished final stanzas also applied to Chicago, the windy city of glass towers, where violence was rampant. The Black Panther Party's militancy frightened white people, whose flight to the suburbs turned inner city neighborhoods Black. Poor people of all colors were evicted from their homes. Poverty gripped the city and houses were vandalized, burned, and boarded up. If unprecedented rises in the price of gasoline and unemployment statistics demonstrated the instability of our 'great republic on its hill,' the collapse of Saigon sent it sprawling. Live coverage in Chicago showed SWAT teams engaging with Black-on-Black gang wars, guns blazing as they battered their way into Southside drug dens. The city had the highest number of civilian casualties in the US. Guns could be purchased cheaply on the street. More than 800 Chicagoans were killed between 1975 and 1976.

To keep our terror at bay, Johanna and I watched *The Mary Tyler Moore Show*, a feel-good sitcom about a TV newsroom in Minneapolis, and we made love incessantly. We screwed our way to New York City in an Amtrak Pullman car and were married in City Hall with the couple in line behind us as our witnesses. Our honeymoon was a quick ferry ride to Liberty Island to scale Bartholdi's colossal, torch-bearing Lady of the Harbor. I felt impaled like a Wolfy's wiener on a two-tined fork; bored with my job as a humdrum junior architect, now at Booth and Nagle Architects, yet reluctant to depend on my art alone. My indecisiveness tested my wife's patience. I signed up for evening courses at the Art Institute of Chicago. I was terrible at painting. I tried sculpture and came close to accidental suicide in the Art Institute's foundry. Late one night, the instructor, several other students, and I carved up plastic foam blocks and wrapped them in plaster, creating molds we could then pour molten aluminum into via holes at the top. The plastic blocks burned when the aluminum was poured in, emitting a dense black cloud of acrid smoke. Coughing, gagging, tripping over chairs, and slamming into tables in our rush to escape, we eventually lay panting on the grass in Lincoln Park as the smoke began to dissipate. I look back on this incident as an inauspicious start to my artistic quest. The following week, the nation's financial downturn relieved me of my job. I accepted an academic position at the University of Wyoming, which I hoped would put me one step closer to my dream

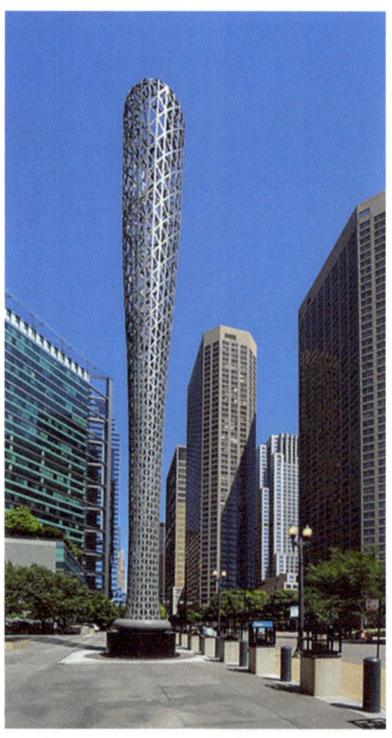

Bat Column, 1976, Chicago, Illinois,
Claes Oldenburg and Coosje van Bruggen

We packed our belongings and loaded our VW into a rental truck, but before we departed, I drove by the site where Claes Oldenburg's *Bat Column* would stand on the edge of the downtown Loop. The site was cordoned off by an obscuring wall with only a poster stapled to the plywood stating that this spot would soon be the location of Oldenburg's bat. In homage to the man who inspired me to pursue my dream, I drew an image of a sculpture for the inegalitarian, violent, merciless Chicago I had come to know. Here is my drawing of a 'Saturday Night Special Memorial' for Grant Park.

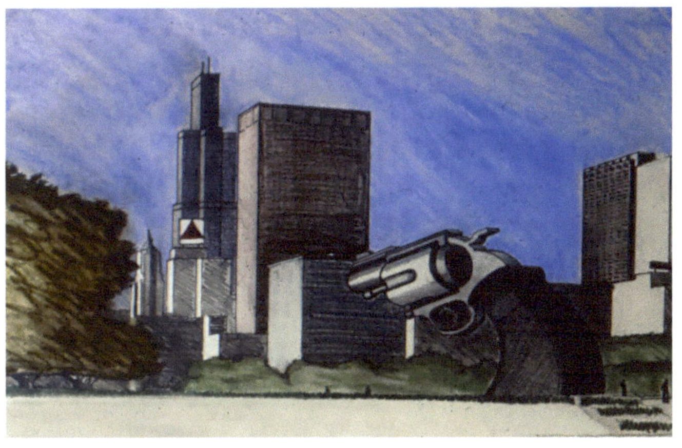

Saturday Night Special Memorial for Grant Park, Chicago 1976. Carlton Davis, pastel and colored pencil, 18" × 26" (45.7 cm × 66 cm), collection of Roberta Kent

We departed the troubled City on the Lake, heading west into what felt like a vast emptiness where relentless winds erased the past. I had accepted a position as an assistant professor of architectural engineering and planned to use my free time to hone my artistic skills.

Our final stop was my favorite eatery. As we noshed, I informed Johanna that Wolfy's pylon wiener sign was iconic because its two-tined fork recalled the farmer and his wife's pitchfork in Grant Wood's *American Gothic* and doubled as a tuning fork vibrating to the nonstop shrill of capitalist culture. She stymied my lecture by saying she appreciated my pole more than Wolfy's and the only vibration she might require could be produced with a personal vibrator. In the twilight, we spotted the first great pylon sign at a gas station on the Iowa interstate. An oblong 'Standard' imposed its luminous presence between two pink cirrus clouds. We stopped for the night at a motel just behind the station. I could see the Standard sign through our motel's window and drifted off into an art-inspired slumber. I wanted my work to be anything but standard.

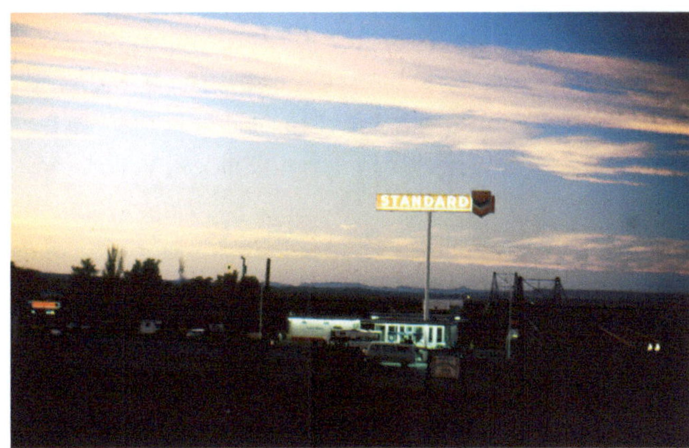

Standard gasoline station, Illinois, photograph by Carlton Davis

The following day, we crossed into what I thought of as Thomas Hart Benton land. Benton was once Jackson Pollock's teacher at the Art Students League in Manhattan. Pollock told an interviewer that Benton's traditional American landscape paintings had given him 'something to rebel against.' We passed Nebraska's endless cornfields on our way to

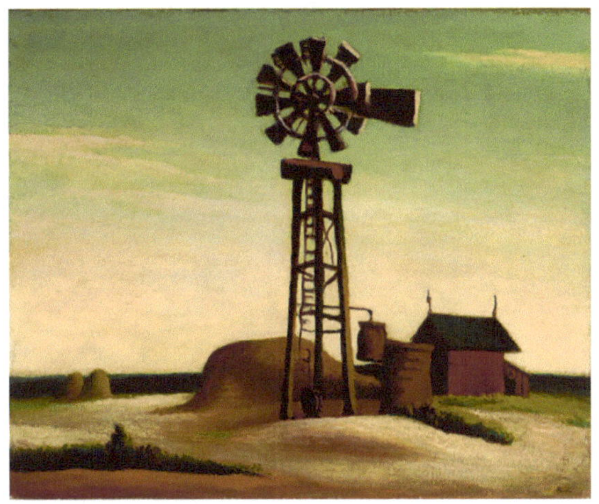

Windmill, Thomas Hart Benton, 1926, oil on board, 19-7/8" x 24" (50.5 cm x 61cm), Birmingham Museum of Art, Birmingham, Alabama

Wyoming. Johanna rolled her eyes when I remarked on the capitalist stupidity of the agribiz. "Please, honey, save your lectures for your class. That way you'll be paid for your time instead of wasting mine." We climbed higher through the plains as I struggled to subdue my irritation. We stopped on Interstate 80 between Cheyenne and Laramie near the great head of President Lincoln. We stood on the far side of the interstate from the 30-foot-high granite pedestal admiring Honest Abe's twelve-and-a-half-foot bronze head, and I told Johanna, "This is the perfect site for my memorial to Jackson Pollock, Wyoming's one and only Art Hero native son. My *Paint Cans for Pollock* would be slightly higher than Lincoln's head across the highway. From a distance, the poured bronze would look like hardened paint flows and be pocked with child- and adult-sized footholds, making Pollock's tricolor paint cans an inviting monument to climb.

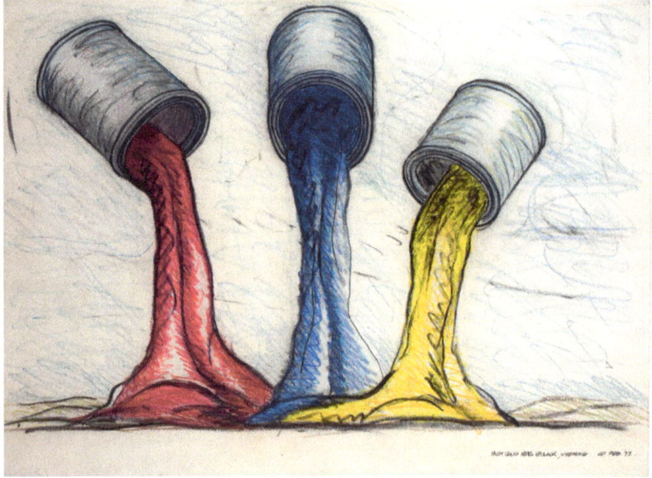

Paint Cans for Pollock, Wyoming 1976, Carlton Davis, pastel, charcoal, and colored pencils on Arches Paper, 22" × 30" (55.88 cm × 76.2 cm)

Johanna looked me straight in the eye as I eagerly awaited her reaction to my dream scheme, which I hoped would be positive. "My dear, I think you're certifiable," is all she said.

We fled to Wyoming to test my ability to be an artist. Johanna was turned off by my self-obsession. My attention was focused on the eyes in the self-portrait I created in this pivotal year. Black shapes created figures on my irises that were mirrored in my glance. The sideways gaze expressed caution and concern. The figures on the irises were phantom judges, evaluating my worth. I stopped myself from explaining that what was recognized as art, let alone fine art, was subjective and evanescent. It was unlikely I would become a well-known artist decades or centuries after my death, like Vermeer. I was painfully aware that my self-centered impositions on our conjugal bliss were products of my deep insecurity. My goal was to make art in the present moment, regardless of the misery and misfortune that might accompany and surround that.

As my buddy Claes Oldenburg reminded me in my imagination, "You think too much!" There was no point stressing over the future. Recalling the unexpected triumph of Clint Eastwood striking out for Italy, I said *sotto voce* to my lonesome cowboy self, "Look out, Laramie, the High Plains Drafter has arrived."

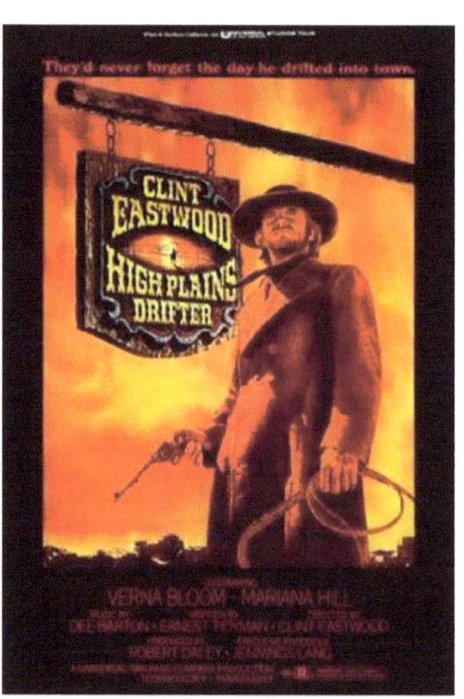

Theatrical release poster by Ron Lesser, film, 1973, directed by Clint Eastwood

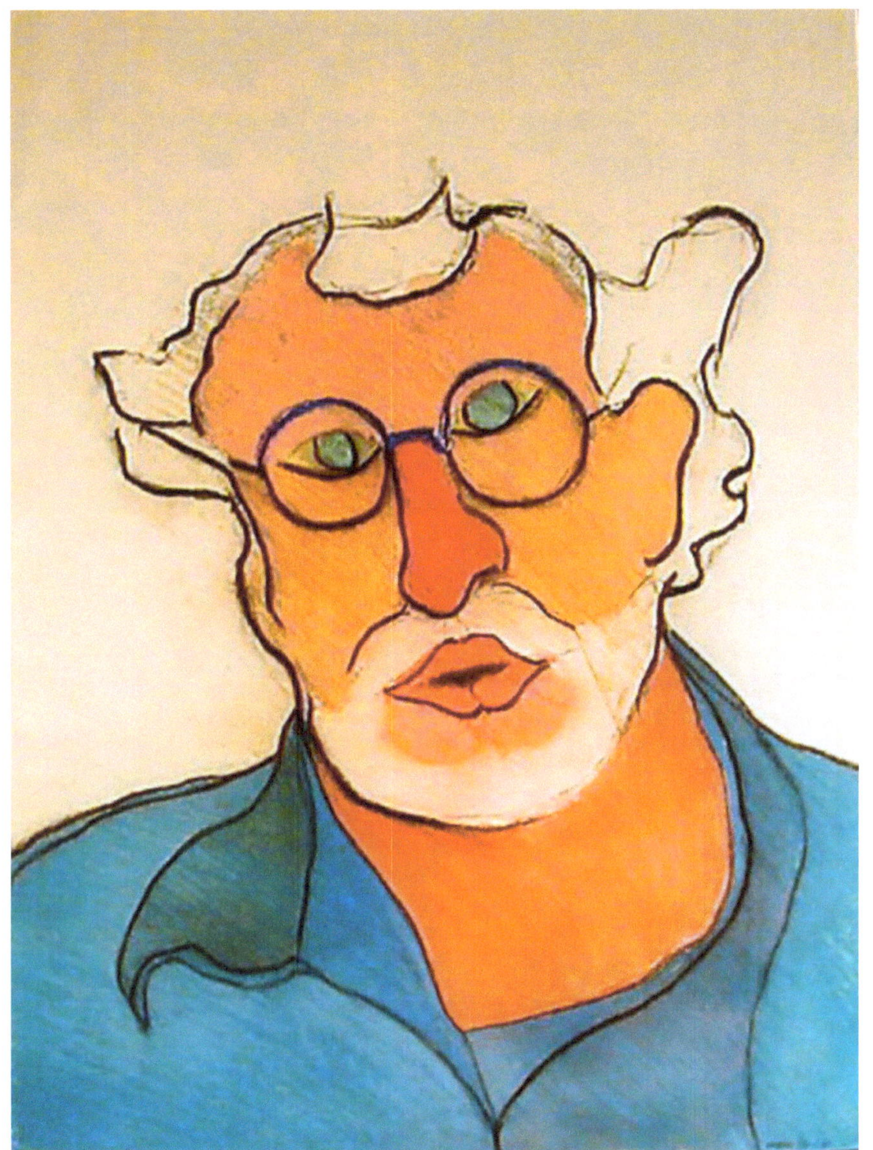

Self-portrait, 1977, Carlton Davis, pastel and charcoal on paper, 24" × 18" (60.96 cm × 45.72 cm)

CHAPTER 4

1977
WITNESS TO THE WEST

Several days and 1,000 miles from Chicago, we ascended the high plains of Western Nebraska, passed the missile silos at Cheyenne, Wyoming, and arrived at our destination: the high valley prairie town of Laramie. In 1977, Laramie had a population of approximately 24,000, of which 3,000 were students. The town was named after Jacques La Ramie, a French-Canadian fur trapper who had disappeared in the mountains beyond the high valley. La Ramie was believed to be the first white man to trade with what were then called the Plains Indians. What began as a frontier encampment evolved into a small town when it was, briefly, the terminus of the transcontinental railroad in the 1860s. The founding of the university in 1886 made Laramie and the university the center of cultural life in the territory and, later, the state.

I had briefly flown there to be interviewed for the assistant professor position and had been picked

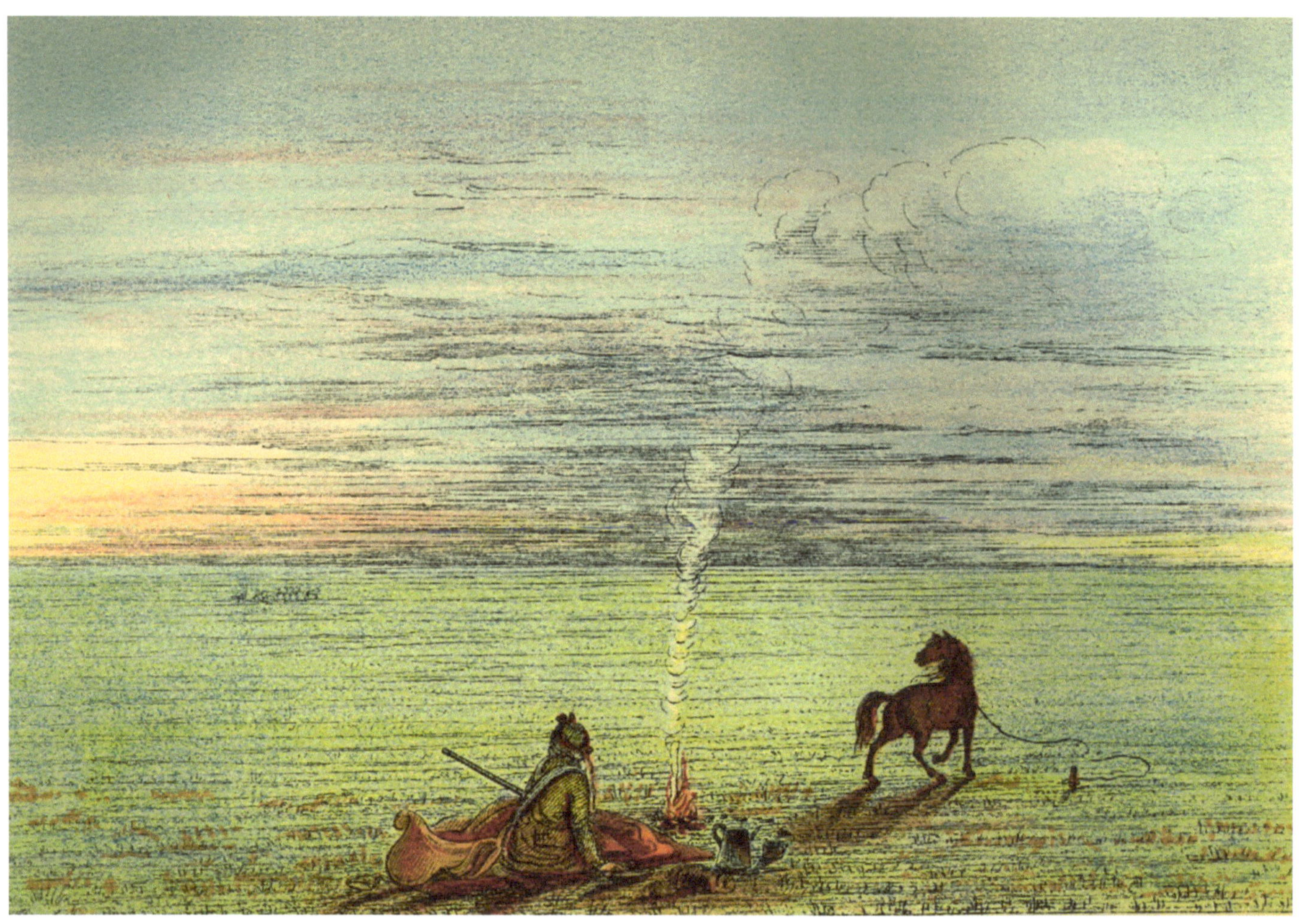

North American Indians, George Catlin, 1926 edition,
Plate 184, published in Edinburgh by John Grant

up at the single-terminal airport, a tiny structure operated by one man who oversaw all activity on the single runway. When I returned to Chicago, I convinced Johanna that living and working in Laramie would be a great adventure.

The University of Wyoming department head wanted me to teach undergraduate students how to prepare construction documents, the ins and outs of professional practice, and a power and lighting course. I was set up to teach the first two classes because I had learned them in Chicago and had reviewed them for the architect licensing exam I had passed the previous year. A power and lighting course was another matter. I knew nothing about the subject. There was only one other architect in town, and I thought opening an office in Laramie might help me establish my presence in Wyoming and generate income. In a tongue-in-cheek homage to Clint Eastwood and Sergio Leone's premier Spaghetti Western, my shingle denominated me as 'The High Plains Drafter.' I planned to pursue my art between prepping for and teaching classes and practicing my profession. I could make art full-time during summer break.

I was fascinated by Native American culture, especially the tribes that inhabited this part of the plains before white people migrated west. My father had learned a few Native American dances as a teenager and collected tribal paraphernalia but showed no real interest in indigenous history or culture. His son cherished both.

I learned that George Catlin was one of the first white men to visit the high plains' indigenous inhabitants. He had been pursuing a legal career in Philadelphia but did not care for the profession and decided to be a painter instead. From 1830 to 1833, Catlin made five trips to lands acquired a mere three decades earlier from Emperor Napoleon by our Francophile president, Thomas Jefferson. Celebrated as the 'Louisiana Purchase,' the deal was consummated on April 30, 1803. The fledgling United States of America acquired 827,000 square miles of land west of the Mississippi River for $15,000,000. This land had previously been claimed by Spain and France and stretched from New Orleans to Canada, nearly doubling the size of the territory we had wrested from Britain in the Revolutionary War.

In the spirit of Jefferson's celebrated 'Corps of Discovery' explorers Captain Meriwether Lewis and Second Lieutenant William Clark, Catlin visited Arapahoe, Blackfoot, Crow, Mandan, Shoshone, Hunkpapa, Lakota, Miniconjou, and Oglala Sioux tribes. He sketched their faces and their horses, recalled in detail what they wore and ate, walked through villages, attended ceremonies, joined hunting expeditions, and, in stunning detail, captured the topography of the lands they inhabited. After each trip, he returned to Philadelphia and turned his sketches into oil paintings that he exhibited salon-style, with pictures mounted close together one above the other, in Philadelphia, New York, Washington, D.C., and Europe. One of my favorites is of a Native American man sitting beside his campfire, his horse bridled and tethered nearby. The man, with a

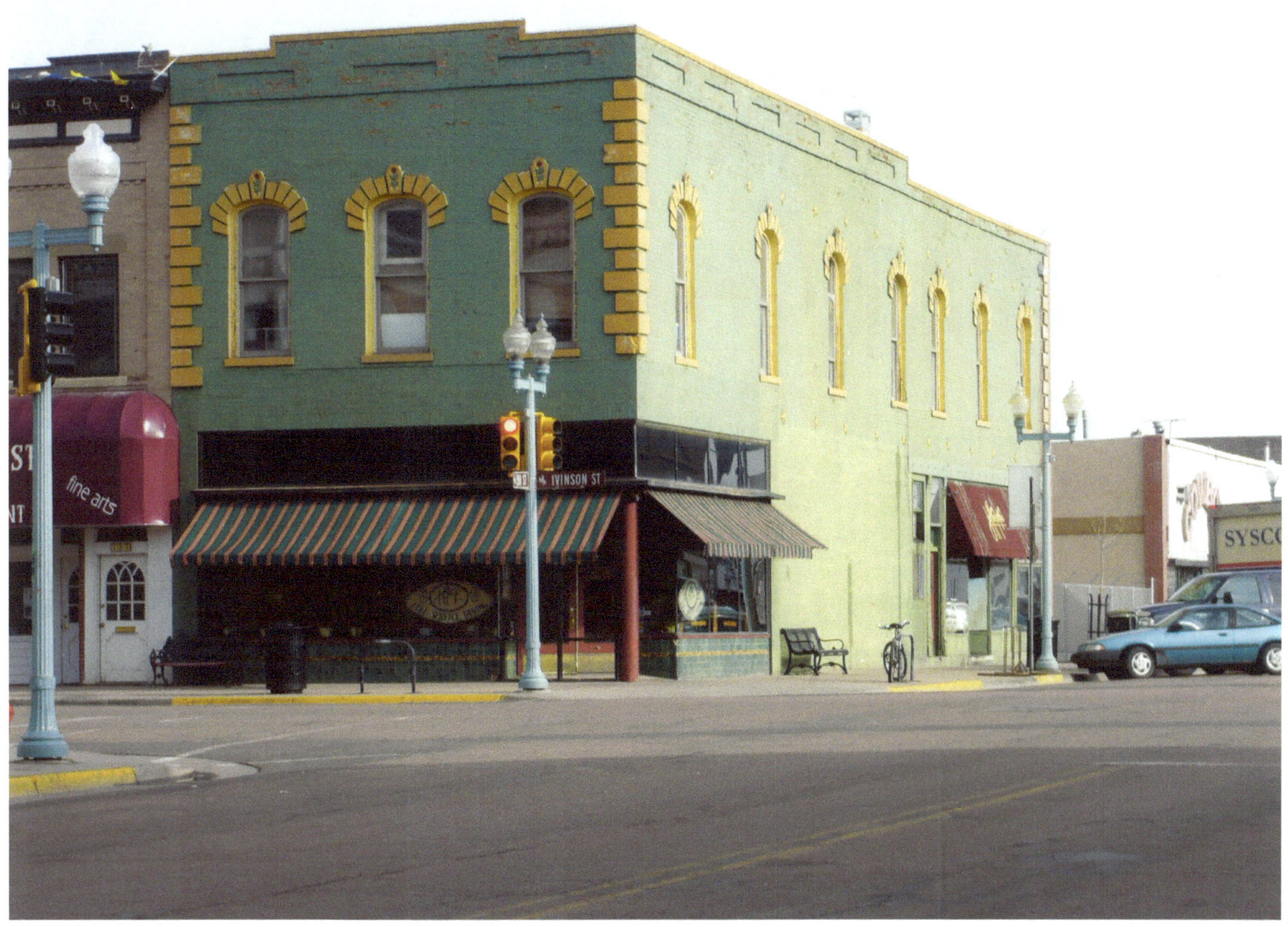

Ivinson and First Street, Laramie, Wyoming, 1977, photograph by Carlton Davis

staff or bow on his lap, is looking out across an empty prairie at twilight. Even as a youngster, I was inspired by Catlin's keen eye and adventurous nature.

Johanna found a suite of vacant rooms in a two-story building on a street corner near Laramie's commercial center. We converted the space into living quarters and a studio for me. We were above an antique shop and next to a store selling what was then considered 'fine art,' namely local mountain vistas, Indian braves on horseback, and Frederick Remington knockoffs. My studio's three windows overlooked the Cowboy Bar across the street, the favorite hangout of college-age cowboys and cowgirls who drank, danced, and flirted, mainly on weekends. Now and then, someone would get ornery and shoot

out the saloon's plate glass windows with a rifle that held pride of place in the owner's pickup truck cab's rear window rack.

You could get a glimpse of First Street's detritus from the windows, including junked cars, twisted signposts of yore, and abandoned heaps of bottle shards. Discarded lumber and decomposing bricks littered the prairie while thunderous 18-wheelers sped down the nearby interstate highway.

We grew bored with Laramie as soon as the novelty wore off. Once, I went for a drink in a country and western joint on 'Frontier Days,' the annual rodeo hullabaloo at the Laramie fairgrounds. With my back pressed to the wall by a horde of inebriated customers, I watched a man in a baseball cap ride his horse into

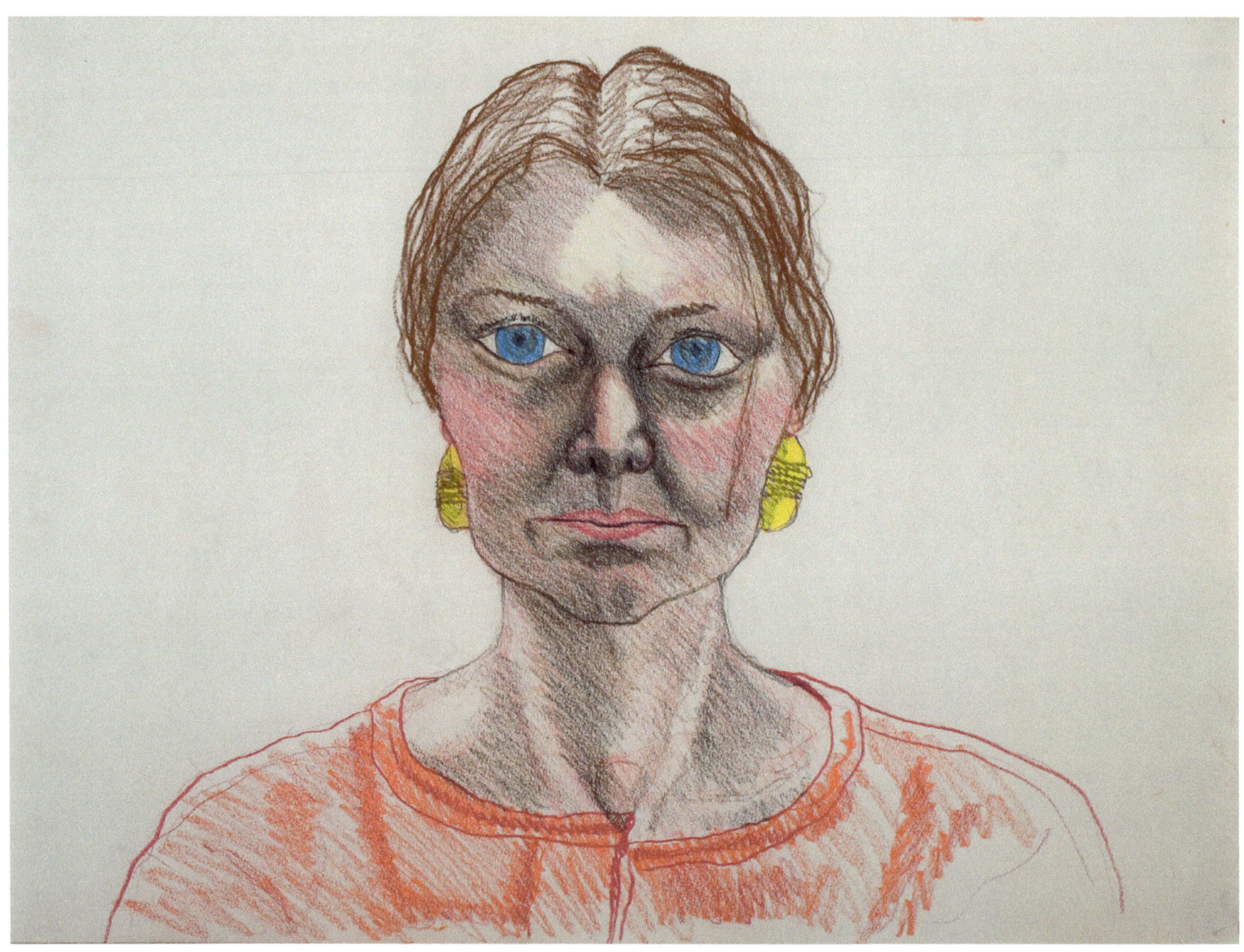

Portrait of Johanna, 1977, Carlton Davis, colored pencil on paper, 22.5" × 30" (57.15 cm × 76.2 cm)

the establishment. No one at the bar gave it a second thought until he tried to get the animal to back out of the doorway. Unused to reversing, the horse freaked and kicked the shit out of the Wurlitzer jukebox.

On another occasion, I witnessed a historic standoff outside a small, turn-of-the-century hotel on First Street. The antagonist was a lone gunman, positioned at the foot of a banister at the end of a corridor and taking potshots at no one in particular. When a combined posse of police and state troopers opened fire from the street, the racket was deafening. The next day, *The Boomerang*, Laramie's local newspaper, reported that the perpetrator had been arrested unscathed. I went to inspect the hotel's lobby after the yellow police tape had been removed a couple of days later. There were at least 100 bullet holes in the wall behind the staircase.

Teaching aspiring architects and engineers how to detail a building and write up contracts was exceedingly dull. I had difficulty relating to my students. They found my smart aleck, Ivy League superiority, born of years of verbal jousting at a competitive, all-male college, demeaning. I needed to communicate, not criticize. My dissatisfaction with how my life was going was taking its toll. My relationship with Johanna was crumbling, as was my interest in teaching. I struggled to stay a few chapters ahead of my students, and the power and lighting course brightened when I dropped my defensive attitude and supported their progress.

People entertained themselves in very few ways in Wyoming. They hunted, which held no interest for either of us, and they fished and tied flies, which was the go-to topic at faculty get-togethers. We enjoyed cross-country skiing in the Snowy Range Mountains 20 miles west of Laramie and birdwatching. We would get up hours before sunrise and drive 100 miles for a chance encounter with a rare specimen. Once, shortly after daybreak at a ranch in the middle of nowhere, I saw a great white owl with a six-foot wingspan! We had been invited to a cattle branding at which I helped wrestle a big calf to the ground, grabbed it by the tail, and put my foot over its anus to protect the man with the branding iron from getting sprayed by the terrified animal. Johanna had a clipboard and kept track of whether the calf was a young cow or a steer-in-the-making that needed to be castrated.

Johanna's work in Laramie was similarly clerical. As in Chicago, she retreated into introspective silence as soon as she came home each day. One day, I took advantage of this to make another portrait. This time, I dared to encompass her eyes, nose, and forehead. What I found there reminded me of Catlin's paintings of Native Americans in which something essential appeared to shift, their souls perhaps, as if they were threatened by the outsiders' scrutiny. In Johanna's case, I slipped easily into the role of outsider because I had provided the pretext for our presence in Laramie, and, other than sexually, I displayed little interest in who or what she was about, i.e., her humanity. I think she felt I was stealing her spirit. My emotional ups and downs

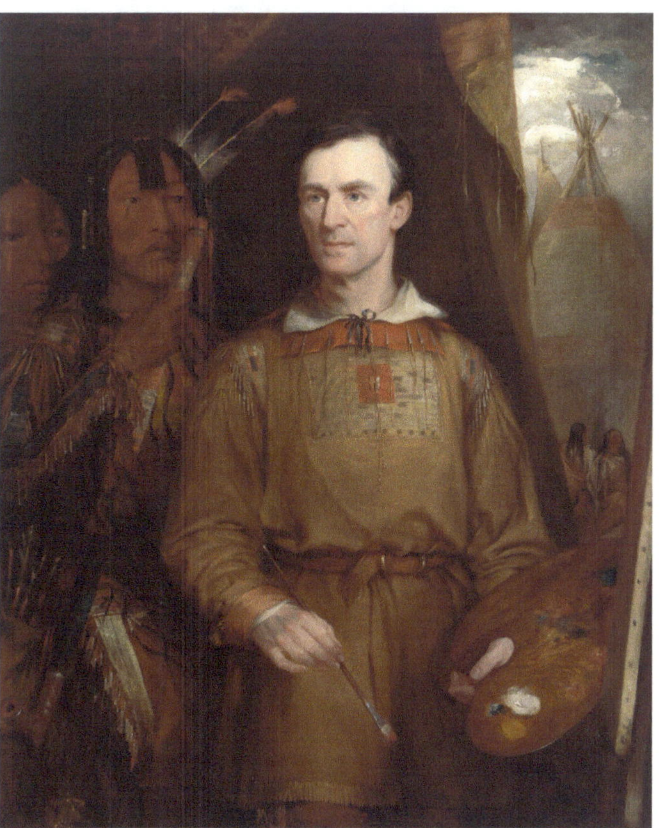

George Catlin, Portrait by William Fisk, 1849, oil on canvas, 62-½" x 52-½" (158.8 cm x 133.4 cm), National Portrait Gallery, Smithsonian Institution, Washington D.C.

were a lot for her to handle, and if I looked to her for empathy, it was wishful thinking.

There was little to talk about now that our lust-hot romance had cooled. We were very different people. She was totally non-committal about my artistic endeavors and uninterested in my theories about anyone else's.

Thus, she remained as flat and impenetrable as her portrait. I did not see flatness as negative *per se*. I attempted to include it in my 1977 self-portrait, knowing that my way of being can be understood over time. One adept at masking their emotions is, by definition, a shapeshifter, a shaman, a hunter, or a warrior. Anointing one's face with daubs and stripes of plant dye creates a living mask that functions as a design for remembering ancestral knowledge, dreams, and portents. So do names like Sitting Bull, Crazy Horse, Black Hand, and Sacajawea (which means Bird Woman). My wife was a force to be reckoned with, but not one I would ever see clearly. I look at George Catlin's portrait at the Smithsonian which seems to focus on his nose, an important organ for one who was accustomed to nosing around in alien cultures. Perhaps to emulate Catlin, my boyhood hero, my 1977 self-portrait focuses on my nose, which follows on from Rembrandt's focus on his nose, and there were other artists' noses to follow. Otherwise, I seem dazed, open-mouthed, hangdog, and indecisive. The worst was yet to come, and maybe I sensed that.

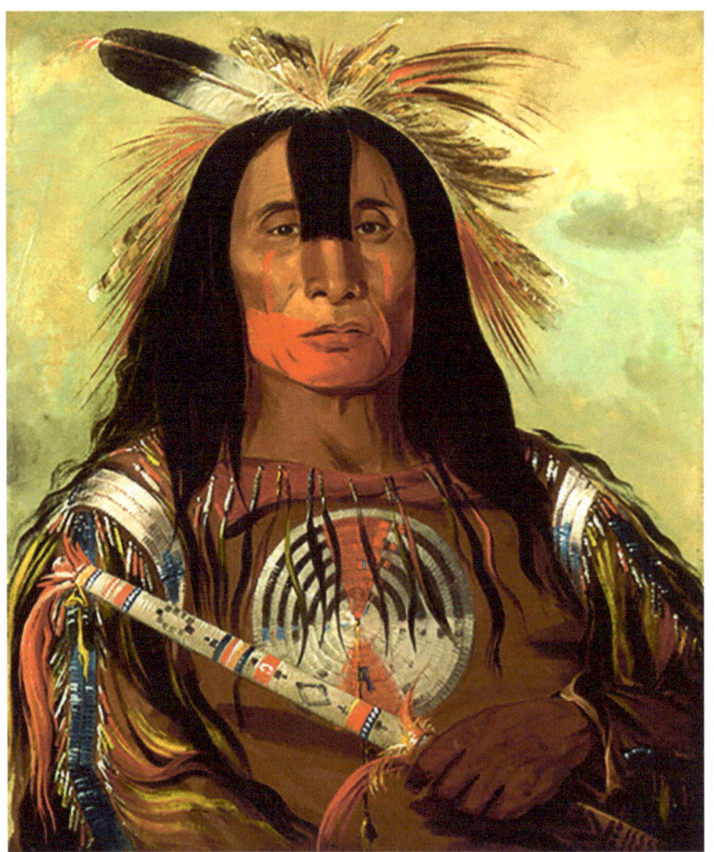

Buffalo Bull Back Fat, Head Chief of the Blood Tribe, by George Catlin, 1832, oil on canvas, 29" x 24" (73.7 cm x 60.9 cm), Smithsonian American Art Museum, Washington D.C.

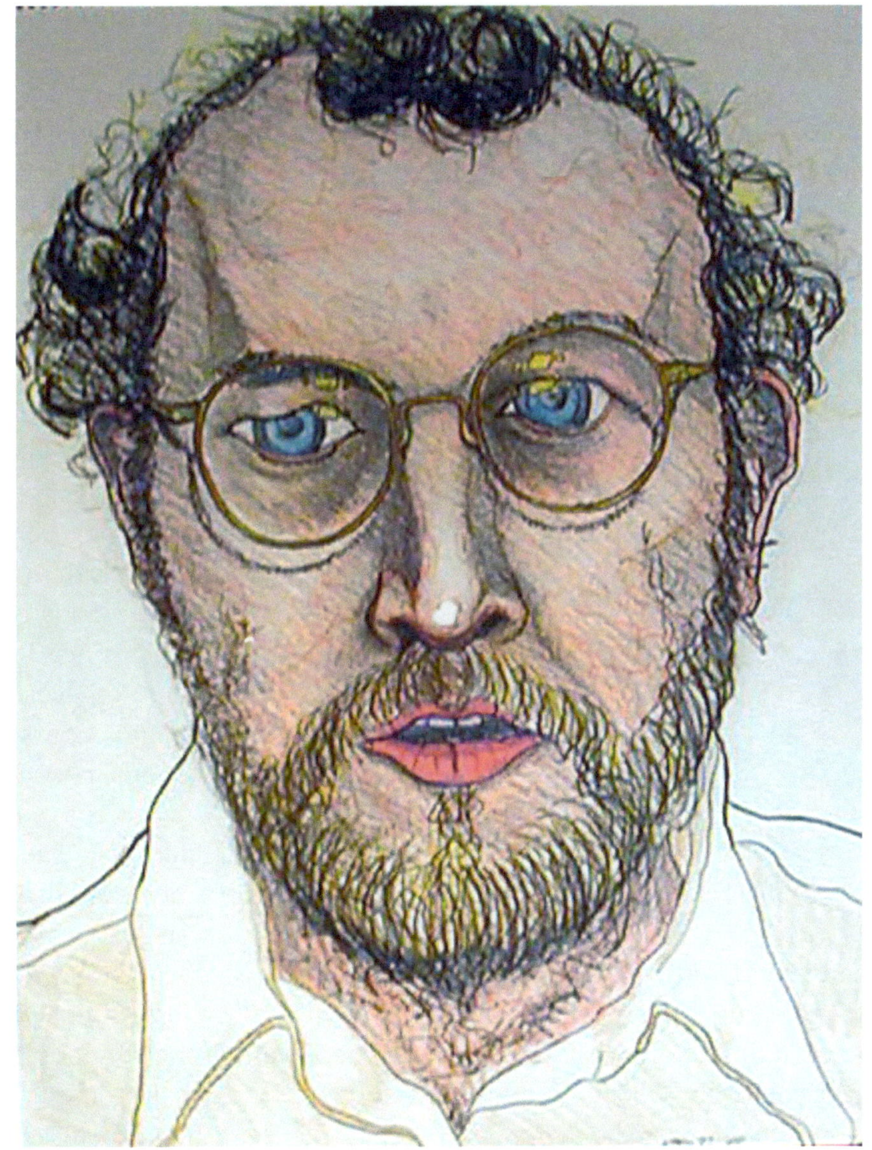

Self-portrait, 1978, Carlton Davis, 18" × 24" (45.72 cm × 60.96 cm) colored pencil on paper

CHAPTER 5

1978
INSIDERS AND OUTSIDERS

n 1977, Gary Gilmore, a convicted murderer, was executed by firing squad at the Utah State Prison. He claimed he'd enjoyed killing and wanted to die as he'd lived, by the gun. "Let's do it," he'd drawled as a black sackcloth hood was lowered over his head. Government gunmen drew a chalk circle target on his black t-shirt, strapped him to a chair, and finished him off with six bullets to his coal black heart from behind a black screen into which they'd cut small holes and inserted the barrels of their military rifles. I imagined joy in the eyes of the anonymous witnesses and the Governor of Utah's delight at the speedy dispatch of a murderous madman. Violence, particularly gun violence, is an outlet for all kinds of internal pressures that most of us hold in abeyance by willful self-control, tranquilizing ourselves with drugs or religion, indulging at our own risk, recanting in the presence of fellow sufferers, and finding ways to assuage them before they become life-threatening to us or the public-at-large.

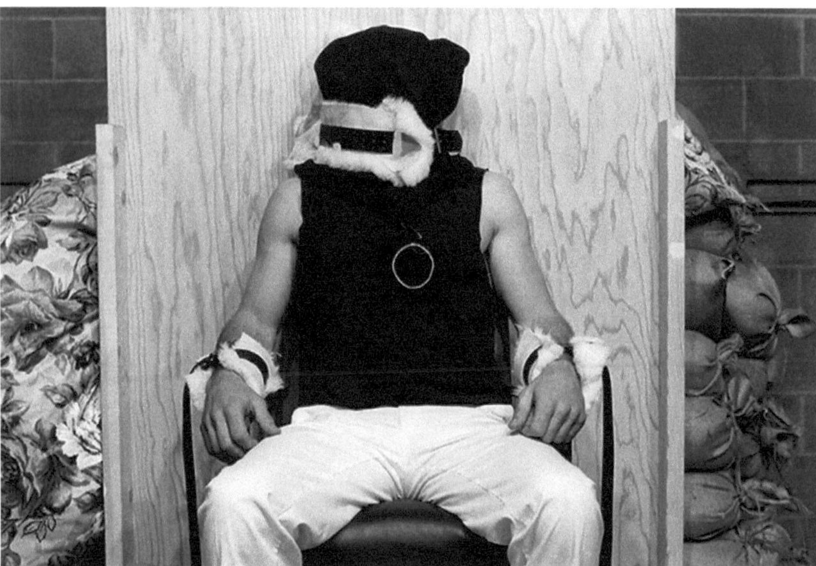

Gary Gilmore's execution by firing squad, 1977, Utah State Prison

Not long after Johanna and I arrived in Laramie, I became aware of the extent to which gun culture and abandonment pervade the forlorn existence of many men in the American West whose firearms provide the antidote to their fears. The *Laramie Boomerang*'s crime column kept me abreast of the body count of men discovered rotting in rented rooms, crumpled beside the railroad tracks, pulverized by high-velocity traffic on the I-80 straightaway, and shot in senseless confrontations with others or themselves.

Laramie residents were divided into two groups: Outsiders and Insiders. Outsiders arrived as visitors or transplants, usually from more densely populated places. Our first contacts with Insiders were generally reassuring. We found them pleasant and accommodating, but their smiles were shields. They resented that we could come and go at will while they remained stuck in the superior boondocks. The prairie beyond Laramie's two-story brick buildings and the I-80 was littered with rusted vehicles, ruined shacks, and bags of trash. A wide railroad freight yard divided the town between the haves and have-nots. The north-south access road was lined with gas stations, cheap motels, and illuminated pylon signs. Romantic notions of beautiful, unspoiled Wyoming morphed into a more violent and desperate reality.

Three events hastened our departure. Every day, I watched an old man come out of the rundown hotel on First Street with a four-step ladder perched over his shoulder and a dog at his side. He set up his ladder beside the tracks just beyond the station house and sat there for hours with his dog watching the freight trains pass. One day, he vanished. I asked people if they knew where he was. No one knew anything, not even his name. Ten days later, I read a report in the *Boomerang* that a rancher had found the body of a man, Eugene German, in a mud-

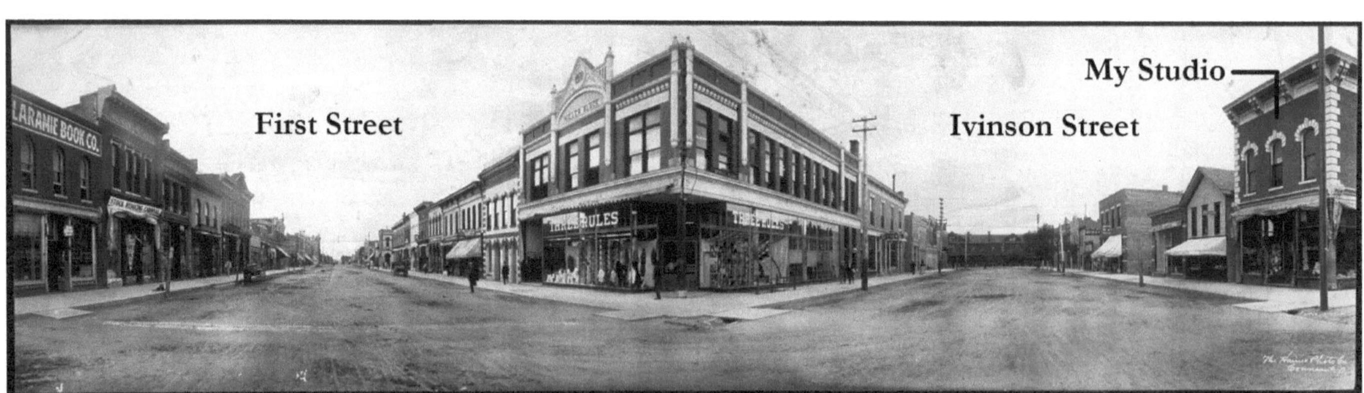

Laramie Wyoming's historic district, 1906, photographer unknown

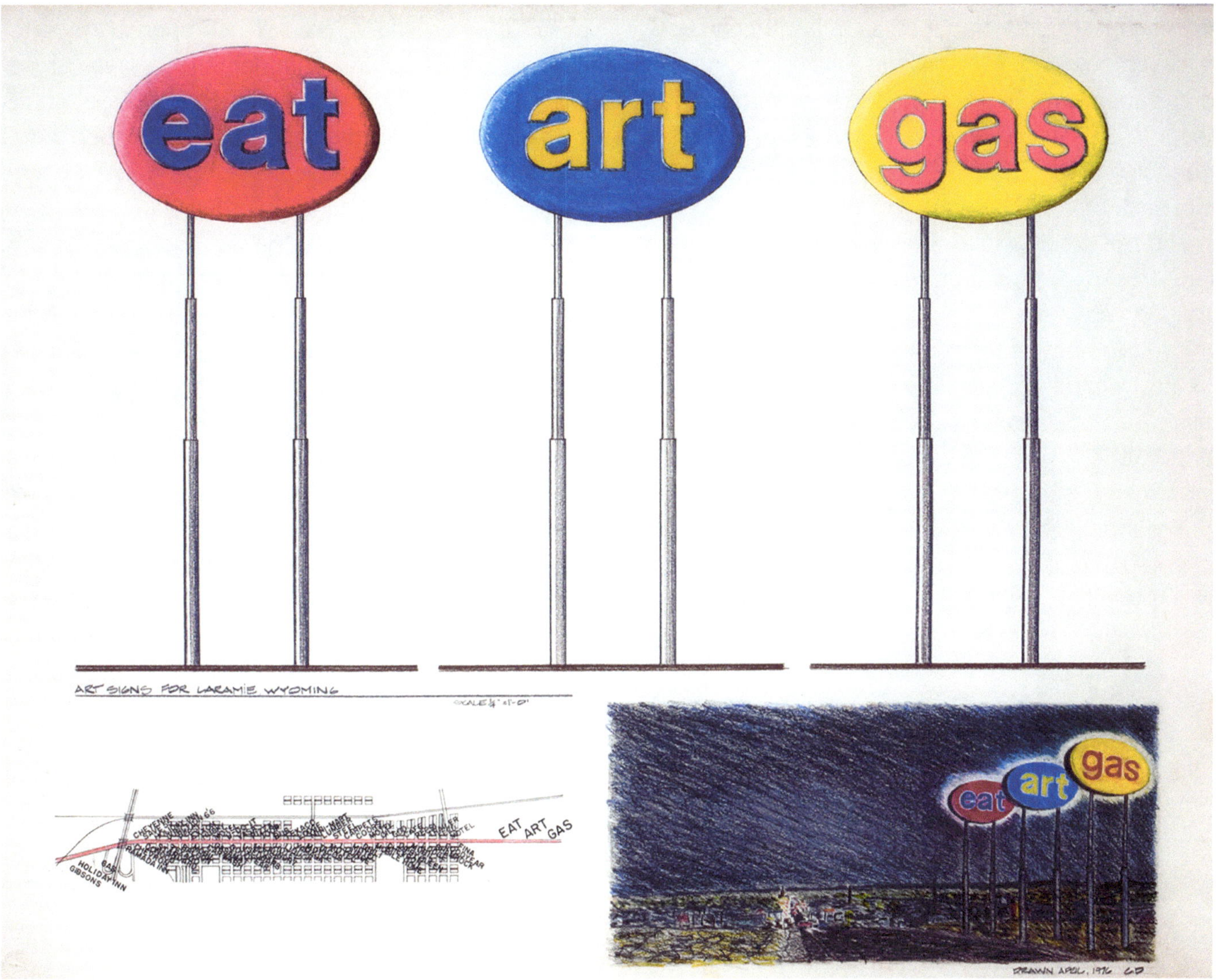

Eat, Art, Gas drawing, 1978, Carlton Davis, colored pencil and rapidograph type on paper, 18" × 24" (45.72 cm × 60.96 cm)

clogged waterhole. It had been partially devoured by coyotes. His dog had disappeared.

Death came one step closer. Kenny Harmes, a sometime bartender, died in a room down the hall from our apartment. He had been reported missing for weeks. When she noticed the stench, Johanna begged me to call the cops. As we waited for them to arrive, I jimmied open his door with a paint spatula. Kenny's remains oozed into the dull brown carpet. His nose had a boil at the tip and his head was a huge beige balloon. Rigor mortis had stiffened his Popeye arms. His feet were translucent and looked like pillows. The two first responders began to argue about how to dispose of the corpse. When they noticed me standing there, gasping and gaping, they ordered me out.

...

Back in my studio, I reminded myself that I was 34 years old and at the beginning of my career as an architect/artist. I threw the windows open to let the cold wind blow Kenny's and Eugene's spirit molecules to nirvana. Despite frequent bouts of anxiety, I had designed and seen into construction my first building, Gem City Bone and Joint Clinic, a clean-lined, solar-heated orthopedic clinic. I had completed two sculptures. The first was *Plow Flower*, a six-feet-high assembly of flat pieces of rusted iron from a junked plowshare. It was a monument-sized paean to old-style agriculture. If I stuck around long enough, maybe I'd find Outsider patrons and become the Henry Moore of Wyoming. My other creation was a prototype made of gridded chicken wire set atop a two-foot-high sheet metal box. It was the first of what would be many attempts to make semi-transparent sculptures out of quarter-inch gridded wire. I learned to solder clean corners and enjoyed the material's malleability. In the process, I created a minefield. If I slipped or stumbled, I would resemble St. Sebastian pierced with tiny wire arrows. It never occurred to me to hire someone to sweep or straighten the place.

The most compelling reason to leave Laramie was captured in a drawing of my pregnant partner. A full-time clerical job well below Johanna's skillset helped keep my 'full-time artist' boat afloat, but it was only possible when she worked. When she was around, her very presence was a condemnation. I was broke, she was fed up, and sex was no longer a fix-all. Time to take the Outsider prerogative: exit.

Not surprisingly, that year's self-portrait felt unfinished. I thought the lines were finicky, the facial rendering had little power, the shading was ordinary, and the expression was bland yet fearful. It was, to some degree, the product of my domestic exile and the deaths of two men whose existences were so inconsequential that they had gone unnoticed. The man whose name was generally unknown died like a dog in a muddy ditch and was cannibalized by coyotes. The other, Kenny, the bartender, went missing in his room and no one cared. The ugliness I had seen down the hall propelled the drawing, which I worked upon feverishly without deliberation. I thought I could erase the odor of rotten flesh, which I believed had penetrated the air, the walls, and my body. The yellow blotches on my glasses were the color of Kenny's corpse. The heart-shaped nasal mark recalled Kenny's boil and was also my salute to Rembrandt. Was I subconsciously mourning the passing of an expendable self?

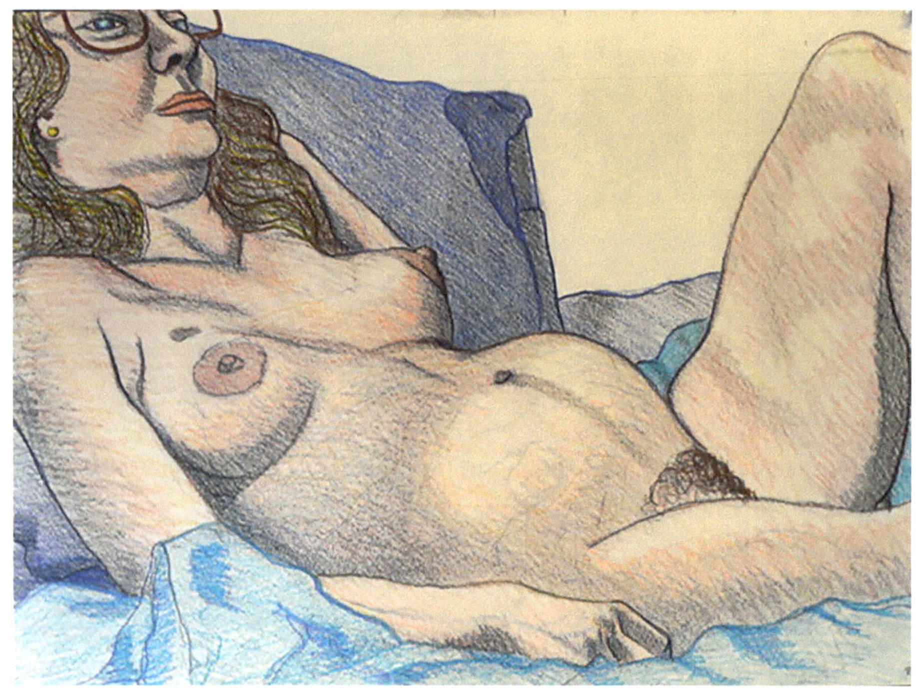

Johanna, 1977, Carlton Davis, colored pencil on paper, 18" × 24" (45.72 cm × 60.96 cm)

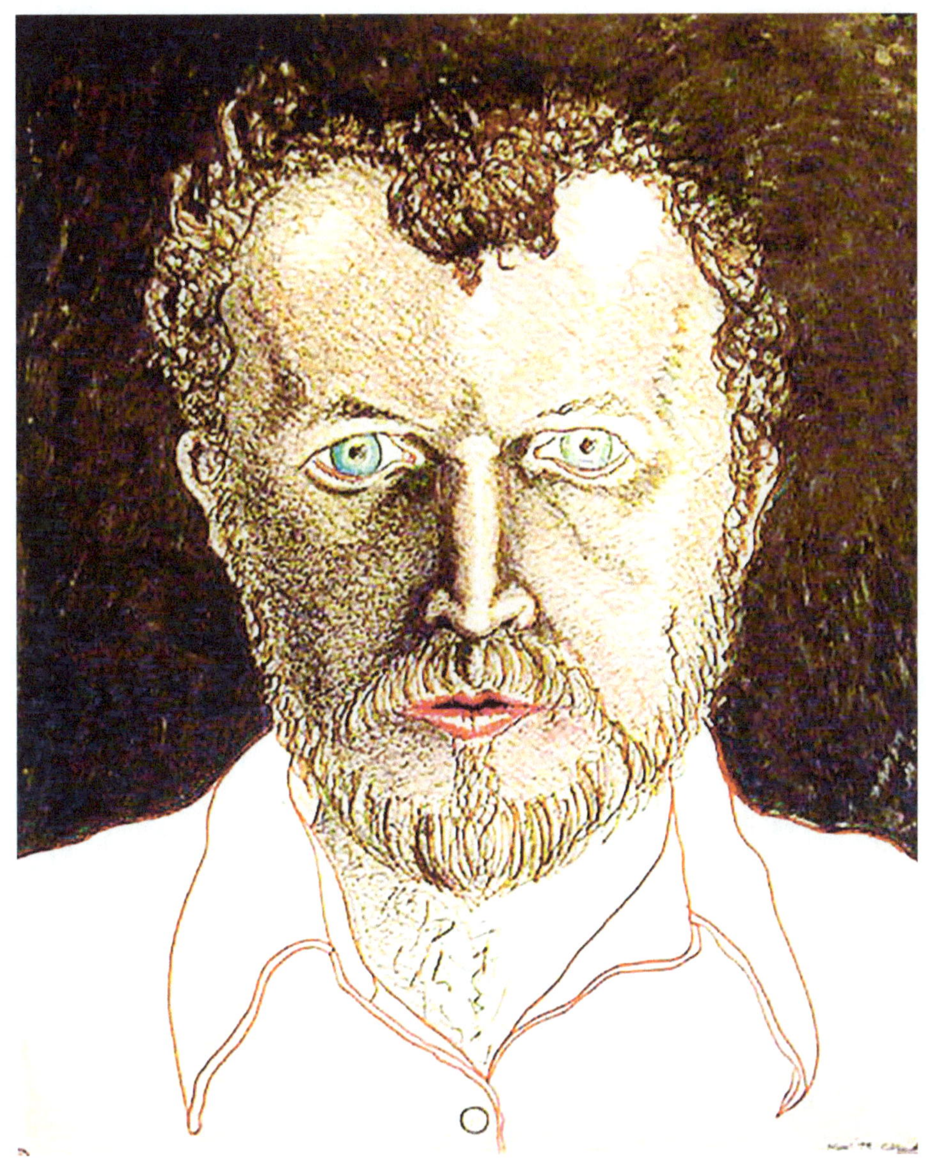

Self-portrait, 1979, Carl Davis, colored pencil & ink on paper, 24" × 18" (60.96 cm × 45.72 cm)

CHAPTER 6

1979
SAN FRANCISCO NIGHTMARES

It is 223 miles from Laramie to Green River, Wyoming. Green River is 169 miles northeast of Salt Lake City, Utah. I stopped at what I imagined as the antediluvian Mesopotamian landscape long enough to photograph Johanna with our beautiful daughter. We were pilgrims in panic and, in my case, psychological disintegration. On the 353-mile leg from Salt Lake City to Winnemucca, Nevada, the silence was broken only by Sarah's vociferous demands to suckle. I observed the nursing couple from the driver's seat and remembered when Johanna's breasts were my delight. The 262 miles from Winnemucca to Reno, Nevada, ground my soul to powder. I slowed down in Reno to photograph two neon cowpokes in chaps with arms folded and attempted to initiate a discussion on illuminated signs, but Johanna would have none of it. On the final 250-mile leg from Reno to San Francisco, my dependents slept.

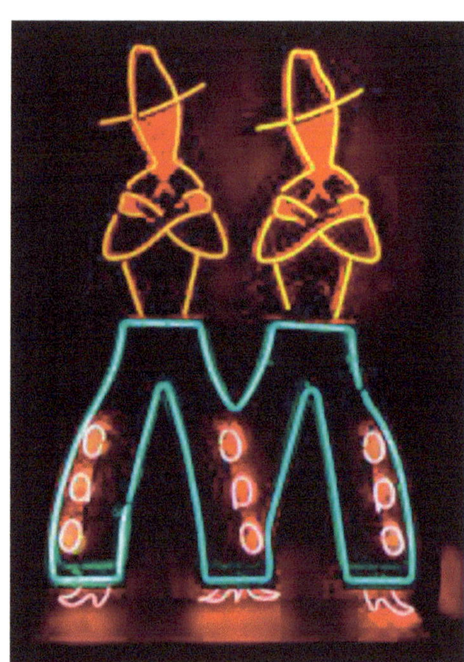

Johanna and Sarah, 1978, Great Salt Lake Desert, photograph by Carlton Davis

We were warned by friends that moving, changing jobs, and caring for an infant at the same time was a recipe for disaster, but I was heedless. San Francisco embodied all my fantasies: the Pacific Ocean, streetcars, jazz and poetry in the coffee houses, and alternative galleries open to new and interesting work. The art museums in Golden Gate Park were warehouses of inspiration. The City by the Bay was the perfect place for my art to bloom.

However, I had mouths to feed. I vowed to give the architectural profession one more shot and soon regretted my decision. The firm that employed me was mediocre and devoted to the 'Bay Area style,' featuring redwood siding and shed roofs, the antithesis of the Post-Modernist design philosophy I had absorbed at Yale. Junior architects worked long hours for a pittance. Most of my cohort spent lunch hours smoking pot and griping in a nearby park.

Neon sign, Reno, Nevada

Much to Johanna's displeasure, I took long, compulsive runs to relieve my frustration and explore the city. We were trapped behind separate fences, like the menacing wire one in sculptor George Segal's installation honoring Holocaust victims adjacent to the Palace of the Legion of Honor. Most of the ghostly white figures were sprawled on the ground within the three-sided concrete enclo-

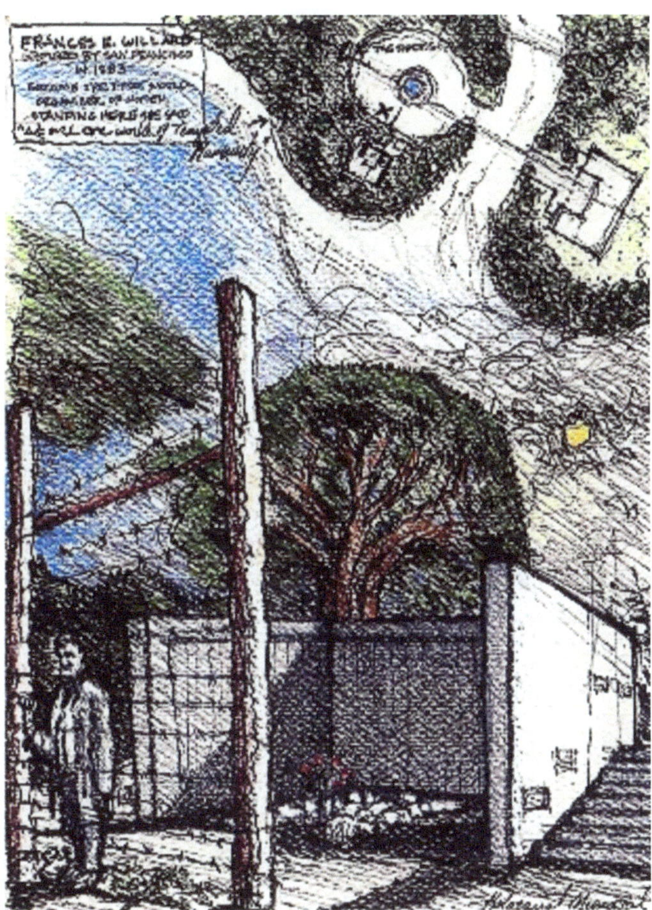

Sketch of George Segal's Holocaust Memorial in San Francisco, 1979, Carlton Davis, colored pencil and ink on paper, 12" × 9" (30.4 cm × 20.6 cm), private collection

Nine days later, Mayor George Moscone and Supervisor Harvey Milk, the city's first openly gay political appointee, were murdered by their colleague, Supervisor Dan White. At the time, I was enrolled in a three-day marathon psychic cleansing known as Erhardt Sensitivity Training (EST), which I hoped would liberate me from the plague of depression. The so-called 'trainers' harangued more than 1,000 participants for hours on end. Bathroom breaks were subject to debate. I was told that the reason my life failed to satisfy me was that I was not 'experiencing my experiences.' I was urged to let go of my mental restrictions and believe that my life would improve if I let myself explore childhood trauma.

The Marin Civic Center resounded with tearful lamentations and manic glee as we EST trainees dredged up disturbing experiences we had buried. I started to shout, "I won't go! I won't go!" at the top of my lungs as I remembered being dragged by the arm, age five, from the back seat of a car and attempting to free myself from my grandfather's grip as he dragged me into a foster home where I was confined for almost a year and repeatedly raped by older boys. After my EST 'graduation,' I went back to our apartment feeling exultant and relieved.

sure, while a lone male figure stood gazing out at the free world.

At the urging of their leader, Jim Jones, more than 900 members of the People's Temple, not far from where we lived, committed suicide in Guyana, a former Dutch colony north of Brazil. While jogging past the cult's abandoned headquarters on my way to the Bay Bridge, I noticed fallen leaves, small cones, and desiccated seedpods underfoot. I gathered three samples of each thinking they could commemorate the victims of Jones's demonic spiritual scam. I had converted one bedroom of our apartment into a studio, and there, I made several sets of character studies of the decaying vegetable matter I had salvaged from the perimeter of the shuttered and boarded-up Bay Area "Temple."

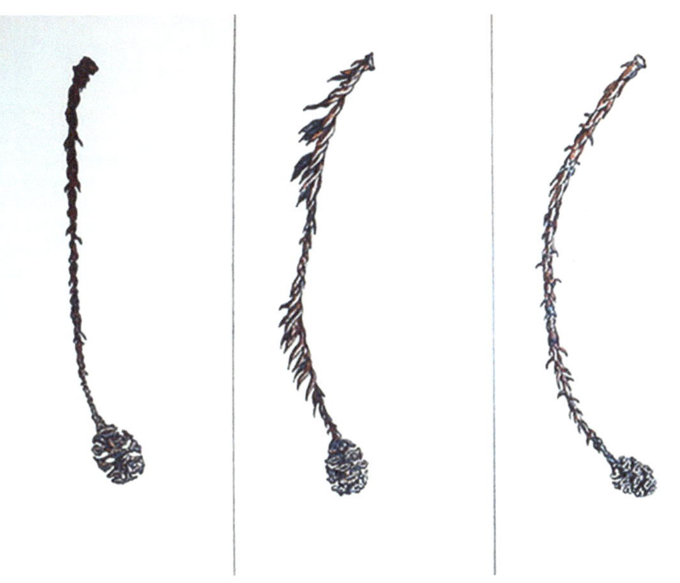

Three Cones, Three Pods, 1979, Carlton Davis, colored pencil on paper, two drawings, 19" × 24" (48.26 cm × 60.69 cm)

The ridiculous aftermath of the murders of Mayor Moscone and Supervisor Milk was their assailant's acquittal by what became known as the 'Twinkie Defense.' His attorneys claimed his uncontrolled consumption of junk food was at the root of his homi-

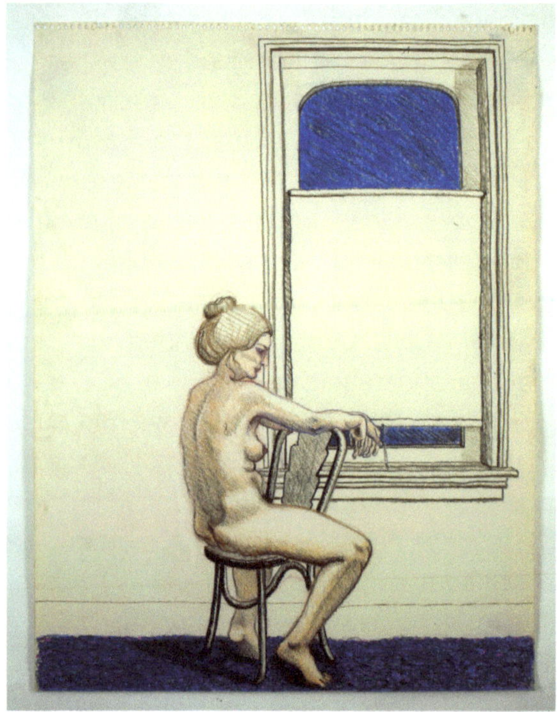

Johanna on chair, 1978, colored pencil on paper, 18" × 12" (20.32 cm × 30.48 cm)

cidal rage. This set off a series of what the press termed White Night riots, in which outraged leather boys and transvestites battled police.

My life as a Bay Area artist was scuttled by the escalating tension between me and my wife. I made her the subject of a final portrait. Johanna's back is turned to me, as it had been for quite a while.

I started having sex with Bonnie, a gracious office colleague. She stayed late to help me with a project I was working on, and we took advantage of the empty office to enjoy each other. On weekends, I abandoned the nursing couple and biked across the Golden Gate Bridge to Marin County where Bonnie lived to enjoy an intimacy that Johanna no longer allowed. Infidelity was the last straw.

I went to Guerneville with my friend Scott to wander among the redwoods. He had a thriving pot garden in the thick of the forest and an Airstream trailer where we could smoke, eat, and crash. But nothing calmed my anxiety. In the fall, I accepted a teaching position in UCLA's Architecture program and a part-time job at the Urban Innovations Group (UIG). I planned to try my luck in Los Angeles

Seven hundred-mile round-trip drives from LA to San Francisco and back every weekend rid me of my last shreds of civility. One day, as we argued by the shallow lake in Golden Gate Park, Johanna tried to yank Sarah from a carrier on my back, dropped her in the lake, and broke her arm. On another occasion, she screamed and spat at me while our toddler trembled at her side. I followed them back to our apartment and, when Johanna tried to take refuge in the bedroom, prevented her from slamming the door in my face. An instant later, my hands were around her throat. She pleaded with me to let her live for our daughter's sake. Reluctantly, I released her.

Years later, I visited a friend in prison who had killed his wife with a kitchen knife he had wrested from her grasp. He was serving a sentence of 25 years to life. I could have been his cellmate. I lived alone for the next decade.

> "I shot the sheriff, but I didn't shoot no deputy
> All around in my hometown
> They tryin' to track me down, yeah
> They say they want to bring me in guilty
> For the killing of a deputy, for the life of a deputy."

I danced solo to Bob Marley's reggae anthem before I made my 1979 self-portrait, feeling as desperate and defiant as Gary Gilmore facing the firing squad. My lips are pursed, not to beg forgiveness but rather to blurt, "I don't give a damn." Violence had invaded my brain and turned my heart to coal. With my ego aflame, I compared myself to Caravaggio the killer, Marinetti the fascist, and the more recent misogynist painters Francis Bacon and Lucien Freud. I would calm my qualms among the pliant palms of La La Land.

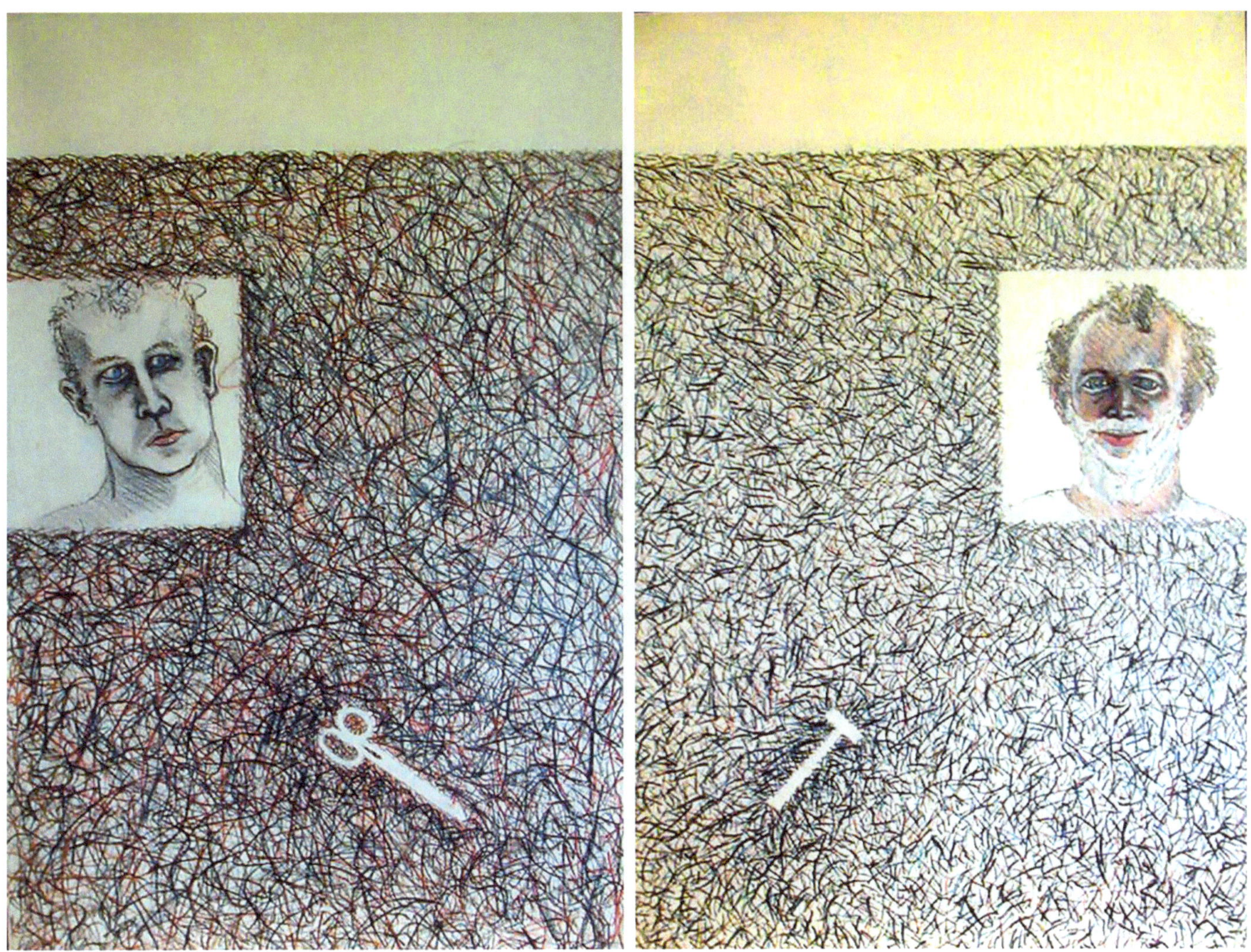

Two self-portraits, 1980, Carlton Davis, colored pencil on paper, 40" × 26" (101.6 cm × 60.04 cm)

CHAPTER 7

1979-1980
TREMORS AND TRANSITIONS

n San Francisco, I spent 1978 and part of 1979 living in the city with my wife Johanna and our baby daughter, and the other part in Los Angeles. I told myself I had not given up on architecture or my marriage, but I resented Johanna's obvious displeasure with everything about me. The divorce bell was tolling and its reverberations in my often-clouded cranium were hard to ignore. In San Francisco, I designed buildings with redwood siding and 45-degree pitched roofs, which was fuel for more disgruntlement.

In LA, I taught at UCLA's Architecture School and coordinated the work of architectural students at the recently opened Urban Innovations Group. UIG was a working office undertaking real projects and competitions and employed students as part of the firm's affiliation with UCLA's architecture program. My job there was to mentor new students who had no idea how to put construction documents together and to ensure they kept up with their coursework.

The biggest plus for me was getting to work with the UCLA architecture dean, Charles Moore. He had

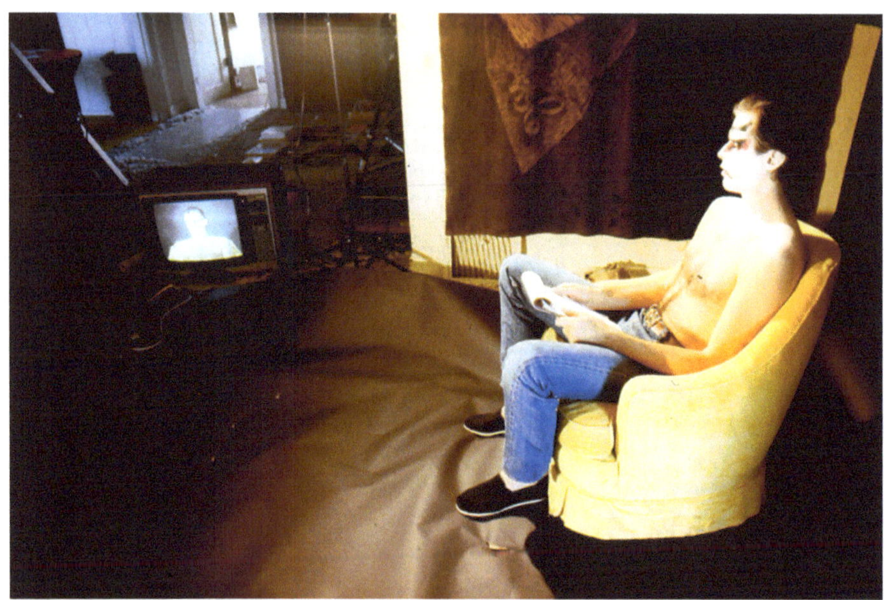

Gary Lloyd rehearsing for his performance at the Long Beach Museum of Art, 1980, photograph by Carlton Davis

been the dean and my favorite teacher at the Yale School of Architecture when I was working toward my master's degree. At UIG, I drew up his conceptual plans for the proposed redevelopment of Bunker Hill, a downtown Los Angeles landmark.

Each weekend, I would fly back to San Francisco and deal with the dissolution of my marriage. I was an oversized jockey on a wooden horse in Golden Gate Park, bobbing and spinning with my daughter in my arms. Johanna had no interest in coparenting if it meant leaving San Francisco. Southern California, especially LA, was hell on earth to most Northern Californians. Who would want to live there?

Two UCLA colleagues, video artist John Sturgeon and his sculptor friend Gary Lloyd, offered to take me in. Torrential rains inundated the usually smoggy city that summer. Our Hollywood bungalow had six-inch-wide exterior cracks that allowed water easy access. John and Gary were rehearsing for roles as Japanese media critics, recording themselves running their lines in ersatz Japanese and staying absorbed in the video playbacks amid a serpentine tangle of electric cords while water ponded in the living room. John's painted Kabuki face was clown white with thick black greasepaint slashes above his eyes and scarlet rouged lips. He was the Japanese Mexican shaman

'Don Alkemiko.' Gary sat shirtless in a chair with script in hand while live wires were about to sizzle in the water near his feet. As someone who knew a thing or two about electricity, I worried that the bungalow could catch fire in the flood.

When I confronted my housemates with my misgivings, Don Alkemiko smiled, bowed, and said,

"Tell me, mighty foreigner, have you lived with artists before?"

"Never. Why do you ask?"

"The artist's life is a twoness. We survive to flourish."

"Then unplug! Right now! This place could go up in flames!"

The Kabuki men were silent, unfazed by my warning. I sped from the site, resolved to return only after the rain stopped and the puddles on the floor had dried.

A day or two later, LA's smoggy summer returned. The bungalow survived intact, and heart-warming camaraderie replaced my housemates' defiant nonchalance. Sturgeon and I decided to take a jaunt to Death Valley, which I had heard about since I was a kid but had never visited. On the way there, I mentioned how impressed I was by Frida Kahlo's double self-portrait *Las Dos Fridas* at the Modern Art Museum in Mexico City.

I drove my pickup and used four-wheel drive to get through what was called the Devil's Golf Course, a super dry, super hot obstacle course of salty hummocks separating us from the Panamint Mountains and a willow grove oasis on a rocky promontory that John remembered from a previous trip. When we arrived, I read a poem written by my friend Peter.

Trova Frideña

Frida Kahlo sprang to life
in her hand a palette knife
brow and upper lip hirsute
Diego Rivera in hot pursuit
a leftist artist of mighty girth
at one glance knew her worth
took her to New York, the vandal
for the Rockefeller mural scandal
then hooked up with her kid sis
and blew their boho life to bits!
A comrade guest gave her the hots
but when old Trotsky plotzed
pickaxed to death in Mexico City
Frida called Stalin "super shitty"
declared his revenge "anticipated"
though her heart was devastated
she soldiered on in her life of pain
with imperious disregard for gain.
Séances, phrenology, aged tequila
absolutamente nada could heal her.
Monkeys howl & parrots screech
Frida managed one last speech
(as an odalisque in Tehuana duds
she bid farewell to her bosom buds)
¡adios mis guapas hermanitas
tengan cuidado pues los fascistas
van comer sus chucheríacitas!
　　　—Poem by Peter Lownds

I understood *Absolutamente nada* and *demasiado* but not the last three lines. John translated, "Farewell, my lovely little sisters! Be careful or the fascists are going to eat your little tidbits!"

My fear and distrust of women had irretrievably damaged my marriage, estranged me from our infant daughter, and hampered my ability to make art, I realized. John and I camped beneath the heat-strangled willows and ingested the psilocybin mushrooms we had brought. I began to hallucinate, watching the rocks turn liquid with seething energy.

The pressure of centuries on the surface pushed and lifted the fault lines in reds, browns, yellows, and blues, which swirled into vortexes

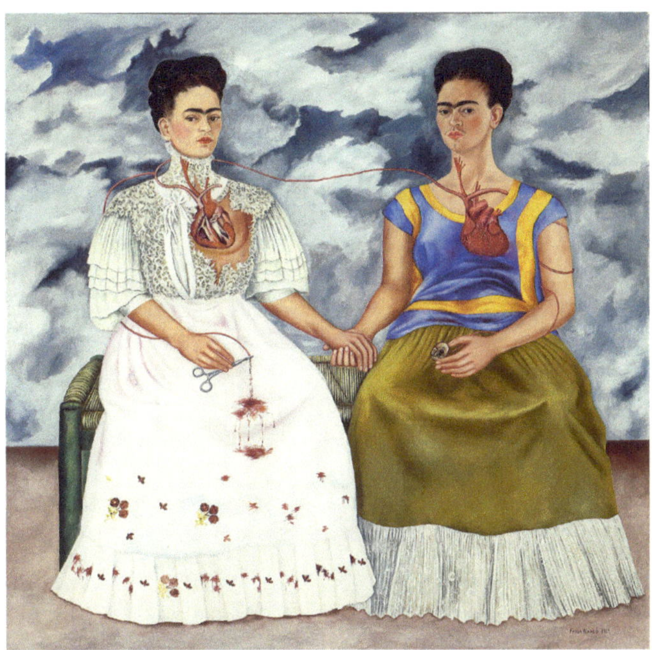

Las Dos Fridas (The Two Fridas), 1939, by Frida Kahlo, oil on canvas, 68.3" × 68" (173.5 cm × 173 cm), Museo de Arte Moderno, Mexico City, Mexico

and pulsated with lava hotspots. The soles of my feet burned as I followed the dry white sand of a one-time creek bed. I removed my clothes and lay down in the sand. The heat entered my heels and spread up through my calves, thighs, buttocks, back, neck, and head. I heard a fluttering in my ears. My guts were churning with excitement and fear. Frida spoke to me then, saying,

"If you look at the sun, you'll go blind!"

"It's fucking hot!" I screamed.

My skin felt like a lizard's and moved of its own accord. I experienced an intense sexual pulsation and rolled over, staring up at the yellow disc despite Frida's warning. I felt two selves inside me. One was a woman. I touched her breasts, pinched her nipples, and felt the molten lava begin to flow. This was what it was like to be at one with nature.

Not long after my experience in Death Valley, Gary Lloyd and I moved downtown into separate lofts. There, I committed fully to living the artist's life. Performance art was all the rage in the early 1980s, so I converted a loading dock that was part of my street-level loft into a drive-by gallery called The Art Dock, where I staged exhibitions and performances, mine and those of artists in the neighborhood whose work I admired.

In 1980, I drew a pair of mirror images of my altered selves. I wanted the portraits to be transitional, so I kept them small and filled most of the background with the instruments and detritus of a self-administered haircut. Frida Kahlo admitted to her "lovely little sisters" that she painted herself constantly because she was the only person she knew inside and out.

At age 36, I drew what I saw in the mirror. What was inside had not yet revealed itself, and part of me believed that might never happen. So, I opted for a squatter's life in what used to be Los Angeles' industrial district. Perhaps surviving its many challenges would firm my resolve, make self-expression more fluent, and allow me to live and create with the unimpaired joy of my artist heroes and heroines.

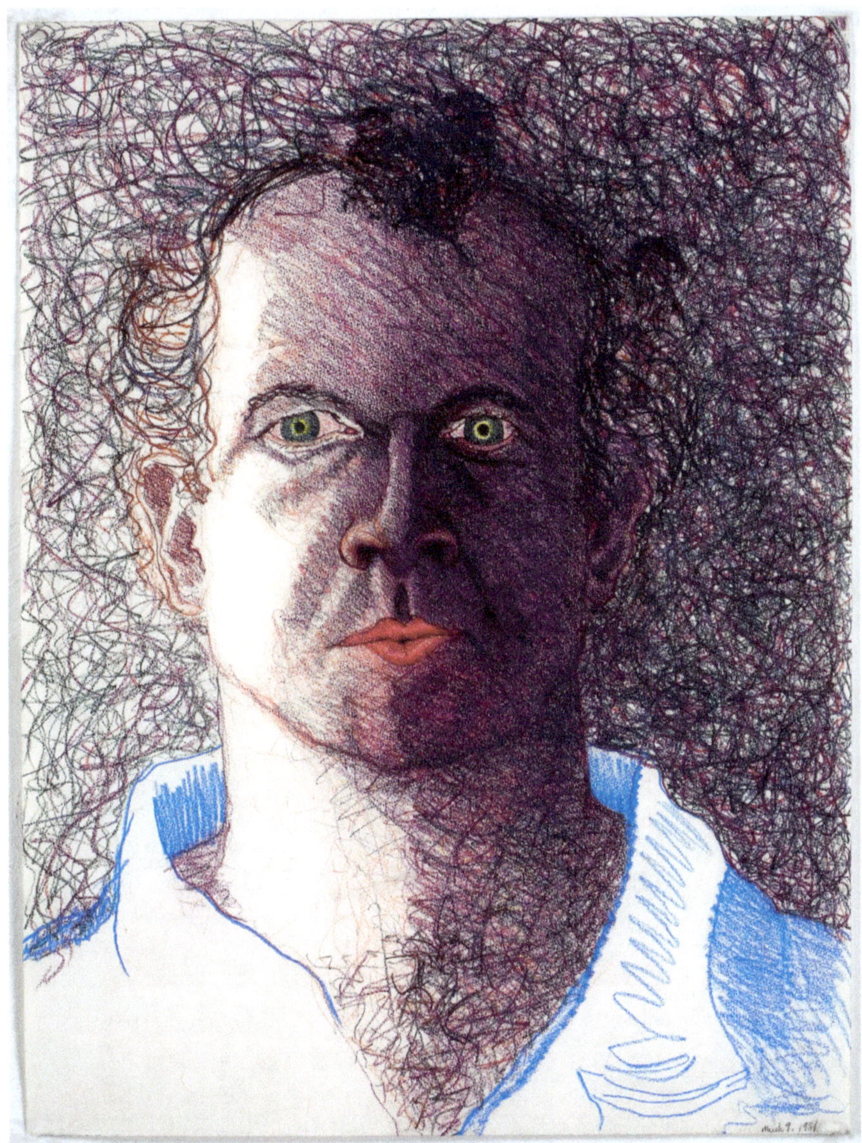

Self-portrait, 1981, Carlton Davis, colored pencil on paper, 30" × 22" (76.2 cm × 55.88 cm)

CHAPTER 8

1981
KNOCKIN' ON THE DEVIL'S DOOR

My life in Los Angeles began with an inner-city real estate deal. My jaw dropped when I first walked into the loft space, one of four on the first floor of 1001 First Street and 112 Center Street, a two-story building constructed in 1881 as a pickle works called Citizens Warehouse. There were 2,200 square feet of space. There was no plumbing, no electricity, and no drywall—just space,

glorious space stripped down to the studs. The rental price was 20 cents per square foot. I signed the lease immediately.

The defining features of what would be my home and studio for the next ten years were a roll-up metal door that revealed a space large enough for men to have loaded and unloaded a railroad freight car, a wooden floor that had lost its luster, six redwood

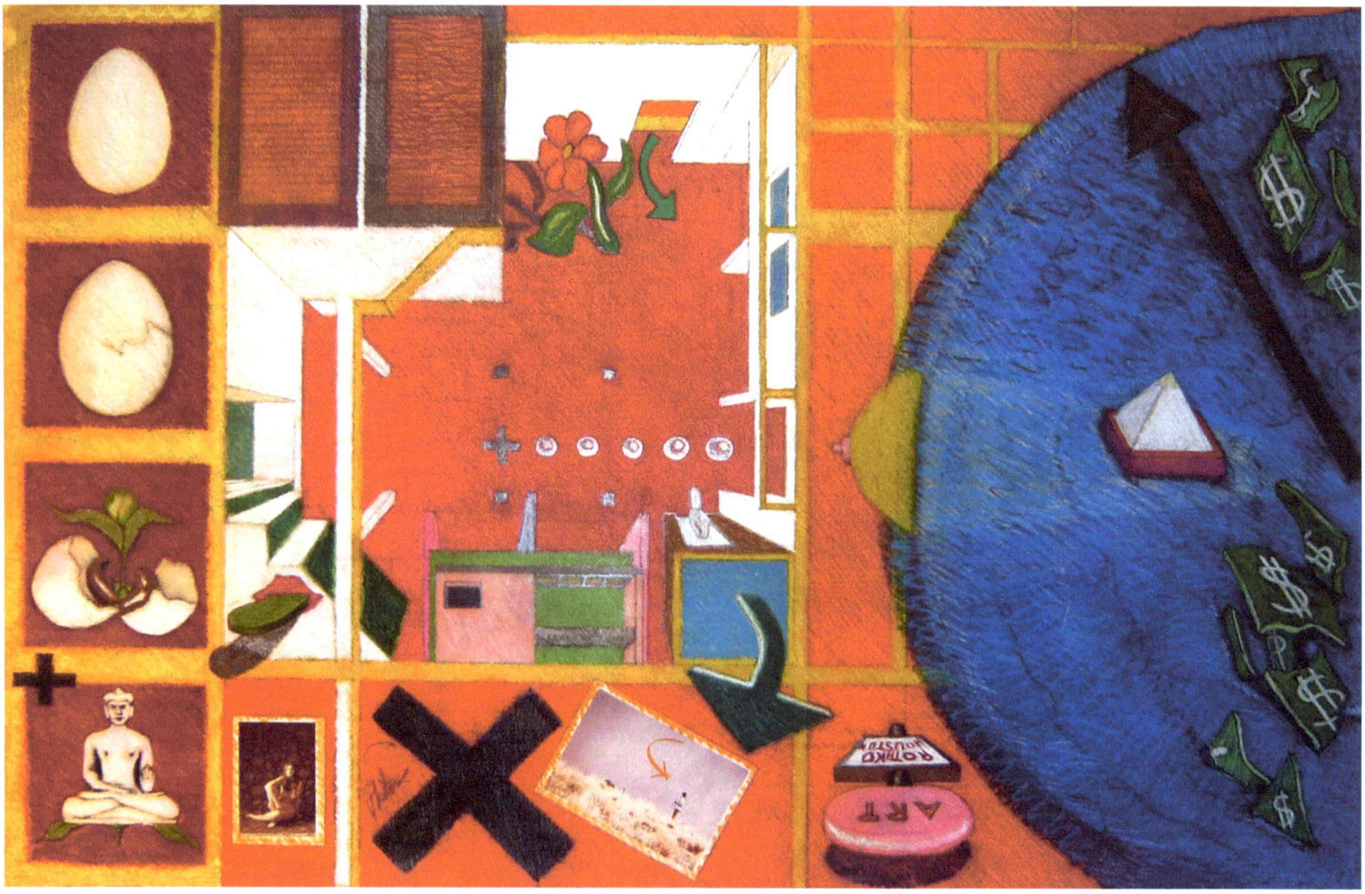

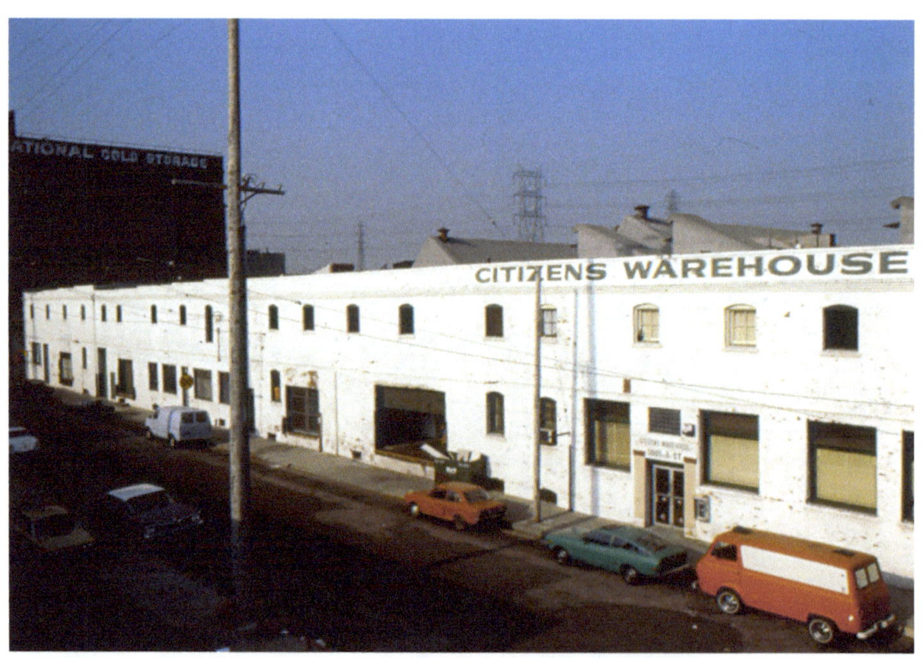

The loft, Los Angeles, 1981, Carlton Davis, colored pencil & photographs, 37" × 24" (94 cm × 61 cm), collection of Elizabeth Des Marais

columns with wedge-shaped capitals, and two staircases, one of which went nowhere; the up-staircase risers were boarded over at the second floor. The other led to a basement full of pickle vats still there from the pickle works days. My primary tasks were to install drywall over the studs, install electrical outlets, block off the stairway to the basement, install a toilet and shower, add batt insulation with aluminum foil for ceiling sound reduction, create a kitchen space, and sand and coat the floor. I had purchased a short section of Christo's Running Fence, an

Citizens Warehouse, 1001 East First Street, Los Angeles, CA, 1981, photograph by Carlton Davis

installation of his in Northern California; this I used as a curtain to make my bedroom space private. I called it my 'auric egg.' My Running Fence enclosure was envisioned as an oracle for dreams.

After taking care of the necessities, I began to

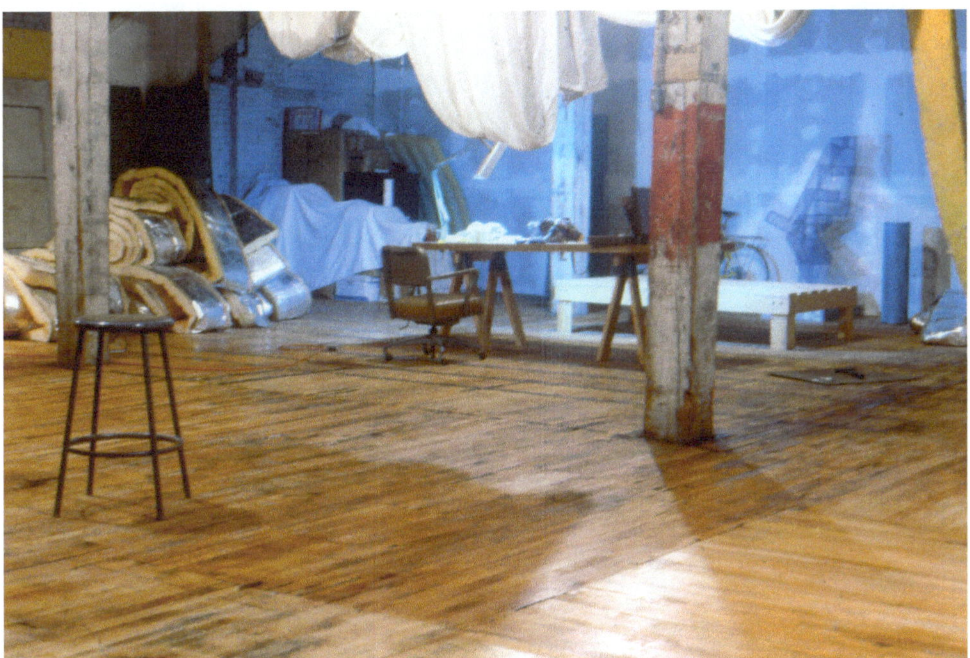

Loft space under construction, 1981, photograph by Carlton Davis

play with the space, built a wall below the stairs to nowhere, and installed a curved plastic laminate tabletop to look like a tongue extending from a curvaceous scarlet mouth I painted on the side of the stair. This is where I placed my phone and answering machine. Next, I created walls without doors to shield the toilet, shower, and kitchen—an assemblage inspired by Gerrit Rietveld, a Dutch architect and celebrated *De Stijl* practitioner. I combined pink and green painted walls with garish wallpaper to create what the French call *quelque chose belle laide*: something so ugly it borders on beauty.

In a state of manic enthusiasm, I made a drawing of the finished studio that included an egg cracking open to reveal a bodhisattva. As a Buddhist seeker following the noble eightfold path, I believed flowers would bloom in my studio and, by practicing daily Tibetan meditation, I'd receive my share of an ocean of wealth sourced by a platform topped with a prismatic pyramid that would deliver it via the bodhisattva's benevolent breast. I attached two photographs to this drawing: one of my wife Johanna, whose return to the family with our baby daughter would augur success, and the other of me standing in the middle of an empty plain with two arrows directing good fortune my way.

The tongue table marked the spot where I exchanged ideas with Giant Jane, the angular 6'-6" transgender singer of the punk band Jane and the Cage. She was an authority on Johnny Rotten and The Sex Pistols, Patti Smith, Robert Mapplethorpe, and the Ramones. Jane let it be known she 'made serious bread' as a dominatrix with an elite clientele. We shared a ceaseless yen for drugs and alcohol. After the bars closed, we went to Zero Zero Club, an after-hours Hollywood bar frequented by the soon-to-be-famous Los Lobos, various wastrels, sycophants, and goths guzzling beer from cans kept in polyurethane coolers. When Zero Zero closed, we went back to my loft to smoke joints, swig tequila, and recall the shenanigans of Grand Guignol-inspired performance artists like Johanna Wendt, who would plunge a butcher's knife into her bulging *cache sexe,* and spewing screams and baby dolls afloat in stage blood. Jane laughed so hard she slid off the chair onto the floor.

"Hey, Jane! Did you know I was once a semi-pro baseball pitcher? Watch this!"

I staggered to my feet, poured what was left of a bottle of tequila down my gullet, and hurled the bottle across the loft, narrowly missing the end of the Christo curtain and penetrating the drywall from which it hung for an instant before shattering on the floor. This is what we called 'wild fun' in

1981. It was also the last time I saw Jane. She called me once from Carpinteria saying she was living in the beachfront mansion of one of her clients and working on her memoirs. People who saw us together assumed we were partners.

My rollicking camaraderie with Jane led me to create Carlotta. Usually, my periods of mania were followed by what I called black brain depression. I possessed two distinct selves. Both seemed to be

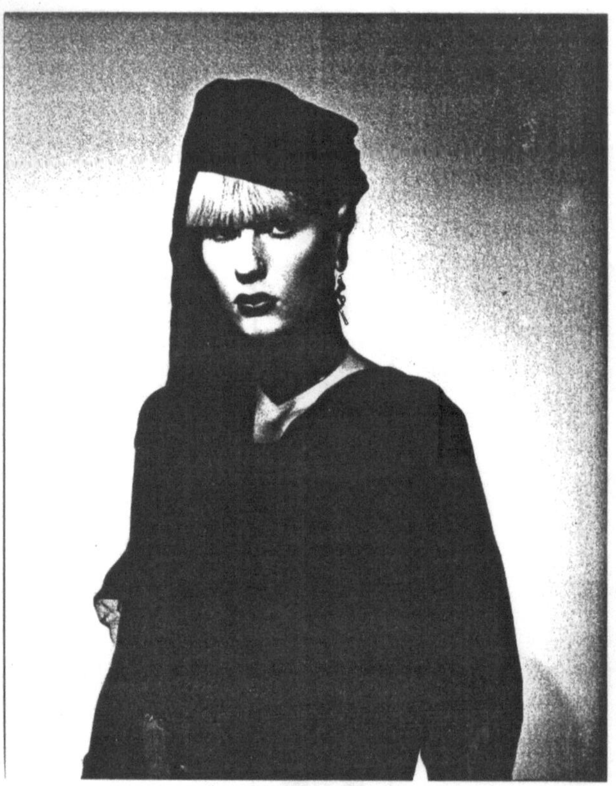

Jane as stern dominatrix, circa 1981 (unknown source)

men, at first, but then it became clear that one was a woman. I called her Carlotta because she was a whole lotta Carl. Carlotta made it clear she wanted to murder Carl because he was a weakling. She dressed in black hose, high heels, a black silk blouse, and a short black skirt. She wore spike-and-chain necklaces and bracelets, a Mao Tse Tung pin large enough to serve as a brooch, and a fluorescent orange wig; she also packed a stainless-steel ice pick in her silver purse. She was far from homicidal, but would not have regretted it if Carl, her deficient

male self, had succumbed to AIDS. Carlotta sprang full-blown from the 'auric egg' in lieu of a merciful and compassionate bodhisattva.

In the early 1980s, the Citizens Warehouse in downtown Los Angeles was a stage set for car chases, arrests, and dramatic confrontations between cops and 'perps' on *Hill Street Blues*. People who seemed vagrant or homeless could be actors or extras made up and costumed to look the part. Beneath the verisimilitude and technical expertise of an Emmy-winning 'cop show' festered decades of police brutality, municipal corruption, and rampant racism.

After the cameras stopped rolling and the trailers and crews departed, degradation remained. The mentally ill and indigent were dumped downtown; they stopped to peer into the murky interior of my street-level loft as they stumbled by. In the reflective glare of a summer afternoon, they did not notice me struggling to meditate. A bag lady in a worn winter coat pushed a shopping cart piled high with salvaged garments. Eight black plastic bags stuffed with crushed aluminum cans dangled from the rigging of her grocery cart. Her partner's left foot had been amputated. With a dingy rag covering his stump, he followed her in a wheelchair powered by his grimy hands, arms, and shoulders. They were on their way to a homeless encampment under the Chavez Street overpass within view of the cold storage building, the duck slaughterhouse, the automobile graveyard, and the LA Piper Technical Center, a fortress at the end of Center Street, three blocks north.

The space left by Giant Jane's departure was followed by the entrance of *latrodectus hesperus*, the western black widow spider. Lots of them. When I moved or lifted materials from the loft's floor, there they were, hanging upside down in the heaps of gridded hardware cloth, the crosses on their abdomens a scarlet warning, "Do not touch!" Acutely aware of the danger within, I wore gloves whenever I lifted my material.

Even scarier were the rats. When I sat on my pillow, folded my legs, and closed my eyes, I tuned

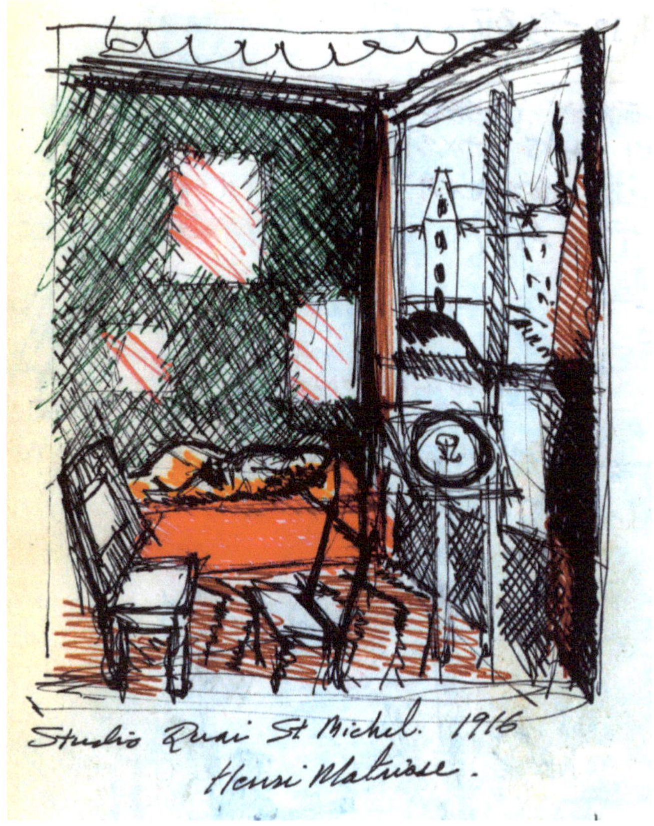

Sketch of Matisse's *Studio, Quai Saint Michel, Paris, 1916*, 1981, Carlton Davis, ink pen on paper, 8.25" x 5.25" (20.9 cm x 12.7 cm)

is focused inward on the disaster that has befallen me. I was beginning to acknowledge the yawning gap between my dreams of glory and my nitty-gritty existence.

In what I hoped would be a therapeutic exercise, I made a sketch of Matisse's painting of his Paris studio in 1916. The painting didn't portray Paris as a 'City of Light,' the capital of the avant-garde. World War I was the main event in 1916 Europe. It was a dark time for Matisse, the leader of the so-called 'Fauves' (the 'wild beast' colorists), whose muted palette reflected his state. His wife and children were trapped in Picardie, close to the carnage of Verdun and the Somme, where hundreds of thousands of French and British troops were machine-gunned, crushed by tanks, bombed from planes, and poisoned by gas. Paris was in mourning during the war. Most art dealers had deserted the city, leaving their former clients to

into their world. Using the rickety cellar staircase to travel to and from their subterranean digs, they were impervious to my existence as they dragged their scaly little feet across the now-resplendent hardwood floor. Their growing ranks were due to the ongoing demolition of the cold storage building next door. I set traps, smearing peanut butter below the steel springs which, I hoped, would function like a guillotine. I baited and set four traps around the studio and resumed my meditation practice. Within moments, I heard a trap snap shut, followed by the high-pitched screams of vermin in agony. Next to a pile of hardware cloth, a gasping rodent stared at me with bulging eyes. It clawed its way out of the trap and began to drag its mangled body toward the cellar stairs. I opened Carlotta's purse, grabbed the icepick, and dispatched the villain. I am visibly shaken in the self-portrait I made in the assassination's aftermath. One eye looks directly at the viewer, while the other

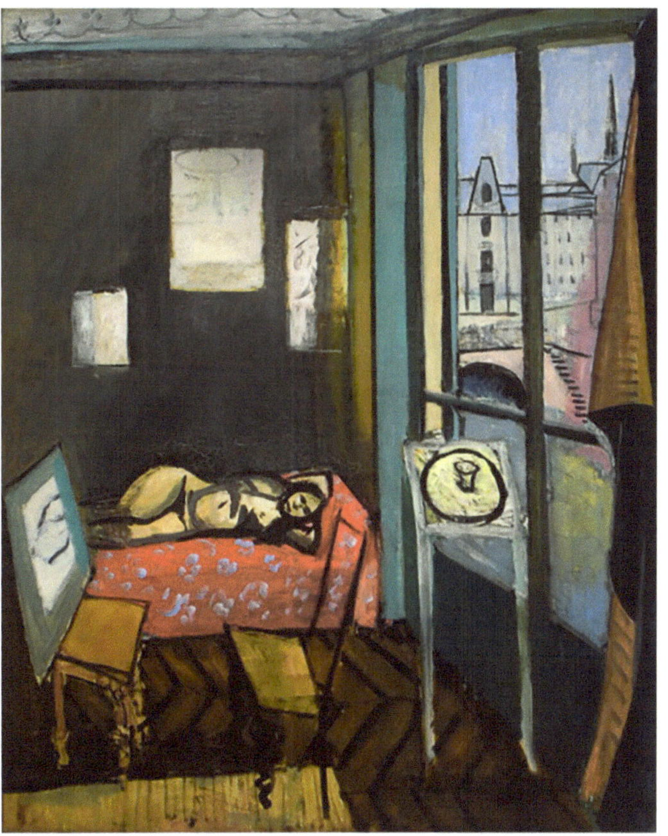

Studio, Quai Saint Michel, Paris, 1916, Henri Matisse, oil on canvas, 58.5" x 46" (147.9 cm x 116.8 cm), The Phillips Collection, Washington D.C.

fend for themselves. Some of Matisse's friends and relatives relocated to New York City, where wealthy Americans' acquisition of their art kept the *avant-garde* alive.

Was I subconsciously mimicking the nadir of my art hero's journey? Endless apprenticeship was a bore. The necessity of supporting myself obliged me to become an employment counselor for furloughed architects. Living in LA's abandoned industrial zone made me aware of the artist's plight in sprawling, smog-choked Angel City. I became a self-appointed spokesperson advocating against a proposed municipal ordinance to ban artists from residing in parking-deficient and code-non-compliant buildings. We would have to bring our lofts into compliance, which was often impossible. My reveries of Montmartre and Montparnasse were interrupted by a panorama of crisscrossing powerlines, blank walls ripe for embellishment, and endless lines of cars parked alongside broken curbs. This was my 'hood,' one I publicly defended and would inhabit for a decade. Meanwhile, I was either high as a kite or stymied by Black Brain. My search for the Buddha's 'middle path' was waylaid.

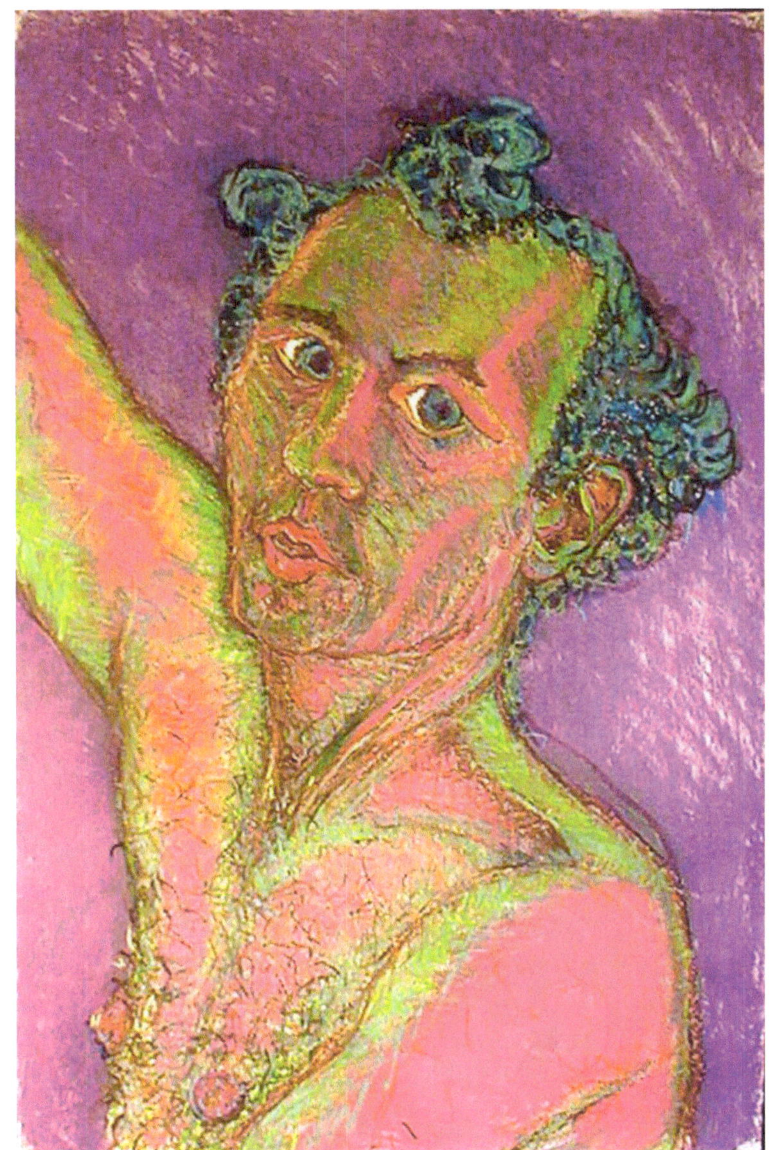

Self-portrait, 1982, Carlton Davis, pastel on paper, 40" × 26" (101.6 cm × 66 cm)

CHAPTER 9

1982-1983
ALLEGORY OF WORMS

"The erect are not eaten by worms," Gary Lloyd proclaimed as he stood next to a monitor displaying a videotape of him bending and gluing metal coins to an armature supporting a human tibia, fibula, and foot. According to him, the most interesting LA artists were denizens of a creative slum located in derelict industrial spaces they were transforming into creative habitats. They would alchemize the moribund lofts of downtown Los Angeles. They were pioneers, alive and erect.

Their art was a radical departure from the chic aesthetic of Santa Monica and Venice Beach where 'light and space' artists Robert Irwin and James Turrell were selling their work nationally and internationally. Downtown LA artists were squatters, scavengers, and survivors at home among the homeless. Jon

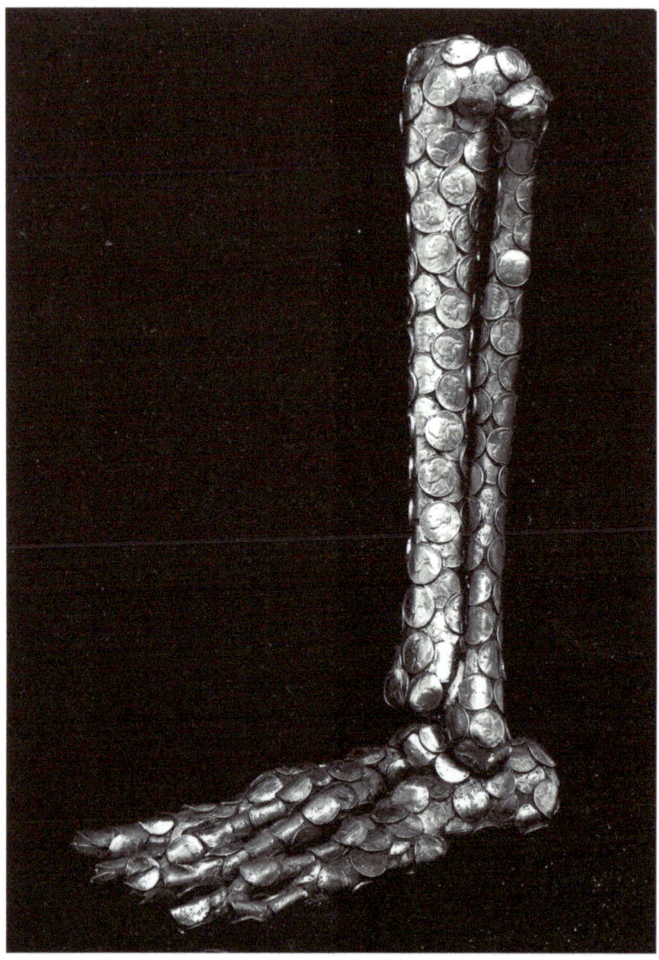

A Lien Leg, 1982, Gary Lloyd, coins over bone

Peterson made sculptural wedges he called 'bum shelters' and propped them up against the sagging fences of the Skid Row on East 5th Street. LACMA's 1982 Young Talent Award winner, Andy Wilf, died of an overdose. The heap of flayed pig and sheep heads he painted were from the abattoir at downtown's Grand Central Market when it was still catering to the Latino community. He took them back to his studio and painted the severed heads with the carnal devotion of expressionist Chaim Soutine and the palette of Rembrandt.

The last time I saw Andy alive, he staggered down Center Street and lay in the entrance of my loading dock like the statue of a medieval knight in a cathedral niche, arms crossed on his chest. His creased and battered cowboy boots watched over him, inches south of his feet. I took his recumbency in the portal of my newfound gallery as an auspicious sign and left him basking in the sun. When I checked twenty minutes later, he was gone. Several days later he died of an overdose. His wake was held at a temple in LIttle Tokyo. He had used the LACMA prize money to purchase heroin. His final painting, a portrait of his head outlined in black shadow, was titled *Better Living through Chemistry*. The illuminated table in the background was covered with narcotics paraphernalia.

Peter Ivers, a Harvard graduate, musician, and host of a popular cable TV show, was the Johnny Carson of the creative arts underworld. His guests were goth and punk musicians, freaky performance artists, and 'Acid King' David Jove. "My job was to provoke them to insanity, to bring out their absolute worst," Ivers boasted. He was beaten to death in his downtown loft. It was front-page news in the *LA*

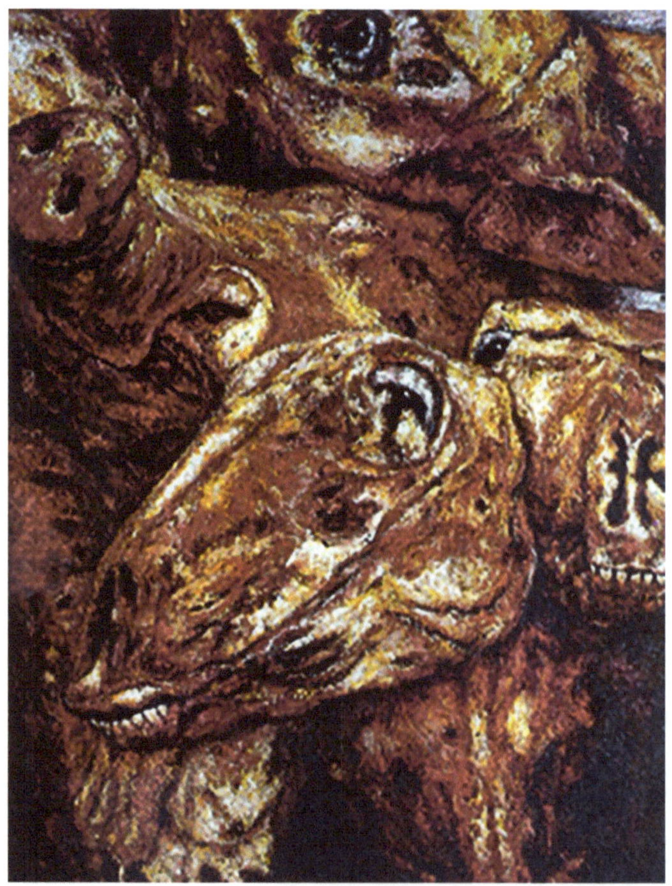

Pig and sheep heads from LA's Grand Central Market, 1982, Andy Wilf, oil on canvas, 48" × 36" (122 cm × 91.4 cm)

Weekly, but the Los Angeles Police Department's

investigation of the homicide was perfunctory. Peter Ivers' assassin was never found, let alone tried.

Downtown artists created impromptu spaces to display their art. These included my Art Dock, AAA Art, American Gallery, Gallery by the Water, and the Exile Gallery started by painters Dennis Goddard, Gary Worrell, and poet Linda Burnham in an abandoned multistory building on Winston Street. They had to displace a huge flock of pigeons that had used the building as an urban rookery. Their gallery space had once been the Canadian Consulate and their stables. I presented two large hardware cloth sculptures in a group show at Exile, one of which I called the *Ironic Column*, a composition of plus and minus shapes hung from a substantial hook.

and Matisse. A decade later, Arnold Schoenberg emigrated from Hitler's Germany to bring his atonal, twelve-tone music to UCLA, where he met Madame Dorland as did fellow emigre Albert Einstein, who brought his beloved violin to the Colony and joined her in duets. I sat with Ellen, as she insisted I call her, on the porch of the Kitchen House. She asked about my work and, when I replied, remarked that the sound of my voice provided antiphonal response to the natural music of the Oak Grove. Despite the idyllic atmosphere of this high desert retreat, one had to remain alert. On a mountain trek to the Far Spring, I nearly stepped on a large rattlesnake sleeping in the shade of a tumbleweed. When I was swimming in the pond, a small fish jumped out of the water to devour a bee that had landed on a lily pad. This glorious setting was the antithesis of the urban gloom that surrounded my loft in downtown Los Angeles.

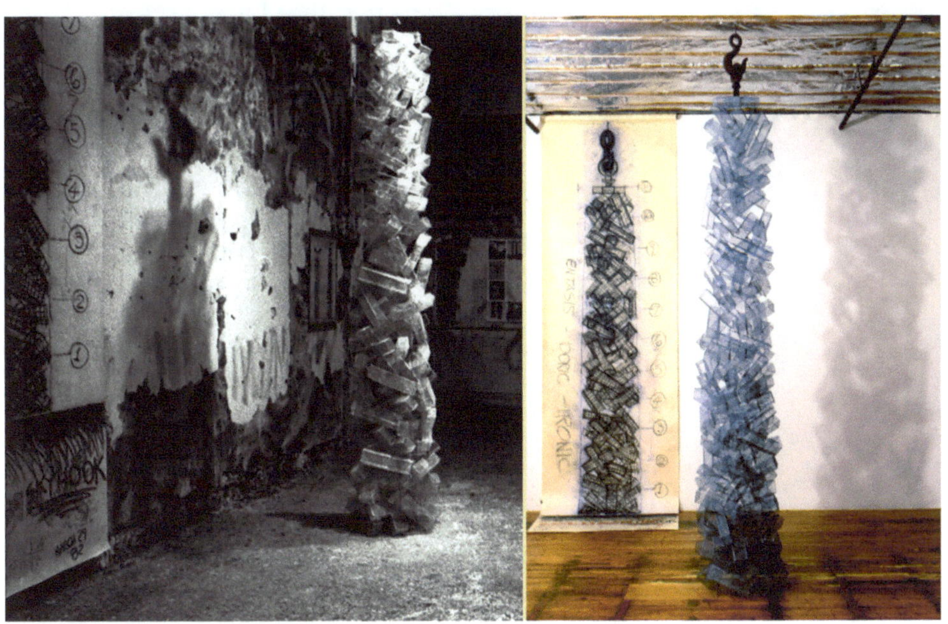

Ironic Column, Exile Gallery exhibition, photograph by Carlton Davis, 1983, hardware cloth and cast iron, collection of Bart and Ildiko Choy

In the historic 1940 feature-length animated film *Fantasia*, Mickey Mouse portrayed the Sorcerer's Apprentice who, with his upraised arm, conjured the magic in the stars and brought forth dancing brooms. When the film was revived in the 1980s, the dancing brooms struck me as the forebears of abstract expressionist 'action painters' splashing their creativity on the studio floor like so many Jackson Pollocks. Los Angeles' Beat poet Charles Bukowski wrote: "Mickey Mouse has a greater influence on the American public than Shakespeare, Milton, Dante, Rabelais, Shostakovich, Lenin, and/or Van Gogh. Which says 'what?' about the American public. Disneyland remains the central attraction of Southern California, but the graveyard remains our reality."

Idyllic Respite

Transported by a two-month residence grant to the Composer's Cottage of the Dorland Mountain Arts Colony in Temecula, California, I gazed at the blooming flowers of Lupine Canyon and took daily hikes through the oaks. The Colony was then the domain of Ellen Dorland who had toured Europe as a concert pianist in the first quarter of the 20th century, where she met Picasso, Braque, Modigliani,

Why was I trying to be an artist in a culture that saw art as just one of many sources of entertainment? On the way home from Dorland, I found meaning and joy in the light rippling through an oak grove on a hillside above Temecula that reminded me that nature is always available as an instructor.

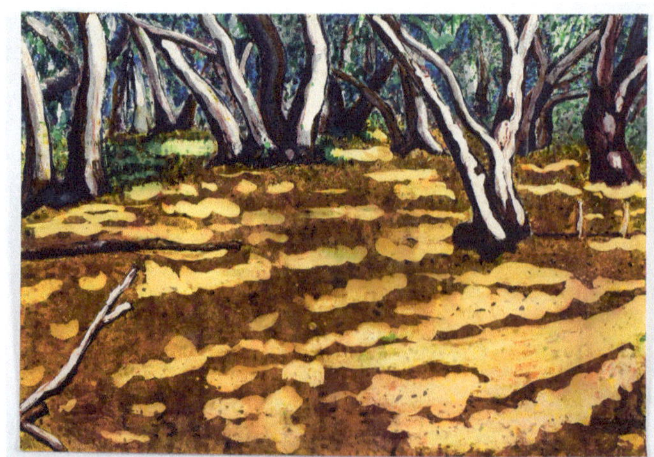

Sketchbook pages, Carlton Davis, three 1983 images, each 11" × 8.5" (27.94 cm × 21.95 cm)

I was an architect, dismissed me as a technician without aesthetic sensitivity.

In 1982, city leaders decided to legalize loft living because they sensed the economic advantage it presented. The first concept proposed was to restrict occupancy to those who could prove they were artists. Of course, defining an artist was impossible. A city council-member stated that "artists are people who throw a lot of parties." His colleagues laughed and approved the ordinance. There was only one provision: applicants had to purchase a license declaring they were artists. The license wasn't worth the paper it was printed on, but it was the only proof I received that I was an artist. Only property ownership counted. The real estate developers had already begun to acquire the buildings the artists had found. Over the next few decades, inner-city Los Angeles experienced a steady resurgence of investment that had nothing to do with the 1980s art pioneers.

Back I went to languish in the boneyard of downtown Los Angeles. My latest self-portrait on paper was garish but larger than its predecessor. Colored pencil lines were replaced by pastels. The eyes that a year before asked, "Who am I?" now said, "Look at who I am." The drawing was looser, and I was more engaged in the act of doing. I no longer stared at the viewer, crazed, pleading, or judging. I began to immerse myself in the pleasure of drawing. I was a worm struggling to emerge from the soil of the grave, an interloper living in a loft that was meant to house a real artist. Some of my neighbors thought I was a spy for the narcs or a lawyer in disguise gathering evidence against the illegal inhabitation of abandoned warehouses and factories. Others, learning

The Oak Grove, Carlton Davis, 1983, watercolor on paper, 24" × 30" (60.96 cm × 76.2 cm)

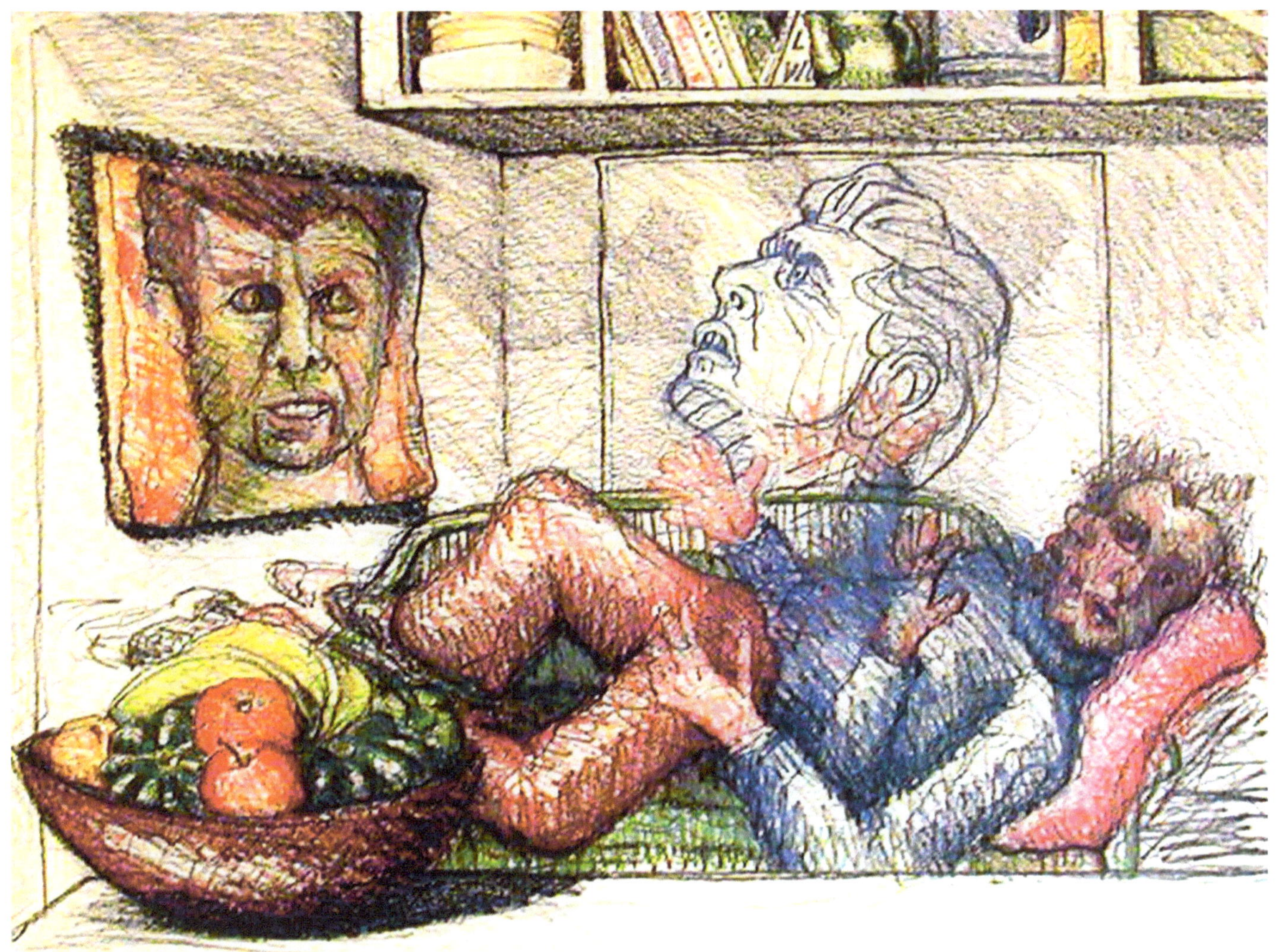

Self-portrait in Victor Henderson's Studio, Venice, CA., 1984, colored pencil on paper, 12" × 18" (30.48 cm × 45.72 cm)

CHAPTER 10

1984
STRIKING IT POOR

Toward the end of 1983 when preparations for the 1984 Los Angeles Olympic Games began in earnest, I was broke. I had spent all my savings on refurbishing my Center Street loft/ studio and paying back the tens of thousands of dollars plus interest I had borrowed to study at Yale Architecture School. I resented paying student loans at age 40 because I derived so little joy from teaching and practicing architecture. I was making monthly car payments and sending Johanna what I could manage in child support. I was often late with the rent. I was super annoyed to have my truck repossessed on a sunny Saturday afternoon while my neighbors gawked.

The Museum of Science and Industry (CMSI) was looking for someone who could come up with a design for an exhibition on comparative economics in time for the Games. Glen Fleck wanted an exhibit that visitors to the museum could play like a giant board game. When they finished playing, they would be awarded a certificate. The exhibit would become permanent when the Olympics ended. The museum was near the Los Angeles Coliseum, which was constructed for the 1932 LA Olympics. The design we worked on compared capitalist and communist economies. The USSR boycotted the 1984 Games, so there was little doubt about which empire would be declared the winner.

The Capitalism vs. Command Economy exhibit was underwritten by IBM and featured the first inter-active computer show in US history.

Had I been an enterprising capitalist instead of a resentful bohemian, I would have worked my ass off, made my talent known to IBM founder Bill Watson, been rewarded with a job designing IBM offices around the world, qualified for a heavyweight 401(k), and invested my profit in IBM stock options. Instead, I grudgingly accepted the gig because I needed to pay my back rent and repossess my truck. My job ended the day the Games began. I borrowed $1,000 from my father to pay my bills and returned to Ellen Dorland's retreat for a couple of weeks to ponder my future.

Once back in LA, I called Glen to see if he had any more work for me. He said he'd recommend me to his friend Frank Gehry, who offered me a job, which I took. I alienated Greg Walsh, Gehry's second-in-command, by parking in his unmarked parking space on day one. Not wanting to rub anyone the wrong way, I inquired about studio space in the neigh-borhood. An artist/carpenter named Victor Henderson was looking for a space where he could build and paint bleachers for a local high school. Bingo! We exchanged studio spaces. His place was on the same street as Gehry Associates, while mine was large enough to accommo-date his goal and materials.

The parking kerfuffle was just the beginning of trouble with Walsh. An architect was expected to work overtime until a project was completed, and Walsh was the office timekeeper. When he noticed I could draw as quickly and efficiently as he could, I became his whipping boy. He never missed a chance to disparage me.

On my own time in Victor's beachside studio, I was making drawings that suggested movement, especially interrupted movement. Reclining on the green wicker *chaise longue* and venting my rage at Walsh's latest indignity, I indicated the movements of my head, hands, and legs in turbulent solitude. I should probably have given up all thoughts of archi-tecture and apprenticed myself to counterculture comic book artist R. Crumb. Underground comics were having a heyday.

Claes Oldenburg was working with Gehry on the *Giant Knife* project for the courtyard of the new Los Angeles Museum of Contemporary Art (MOCA) on Grand Avenue, catty-corner to Disney Hall. I ran into Claes after work and handed him a flyer for my gallery. Although he never showed up there, our imagined Chicago dialogue (viz. Chapter 2) was sacrosanct.

As Glen predicted, I didn't last six months at Gehry Associates. I would have loved to stay longer. I learned a lot from seeing how Gehry worked. He

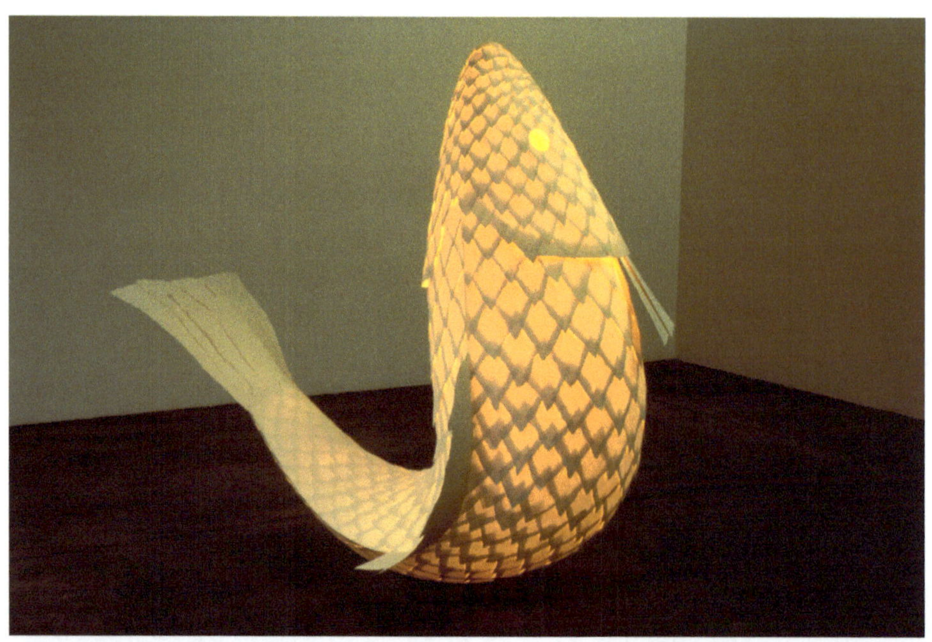

Fish lamp sculpture, Frank Gehry, 1984

allowed his junior architects to solve most spatial problems, then he would play with the forms until they became sculptural. Before I left, I designed a decorative fish column for the end of a swimming pool and a tennis court wall that rose from the sand for a Malibu Beach house. In the early 1980s, Gehry was also known for his fish lamps and sculptures.

I left Gehry Associates because my relationship with Greg Walsh continued to deteriorate, and I had the chance to design a project much closer to home. An old factory across the LA River from the Citizens Warehouse was being considered by the Community Redevelopment Agency as its first foray into specialized housing for artists. The project didn't progress beyond the funding phase and Davis, Fonseca, and Kyrk Architects, a firm I formed with a couple of architect friends to design the project, did not survive.

I registered for unemployment based on my earnings at Frank Gehry Associates and Glen Fleck Incorporated. I was the lone white man in a long line of unemployed Black and Latino people, and I had time to record my many short-term jobs, one of which was as an adjunct assistant professor at UCLA Architecture School. When I finally reached the clerk's window, she assumed I meant to write 'LAUSD' (Los Angeles Unified School District). In either case, I needed an Employment Registration Number (ERN) to verify my claim. When it turned out I didn't have one, she suggested I call my former employer and return to her window when I had the number. I

went to the bank of phones near the door and waited. When my turn came and I picked up the phone, I discovered I only had a dime in my pocket, not the requisite quarter. I slammed the receiver down and smacked the glass doors to the street with such force that they shattered. A uniformed LAPD officer ran up to me and asked if I was hurt. He didn't ticket or arrest

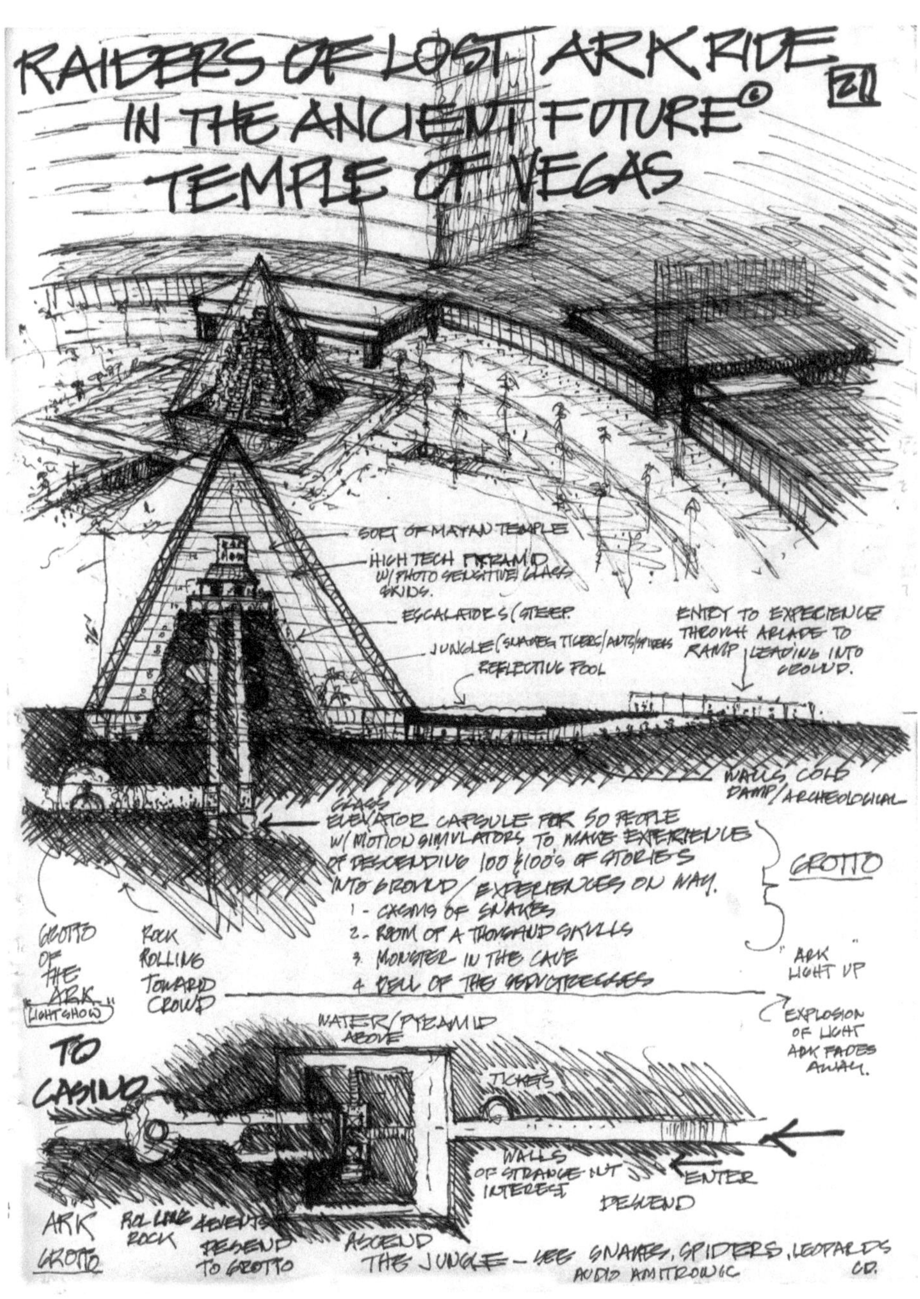

Sketchbook drawing, 1985, Carlton Davis, ink on paper, 8.5" × 11" (21.6 cm × 28 cm)

me for destruction of public property, but he took down my name, address, and telephone number.

The next day, I got a call from NBC News. They were contemplating a feature on the effects of the financial downturn. I agreed to what turned into a long interview with Furnell Chapman, a local NBC newscaster. Yes, I had been an instructor at UCLA, but now, I was a full-time artist, and artists are inured to financial upturns and down-turns. I was preparing to cite Gauguin, Van Gogh, and Modigliani as examples of this when Furnell abruptly ended the interview. He wanted to send a video cameraman to shoot me kicking a can down the freight train tracks behind the Citizens Warehouse. The segment *Striking it Poor* aired the following day. My diatribe about the precariousness of the artist's life was excised. Furnell called me "an ex-UCLA professor down on his luck." The image of a solitary white man kicking a can down a forlorn stretch of tracks was more powerful than a discussion of impoverished artists whose post-mortem work was worth millions.

Naturally, Glen Fleck caught the 'Carlton Kicks a Can' newscast and offered me work on several prospective exhibitions: *The Road to Utopia* for Disney, a *Computer Garden* for IBM, and *Raiders of the Lost Ark* for the Hilton Hotel in Las Vegas, none of which proceeded due to the rapidly expanding financial bubble.

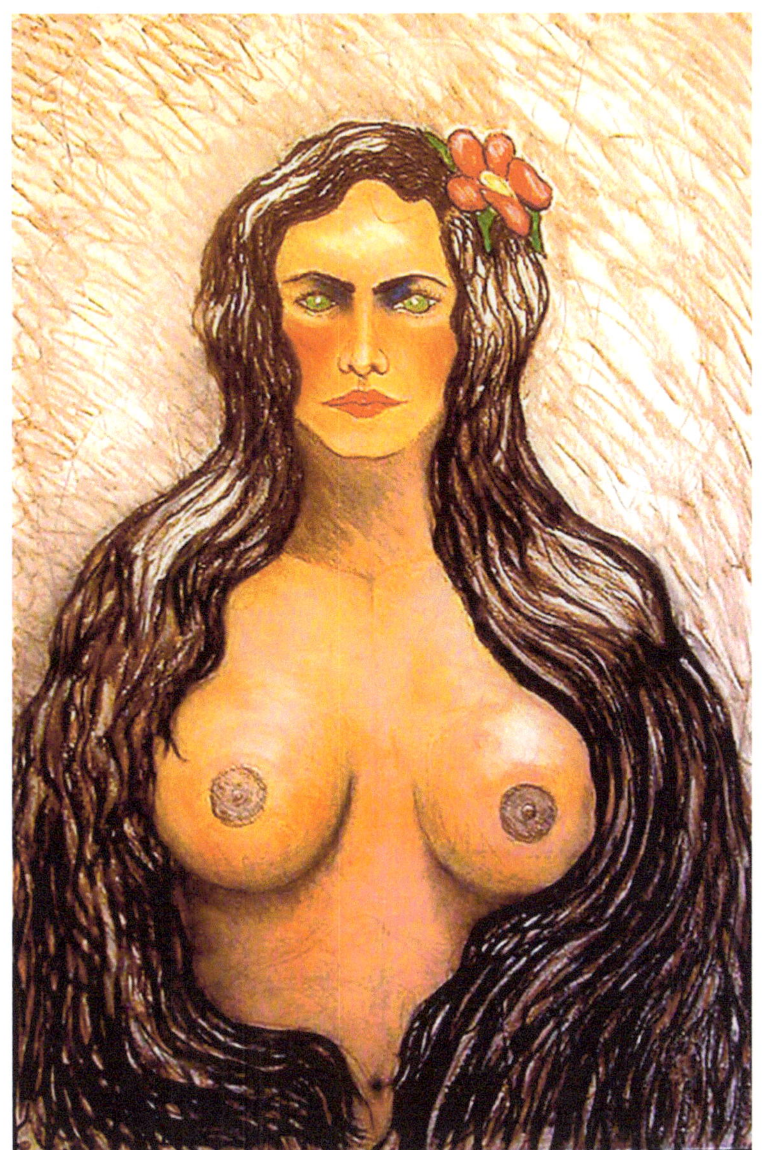

Self-portrait, Carlton Davis, June 5, 1987, pastel and colored pencil on paper,
40" × 26" (101.6 cm × 66 cm)

CHAPTER 11

1987–1988
THE YEAR OF PERSONIC CONVERGENCE

With the Sun, Moon, Mars, Venus, and Mercury all in alignment, 1987-88 was supposed to be a year of 'harmonic convergence.' From my vantage point, things worsened steadily. Andy Warhol died at 59, twenty years after Valerie Solanas's unsuccessful attempt to kill him in 1968, and New York artist Andrés Serrano immersed a plastic crucifix in a bubbly yellow liquid, photographed it, framed it, and called it *Piss Christ*, creating a potent statement about the commercialization of religion and an immediate scandal. This was affirmed for me when Pope John Paul II visited Los Angeles, staying in the rectory of St. Vibiana's de-consecrated cathedral not far from my studio. The 19th-century landmark had been transformed into a performance space by the downtown arts community. For the Pontiff's stay, the cathedral was repainted and altar flowers were wired upright to withstand the September heatwave. While feminists, gay and lesbian people, AIDS workers, and artists picketed the historic site, entrepreneurs sold halo-sprouting headbands with lawn sprinklers labeled 'Now Let Us Spray.'

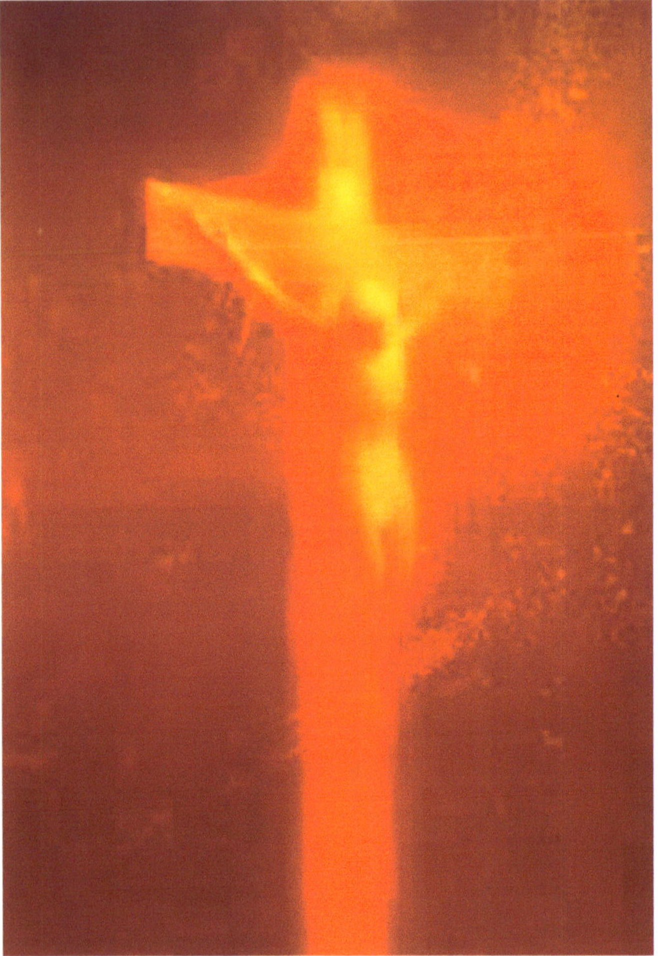

Piss Christ, Andres Serrano, 1987, Cibachrome photograph, 60" × 40" (150 cm × 100 cm), public and private collections

That year's self-portrait presents the feminine side of what I called my 'personic convergence.' Carlotta was a revelation to my friends and acquaintances and, no doubt, a source of amusement/amazement to strangers, although she generally appeared after dark. My therapist saw the drawing as a manifestation of an illness. It was inspired by Albrecht Dürer's 1493 self-portrait as a woman.

Dürer may have had misgivings about displaying this image. His patrons might misunderstand it and withdraw their support. The female version of Dürer holds a thistle, a spike-leafed weed associated with the Virgin Mary's agony. Perhaps his self-confidence was buoyed by religious faith.

Sick of grim downtown Los Angeles life with its profusion of homeless men and transvestite prostitutes in the area I inhabited near Skid Row, I swapped my studio with Lloyd Hamrol, an artist who needed a big space to build large wooden platforms for a beach in Isla Vista. I moved into his small studio near Venice Beach. On September 30, 1987, I felt a premonitory earth tremor. A day later, the Whittier Narrows quake, Mercalli scale 7, destroyed buildings in Puente Hills and Whittier and gave Los Angeles a good shake. This was followed by the stock market crash in mid-October. On October 28, the sewer line erupted beneath the small building of studios on the corner of Brooks Street and Pacific Avenue where I was staying. The landlord began to make repairs. That evening, I biked home from Glen Fleck's office in Santa Monica to find my toilet perched atop a huge pile of foul-smelling dirt. I trance-walked down Brooks Street to a beach pavilion where homeless people camped next to the public restrooms. I watched the haggard group with their shopping carts piled high with filthy clothes, crushed soda cans, discarded small appliances, and garbage bags full of junk. They were passing several bottles of cheap Tokay wine hand to hand. I took it as an omen. The dirt pile with its toilet tiara was a *coup de grace*. There was no escaping my downward momentum. I was homeless. An outcast.

The planetary line-up that was supposed to herald the beginning of the end of wars, materialism, injustice, and oppression did not deliver. I found temporary housing in Virginia (Ginger) Tanzmann's house before moving to Shinzen Young's Community Meditation Center in Koreatown for a six-month residency. Vipassana meditation, or insight meditation, focuses on seeing things as they are. It comes from Theravada, Buddhism's oldest school of thought. Vipassana helped me clean my life up and begin a romantic relationship with Ginger. My life there was organized, monk-like, and placid.

Shinzen taught Vipassana meditation from a

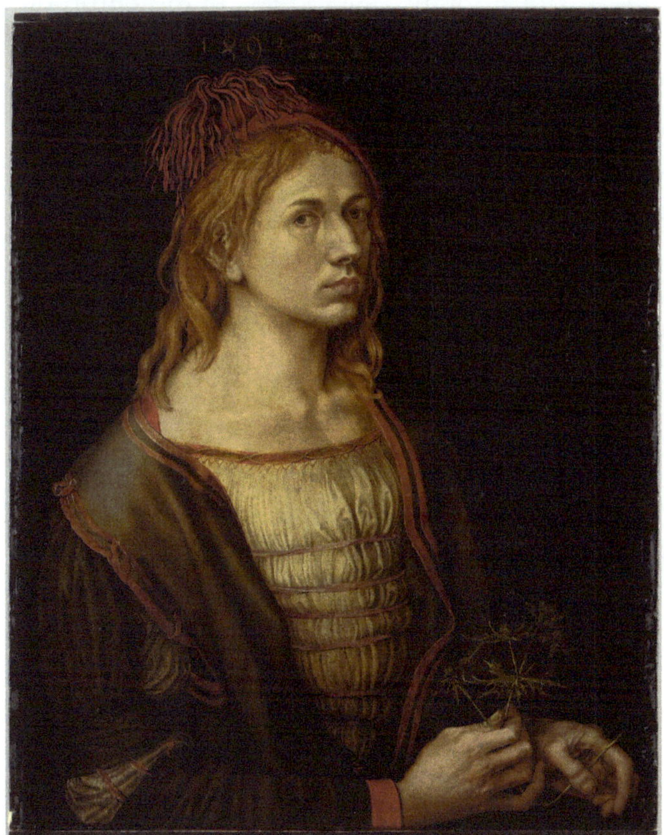

Self-portrait with sea holly, Albrecht Durer, self-portrait, 1493, oil, 22.25" × 17.25" (56 cm × 44 cm), Musée du Louvre, Paris, France

Western, scientific perspective. I was asked to scan my body from head to foot, and wherever I located points of stress or tension, to focus on them until they dissolved. I spent much of the day at the Buddhist meditation center sitting on a black cushion in the communal living room practicing mindfulness. After each sit, Shinzen would ask us to describe what we had experienced. I developed a sharp pain in my left shoulder. The more I sat, the worse it got. Shinzen drove me to a nearby hospital, but the doctors found nothing amiss.

One of Shinzen's associates, Robert Hover, led a week-long retreat. When I told him about my shoulder, he suggested I sit with it long enough to observe how it dispersed; was it in one or more than one direction? If all the pain was focused on my left shoulder, I should visualize pushing it in whichever direction was open and available. He had me practice this in several sessions, and it worked until one day, the pain was unbearable. While Shinzen believed my left shoulder was the focal point of all the poisons in my body, Robert Hover explained that a knot of energy could be a repository of poisons preserved from past lives. He encouraged me to return to this point again and again and pay particular attention to the images that arose in my mind. He assured me it was possible to recall pain and suffering from past lives.

I tracked my inhalations and exhalations. My shoulder pain would fade to be replaced by cramps spreading from my feet to my crown chakra and out through the top of my head. This was followed by a welcome stillness. When the pain recurred, it was even more intense and followed the same course through my body to my head and back down through my shoulders to my groin. Greeting the pain like an old friend from earlier sits, I felt lighter, clearer, and more balanced. I began to smile. Three days later, the pain returned stronger than ever, followed by uncontrollable trembling for the rest of the retreat. I felt like two different people. One was bold, energetic, and angry, the other depressed, sullen, and fearful.

When I moved downtown in 1980, I had my first inkling of a split personality. In 1986, I made two drawings and a small wire sculpture. Each had my male face looking at a two-sided image painted on the wire screen with marbles for eyes. On the left side, my male face with glasses looked at a female image that had the same marble eyes. My face on the left side of the drawing was round and smiling, while on the right side, my face had no glasses. The ocular marbles made the connection between the two. My insight regarding the two 1986 drawings followed the onslaught of divine shakes at the meditation retreat. One self was female, and the other was male. The selves had different expressions. The male shoulder-to-shoulder with the female seemed pensive, while the male shoulder-to-shoulder with the male seemed surprised.

During my meditation, my mind flashed on Ellen Fitzpatrick, called 'Ganga Ma' because she was as large and mysterious as the River Ganges. She lived at the far end of the corridor, beyond my studio, in a studio larger than mine. Ganga Ma worked for Mattel, the toy company that produced Barbie. She wasn't an artist, but she wanted to live like one, so she had an artist/contractor drywall her studio and install a bathroom, electrical wiring for lights and outlets, a kitchen stove, sink, countertop, and long, artful, straight wall in front of the bathroom with a sturdy rod of equal length for her costumes. Ganga Ma was as inspiring to Carlotta's foundation as Giant Jane had been. She had worked at the Nixon White House and witnessed a lot of what she called "cocainery" there. When I finished my place, I walked to the other end of the building to introduce myself. The door was ajar, and I saw a woman with long dark hair attired in a flowing dress, scarf, and high heels struggling to operate a giant belt sander. I offered to finish the job.

Her studio was sparsely furnished. A small dining table with two chairs, a movable bed, and an altar to Muktananda were the focal trinity. The altar was surrounded by numerous lit candles, incense, and offerings of fresh fruit. The centerpiece was a large, framed color photograph of Swami Muktananda Paramahansa, the founder of Siddha Yoga, draped in scarves with an ecstatic smile on his face. She and I attended meetings in Muktananda's enormous Ocean Avenue ashram in Santa Monica. He performed *darshan* at those evening programs, a vision of the deity, with his peacock feather as a wand. Anything was possible. It was meditation with music, dance, and drums and my introduction to the seven chakras and the Hindu path to enlightenment.

Ganga Ma meditated in front of her altar, danced with a peacock feather in her hand, and sat at the open door of her loading dock playing the sitar. When I returned from my summer at Dorland, she had sublet her space. It was rumored she had returned to Benares,

Two self-portrait drawings, colored pencil, 1986, Carlton Davis, each 22" × 30" (58.88 cm × 76.2 cm)

Ganga Ma, 1985, Carlton Davis, colored pencil on paper, 22.5" × 30" (57.15 cm × 76.2 cm)

today's Varanasi, with the swami. I never saw or heard of her again.

I visited many museums to observe the sculptures of Hindu and Buddhist women. The carvings of Tara were all voluptuous. They had large, orbital breasts, narrow waists, broad hips, and smooth surfaces. The 8th-century *Green Tara* at the Brooklyn Museum had a damaged face with no nose or mouth. This destruction focused attention on her large breasts. Above them, a chain draped over her shoulder and looped below her waist resembled a bracelet on her outstretched right hand. The hand directed the seeker to the path of purification. In her left hand, Tara held a long stem that terminated in a closed lotus flower. I couldn't decipher the iconography until I sat on a bench at Echo Park Lake and examined the stems that supported the lotus flowers and fronds bobbing on the lake's surface. Meditation is an aid to cleansing the impurities of our mucky bottoms. Our energy arises from a miasma of life experiences. The water supports the floating lotus in seeking the light. I had turned toward enlightenment and away from the dark. If I continued on the spiritual seeker path, I would one day experience the bliss of creative fulfillment.

I made my 1987 self-portrait female, but there is an explosive male presence lurking behind her plasticized breast and belly plate. Despite his strenuous effort to tranquilize his demons through the instructive moment-to-moment practice of guided Vipassana meditation, he would take decades to be recognized as an artist. What Gautama Buddha called "the middle path" was not an easy one for a labile, 44-year-old to walk.

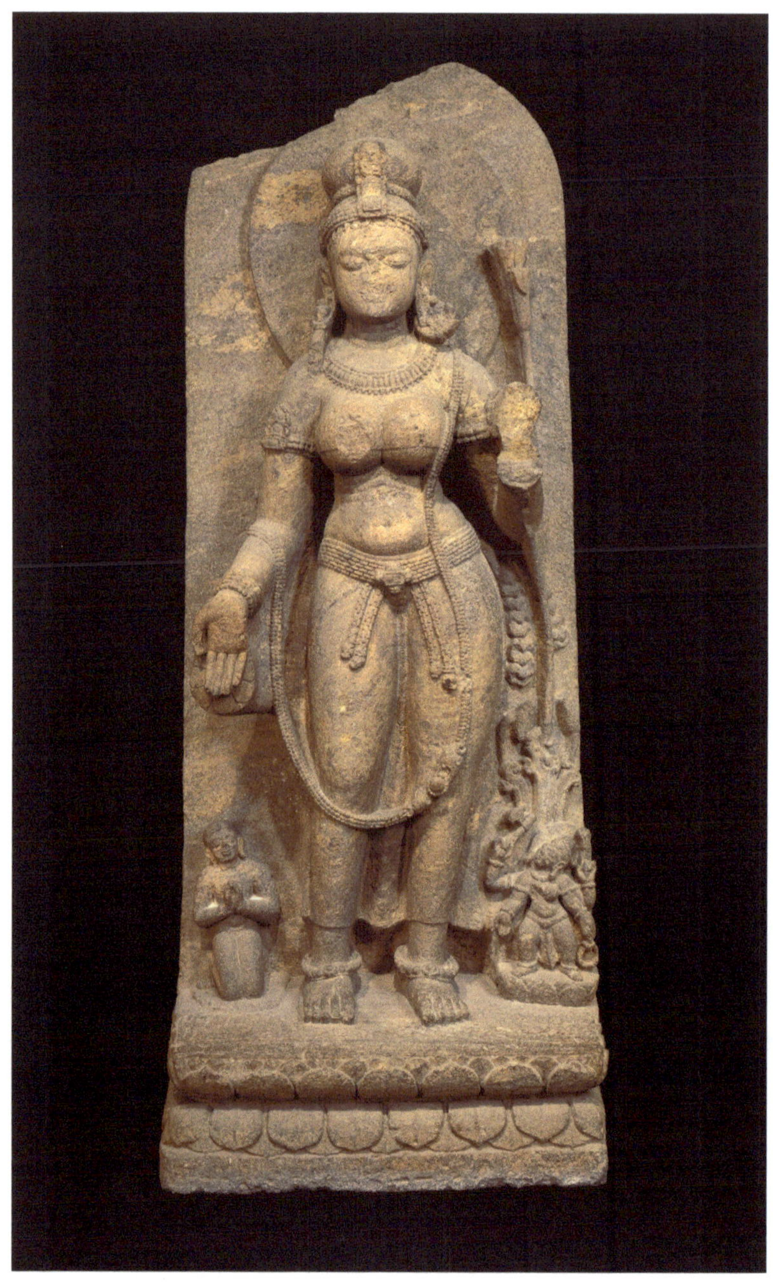

Green Tara, 8th century, khondalite,
67.4" × 26" × 17.5", 1,109 lb,
(171.2 cm × 66 cm × 44.5 cm, 503.04kg), Brooklyn Museum, NYC

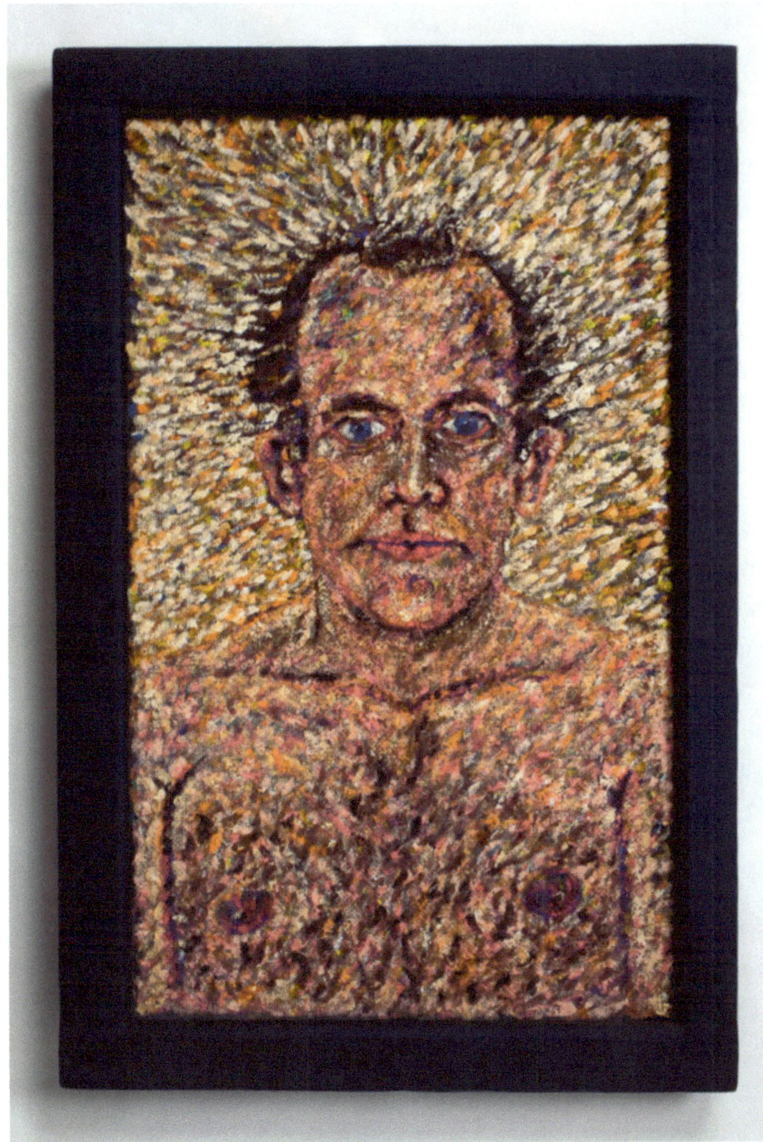

Self-portrait, 1992, Carlton Davis, acrylic on wood window screen, 28" × 18" (71.12 cm × 45.72 cm)

CHAPTER 12

1992
STRAIGHTEN UP AND FLY RIGHT

A buzzard took a monkey for a ride in the air
The monkey thought that everything was on the square
The buzzard tried to throw the monkey off his back
The monkey grabbed his neck and said, "Now listen, Jack…
Straighten up and fly right, Straighten up and stay right
Straighten up and fly right
Cool down, Papa, Don't you blow your top
Ain't no use in diving

What's the use in jiving? Straighten up and fly right
Cool down papa, Don't you blow your top
The buzzard told the monkey you are choking me
Release your hold and I will set you free
The monkey looked the buzzard right dead in the eye
and said, "Your story's so touching, but it sounds just
like a lie."

— Poem and song by Nat 'King' Cole

My first notion that a Chinese zodiac existed came via a paper placemat under a bowl of chow fun noodles. The animals in the Chinese zodiac comprise a twelve-year, rather than a yearly, cycle, and their personalities are reflected by one of five elements: wood, fire, earth, metal, and water. I was born in 1944, a Wood Monkey year. My self-portrait, the sole non-architectural project I completed four cycles later in the Water Monkey year of 1992, was painted on the wire of a wooden window screen. My apparent equilibrium, ease, and openness were benefits of my daily meditation practice.

This chapter opens with the lyrics to *Straighten Up and Fly Right*, composed and sung by Nat 'King' Cole. Before the 'signifying monkey' takes off, he wraps his prehensile tail around the buzzard's neck. The Nat King Cole Trio's bebop version of a Yoruban fable sold a million records in 1944.

My mentor in all things African, video griot and performance artist Ulysses Jenkins, equates the signifying monkey with the Ibo-Yoruba orishá Eshu-Elegba, who must first be propitiated for the ritual to begin. His aspect can be Christ-like or Satanic. Often compared with the Greek god Hermes, he acts as both a messenger to the rest of the pantheon and an overseer of the uncontrollable, including natural disasters, accidents, and violence. In this capacity, he reigns over crossroads, cemeteries, and highways.

On March 3, 1991, LAPD officers beat Rodney King, a 28-year-old Black parolee who was stopped after a high-speed car chase on the 210 Freeway. When he shook the two officers off his back after being tasered, they called for reinforcements, who arrived within minutes and moved King and friends off the freeway shoulder into a nearby suburb. There, eight officers 'swarmed' him, clubbed him 58 times, kicked him repeatedly, and tasered him again as he lay prostrate on the poorly lit street. But the spirit of Eshu was present. A man on his apartment balcony across the street had a camcorder and taped nearly a minute and a half of King's brutal comeuppance, which he sent to the LAPD and Eyewitness News. The police department was slow to respond, but America got to see Citizen King's punishment played and replayed on network news across the nation for what seemed like weeks.

Not quite 14 months later, three of the four officers responsible for the violence were acquitted of all crimes by a white jury in the majority-white community of Sylmar. The news spread like the plague, and the Black majority population of South Central Los Angeles took to the streets. LAPD Chief Daryl Gates decided not to send his men into the melee. The LA riots in 1992 lasted for six days and caused 63 deaths and 2,383 injuries.

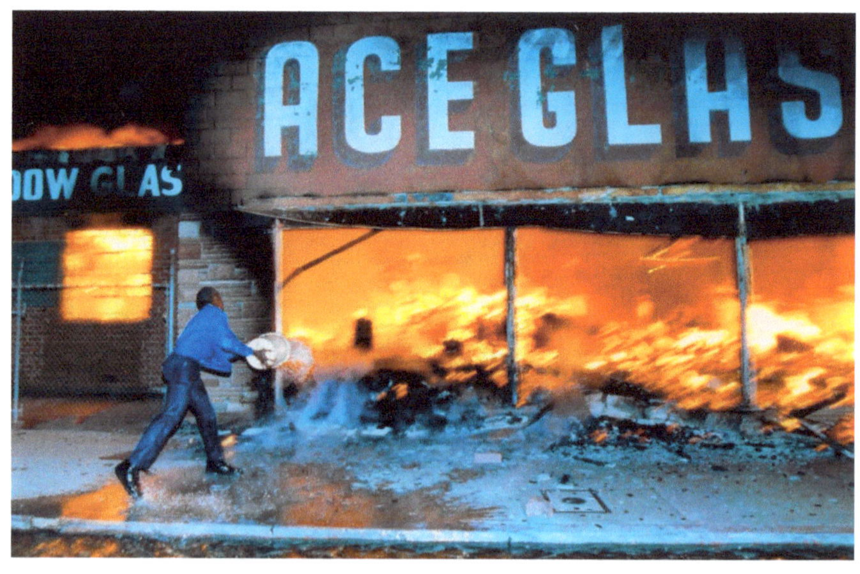

LA riots,1992, photograph by CNN

Widespread arson and looting resulted in 7,000 fires, damaged 3,100 businesses, and cost close to $1 billion in financial losses. It was the largest, most destructive race-based disturbance in US history and required the National Guard, dozens of fire departments, and Army and Marine troops to end it.

I had worked for The Tanzmann Associates briefly in 1984, reviewing a set of drawings for the Los Angeles County Metropolitan Transportation Authority. Mervyn Fernandes, a college friend, was working there and recommended me. I biked to the historic Bradbury Building from my studio at First and Center Streets. I was there long enough to notice that Virginia, the boss, was attractive and smart as a whip. At the time, very few architectural firms in Los Angeles were led by women. I worked for two of them. Ginger's clients were not as high-profile as those of her male peers, and her projects tended to be infrastructure instead of glamour, but I felt comfortable working there. When I called her after the Venice studio fiasco, a spare room at her place in Pasadena was available. The house was old and what my friend Ulysses would call 'funky.' It looked like a Greene and Greene house (there were quite a few in the neighborhood), but it was even older, dating back to the late 19th century. The room for rent was upstairs, spacious, and right across from her bedroom. I rented it on an emergency basis. I considered myself too screwed up to be romantically involved with anyone ever again. I lived there for just one month before my resolve dissolved.

Ginger had been living in LA since finishing grad school in 1969. She was a year younger than I, had graduated from Syracuse University with two architecture degrees, and had been married. Her warm and generous nature morphed our rental arrangement into a trial cohabitation, which was prelude to the best decision I ever made. After a month, I suggested that I move back to my studio to get some perspective on our burgeoning romance. Ginger understood. This lasted the better part of a year. We dated, for the most part dining out together. Neither of us is much of a cook. I was working for another architect on multiple restoration projects, including the Bradbury Building, the Grand Central Market, and Million Dollar Theater.

I had temporarily tamed the Black Dog of depression by committing myself to a daily regimen of meditation and sobriety for the better part of three years, but I was still susceptible to relapse. By 1992, I had a steady job, a new studio, and a safe place to live in Pasadena. Ginger and I had been married for three years when she offered me a management position in her firm. Soon though, I had difficulty coping with the stress of an architectural office and began to use drugs again, first marijuana, then crack cocaine.

After our wedding in 1989, I joined Ginger's firm. In 1991, we enjoyed a 'second honeymoon' in Baja California at a hotel that was so new that workmen were still building the room next to ours, and we had to contend with a leaky shower. Yet we were having a great time exploring Cabo San Lucas by motorbike.

Impulsively, I decided to swim across the bay to El Arco, a huge offshore rock adjacent to the beach in Cabo San Lucas at the southernmost tip of the Baja California península. It had been hollowed out over the millennia and had the sculptural magnetism of Stonehenge on the Pacific. I handed Ginger the binoculars so she could watch my progress. I dove into the bay in my trunks, mask, and snorkel, knowing nothing of what was in store, which included strong undercurrents, barges to be dodged, and the whitewater wake of speedy powerboats. By the time I reached the far shore, my heart was racing as if I had been snorting cocaine. I was astonished by my recklessness. What made me do this shit? Mania is more perilous than stultifying depression. I couldn't ask or rely on Ginger to stop me. She was my wife, not my nurse. I adjusted my mask and blew spouts of water out of my snorkel like a whale.

At 260 pounds, I was a whale! I devoured cherry bonbons at every opportunity. Sometimes, I ate them in the dark after Ginger had fallen asleep. Whenever I walked our dogs, I lit up a joint. One day, Niki, my favorite, who sashayed like Mae West, freed herself from my grip long enough to pursue a possum. I stood there like a doofus, too wasted to respond. I did no exercise and had no self-discipline or urge to meditate. All I did was work. During my big swim in Cabo, I was so busy berating myself that I forgot to wave to Ginger. Amid my waterlogged reverie, my mind flashed to Gertrude Ederle, the first woman to swim the English Channel in 1926.

"At least you didn't have to smear your body with bear grease," I murmured to Carlotta.

"Self-torture's not my bag, babe. My unguent of choice is Chanel No. 5."

The Los Angeles Mission, surrounded by and catering to homeless people, stands at 5th and Wall Streets, at the heart of LA's Skid Row, three long blocks west of Alameda. Ginger and I held hands as we toured the site, beaming at each other and realizing that this was our giant wedding cake. Saving a building in trouble is every architect's dream scenario, and good fortune smiled on us when the Nazarene-affiliated mission hired The Tanzmann Associates to restart the project, which had ground to a halt due to the previous architect and builder's errors in the erection of the steel frame and their startling proposal to make the circular, sloped roof of the chapel out of cut concrete blocks. We redesigned the project, adding a gym with a basketball court to the topmost floor, reconceiving the chapel's interior to include a frieze with Biblical verses, and crowning it with a bright copper sheet-metal tiara topped by a white cross. It overlooks 5th Street and a park where homeless people gather. Made of flat sheets of copper-colored metal, it has become a downtown landmark. At dawn and dusk, the Mission's tiara glistens like gold!

The cast of The Tanzmann Associates was varied and unforgettable. There were five Black people, two of whom were from Africa. There were also three Mexican-Americans, two Chinese-Americans, two Japanese-Americans, a Filipino-American, two Ukrainian refugees from Odesa being settled in the US through sponsorship from a Jewish relief agency, a gentleman from Brazil, and eight white folks, including Ginger and me.

Ginger was the undisputed, round-the-clock leader, the unflappable one who could calm and reconnect all the

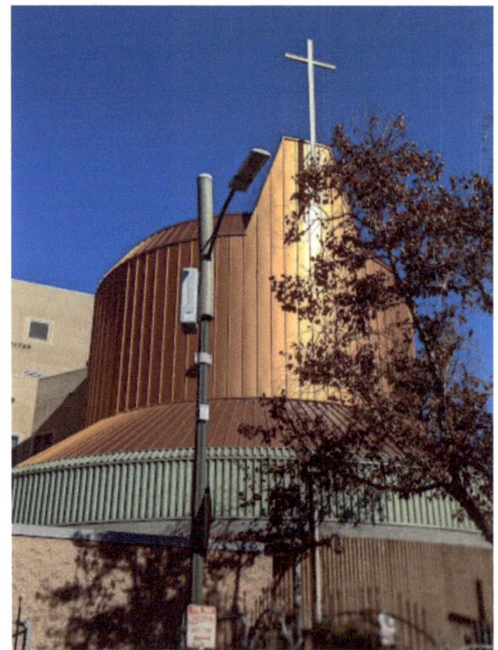

Los Angeles Mission, 1992, The Tanzmann Associates, photograph by Carlton Davis

human elements. She ran the business, and I supervised the staff. The work environment was warm, friendly, open, and accepting to all. The petite Creole woman who ran the welcoming front desk often treated the entire office to her delicious red beans and rice. But not every day went smoothly. The two Africans, both Nigerians, had problems with each other. One was a large and jovial Ibo, while the other was a Hausa from the Muslim north. They rubbed each the wrong way and I had to be vigilant, or they would quarrel. One of the architects made the sign of the cross after every interaction with me. One woman wore headphones the whole day. When I tapped her on the shoulder, she said, "You should know better than to touch me, old man! Aren't you married to the boss?" The architects from Odesa worried about the safety of their relatives in Ukraine. The Brazilian architect was assigned the task of laying out all the bathrooms and stairs. We found numerous errors in his drawings. When I took him to task, he said something in Portuguese I could not understand, but the words were always the same. My translator friend told me what he said: *"Sou apenas um humilde membro da tribu, senhor. Você é o cacique!"* (I am only a humble member of the tribe, sir. You're the chief!)

One day, the most experienced architect on the team made a presentation to the client about the progress of the chapel work when Ginger and I couldn't be there. He swore several times. Ginger received a call the next day from the Mission's leader, a minister, who said he found our employee's language offensive. She managed to assuage him. As the team leader, I sometimes felt like a kindergarten teacher. I was sad to see them go when the team members disbanded at the end of the Mission project.

Ginger and I drove to Montalvo's Grove, a redwood forest in northern California. There, Ginger danced and waved her arms over her head in celebration of the beauty of the redwoods' peeling bark, the lacy closure of the leaves, the patchwork of needles in the dappled sunlight on our trail, and our first resounding business success. As we sat on a large, inviting boulder, red-tailed hawks soared above us. I took my guide and partner in my arms and breathed as I had learned to do on my cushion in the meditation center.

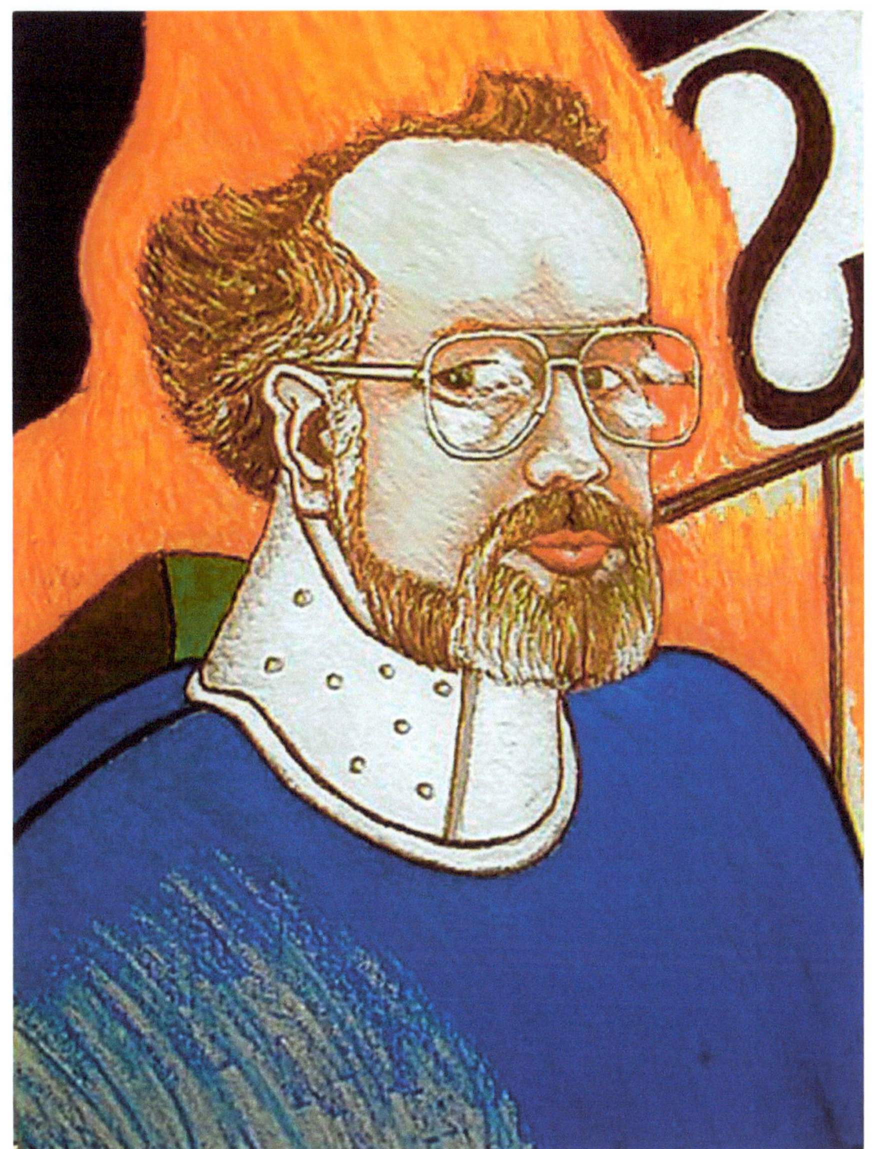

Self-portrait, 1993-1994, Carlton Davis, oil stick on paper, 30" × 22" (76.2 cm × 55.88 cm)

CHAPTER 13

1993-1994
INQUIETUDE

My 1993-1994 self-portrait shows me in a neck brace after a 1993 discectomy. When I was 17, my father, Carlton Davis Sr., pulled me out of Lexington High School after my junior year and sent me to Mount Hermon Academy, a boy's boarding school in the boondocks of western Massachusetts. He thought if I studied and played football in a monastic setting it would improve my chances of continuing the multigenerational Davis presence at Yale. I was a big, strong kid, over six feet tall and 180 pounds, but I shunned all contact sports. Baseball was my game. I was a fast-balling southpaw slinger, protecting my shoulder, arm, and hand until spring when I'd put them all to good use. As a third-string lineman, I felt safer sitting on the bench. My flippant attitude raised everyone's hackles, including the coach's. I was there for just a year, devoid of the requisite spirit and without a single ally. In other words, I was a sitting duck. I had one valuable skill: snapping the ball to the punter with speed and accuracy. The coach would yell, "Davis, get your ass off the bench and make it snappy." I'd pull on my helmet, which, in those bygone days, had just a single arc of face guard, trot to the center of the offensive line, put both hands on the ball, spread my legs, bend my knees, and hang my head until I could clearly see the punter five yards behind me. When the punter yelled, "Hike!" I'd pass the pigskin from the ground through my legs in a spiral with sufficient momentum to lodge, an instant later, in his hands. When our team switched to defense, I'd return to the bench. On a Friday scrimmage the day before the Deerfield game, our season finale, Mt. Hermon's coach ordered a pair of robust linemen to cream me. As I straightened up to block, both hit me above the shoulders. I conked out and came to with what felt like a mouthful of loose or fractured teeth.

A Mt. Hermon faculty member drove me straight to the dentist, who shot me up with novocaine and capped what was left of my front teeth. The pain increased as the drug wore off and soon became unbearable. I begged the school nurse for more novocaine but all she had was aspirin. I phoned my father. He told me to hop on the next bus from Greenfield to Boston where he would be waiting to take me to Mass General. The bus made dozens of stops along the way and the journey took hours. I sat in the back, slid to the floor so the driver couldn't see me, and banged my head on the inside of the bus below the window to distract me from my aching mouth. My father met the bus in Boston and drove me to the hospital where the caps were removed, emitting a stench. An oral surgeon operated on my gums, relieving the pressure and stemming the infection. After several days and nights in the hospital, they put a custom-made bridge in my mouth with two false teeth. I was informed that had I waited a day longer the infection would have invaded my brain and ended my life. I begged my father to let me

return to Lexington High, where I had friends of both sexes and felt at home. He said he'd paid for a full year at Mount Hermon, so I had to go back.

Fast forward 31 years. An orthopedic surgeon at Huntington Hospital in Pasadena focused his laser pointer on an X-ray of my upper spine. "Mr. Davis, the cervical disc between vertebrae C4 and C5 has collapsed and needs to be fused. Have you ever suffered a head injury?"

At the registration desk, the registrar showed me the surgeon's orders, which called for a "discectomy and fusion of discs C4 and C5 with bone marrow from the iliac crest." I envisioned helmeted Greek soldiers invading Troy. Ginger vetoed my decision not to be operated on.

"You'll be a big pain in *my* neck if you don't take care of this. Fix what needs to be fixed."

The next day, she drove me to Huntington Hospital before daybreak. The nurse practitioner administering my electrocardiogram yawned as he removed the electrodes from my chest. A phlebotomist drew my blood with neither a greeting nor a smile. "I have no idea what's happening here!" I thought. I was prepared to exit.

When I asked the registered nurse for the surgeon's office phone number, she sighed and shook her head. He appeared half an hour later and put his hand on my shoulder. Then, he turned to the nurse and two guys in surgical togs next to my gurney.

"We aren't going through with the procedure until Mr. Davis is confident that he is fully informed."

My fear subsided when the surgeon connected the trauma of the gridiron incident at Mount Hermon with the surgical procedure I was about to undergo. I took a deep breath, exhaled slowly, and suspended all resistance to being healed. Four hours later, I awoke in the recovery room, groggy but whole and without a tube in my throat. After an hour or so, they pushed me into an elevator and brought me up to Room 1820. Ginger was happy to see me.

I had an IV and I was handed a device with a button to push for morphine. A nurse appeared every so often and asked, "On a scale of 1 to 10, how much pain are you in?" I would answer, "Seven or eight" and push the button – I was as high as a hamster on its wheel.

I had been hiding my drug and sex addictions from Ginger, but she was not blind to their consequences. She convinced me to go to Las Encinas Hospital, where Hollywood had sent its struggling stars since silent movies became talkies. W.C. Fields went there to dry out after drunken binges, as did Marilyn Monroe when her struggles with fame and miscarriages brought her down. They told me the room I was assigned had once been hers. Convalescing in such privileged surroundings, I decided my mental aberrations were the consequence of having spent too much time and put too much faith in the utopia of an artists' ghetto and my espousal of what, a decade later, seemed their lost cause. Whatever ailed me was compounded by my addiction to marijuana and an undeniable urge to smoke crack cocaine. I drew and described 'The Big Orange Splits' in my sketchbook. The split was male/female. The male persona was the orange's rind; subdued, confused, and defeated by life. The female alter ego beneath remained juicy, decisive, and desirable. It burst through the rind whenever the male was inebriated. Carlotta bursting forth had the power of a psychic earthquake.

Carlotta claimed she knew she was about to be born when, in 1992, I depicted myself as a curvaceous, balloon-breasted woman whose inner male lurked anxiously within. She pointed out that the situation was now reversed. My masculine rind had split to reveal her. When my therapist asked me to introduce him to Carlotta, I jumped to my feet and punched a vacant leather chair so hard it crashed into a bookcase on the other side of the room. "We've been talking about your mother. How did that feel?" he asked. "It was as if I had smacked my mother for abandoning me.," I replied.

My father, who was known as 'Cock' Davis at Yale, met my mother, Lynn Quinn, a New Haven nightclub singer, around the time the Japanese attacked Pearl Harbor. They married when she got pregnant with my sister, and my father took his wife to an Army Air Corps Bombardier Training site in Texas when he was kicked out of Yale. My grandmother, Nonnie, the imperious matriarch of the Davis clan, considered my mother a lowlife hustler. She accused my father of having impregnated her the night they met, drunk and rutting like dogs in the road. She pressured them to bring their infant daughter, Carolee, from Texas to Rochester, New York, where she would be safe should my father be shipped overseas.

My female self emerged at night with a crack pipe in her mouth. One thing we shared was a willingness to take risks. Smoking crack summoned her like a genie. I would make myself up as a transvestite hooker in black nylons, vinyl high heels, a skirt, and a clingy black blouse, and when Carlotta appeared, I blotted out my hirsute masculinity with a pancake base, highlighting my cheekbones with rouge, swelling and shaping my

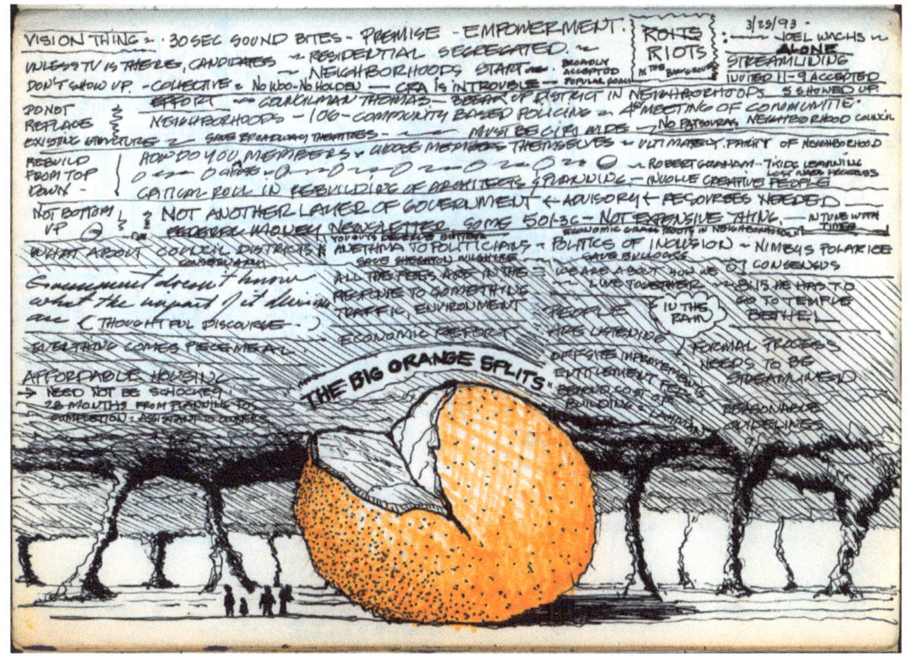

Sketchbook page, 1993, Carlton Davis, ink & colored pencil on paper, 8.5" × 11" (21.59 cm × 27.94 cm)

lips with scarlet gloss, adding long black lashes and a blue and silver hue to my lids, and covering my receding hairline with a reddish-orange wig. My garish attire was replete with silver costume jewelry and I wore a leather collar around my neck studded with silver spikes, which gave me more support than my neck brace. Warhol would have welcomed me to the Factory. I was a swishy, campy creature who fancied herself a femme fatale when her head was full of smoke. After a late night out, I would return to the studio behind our office on Traction Avenue, remove my costume jewelry, cold cream off my makeup, and return home to Pasadena. When I was on a sex safari, I had no empathy for anyone, even my wife who kept the home fires burning, the business profitable, and me alive.

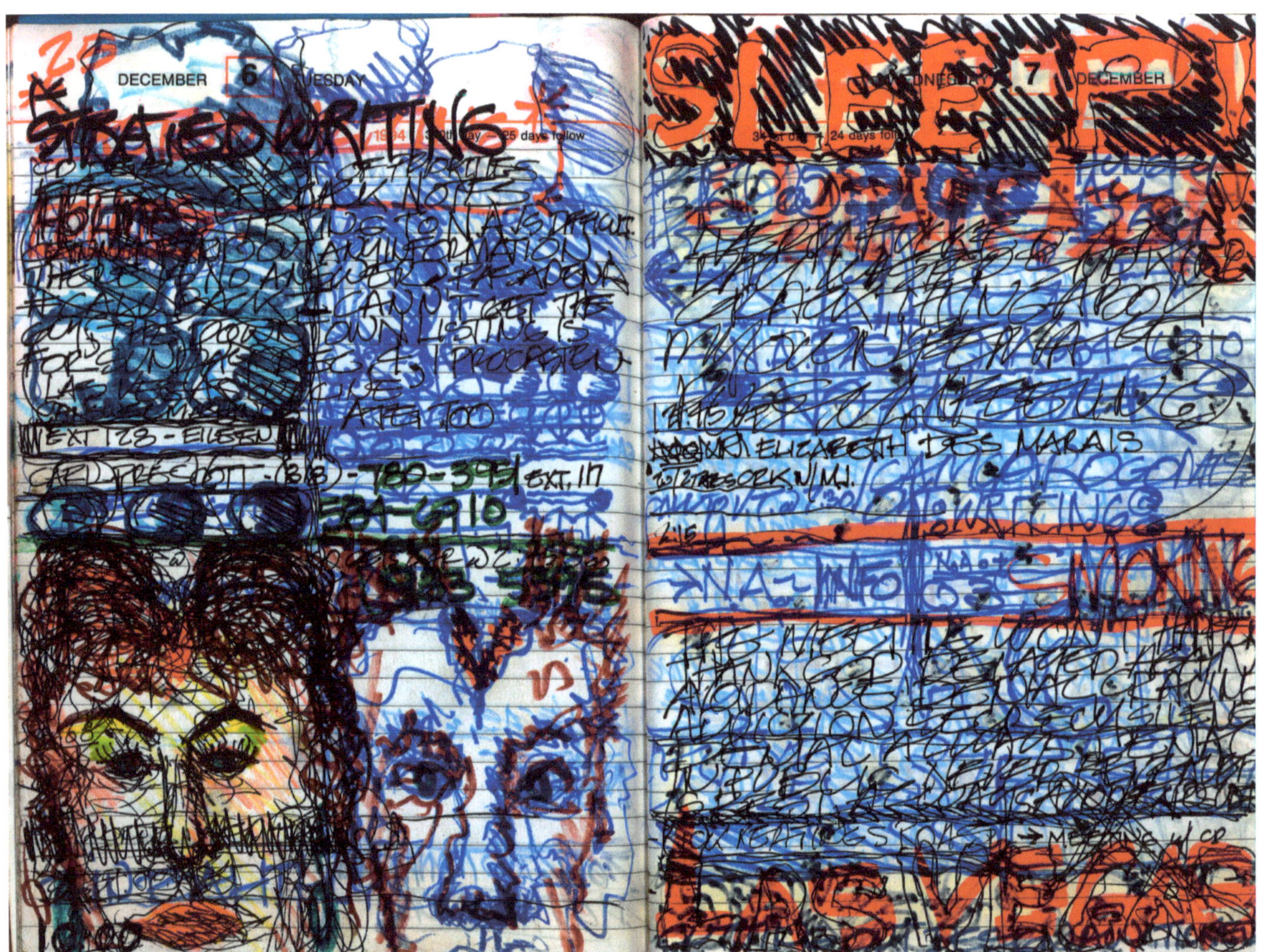

Daily diary pages, December 6 & 7, 1994, Carlton Davis, marker and pen on paper, 8.25" × 11" (20.95 cm × 27.94 cm)

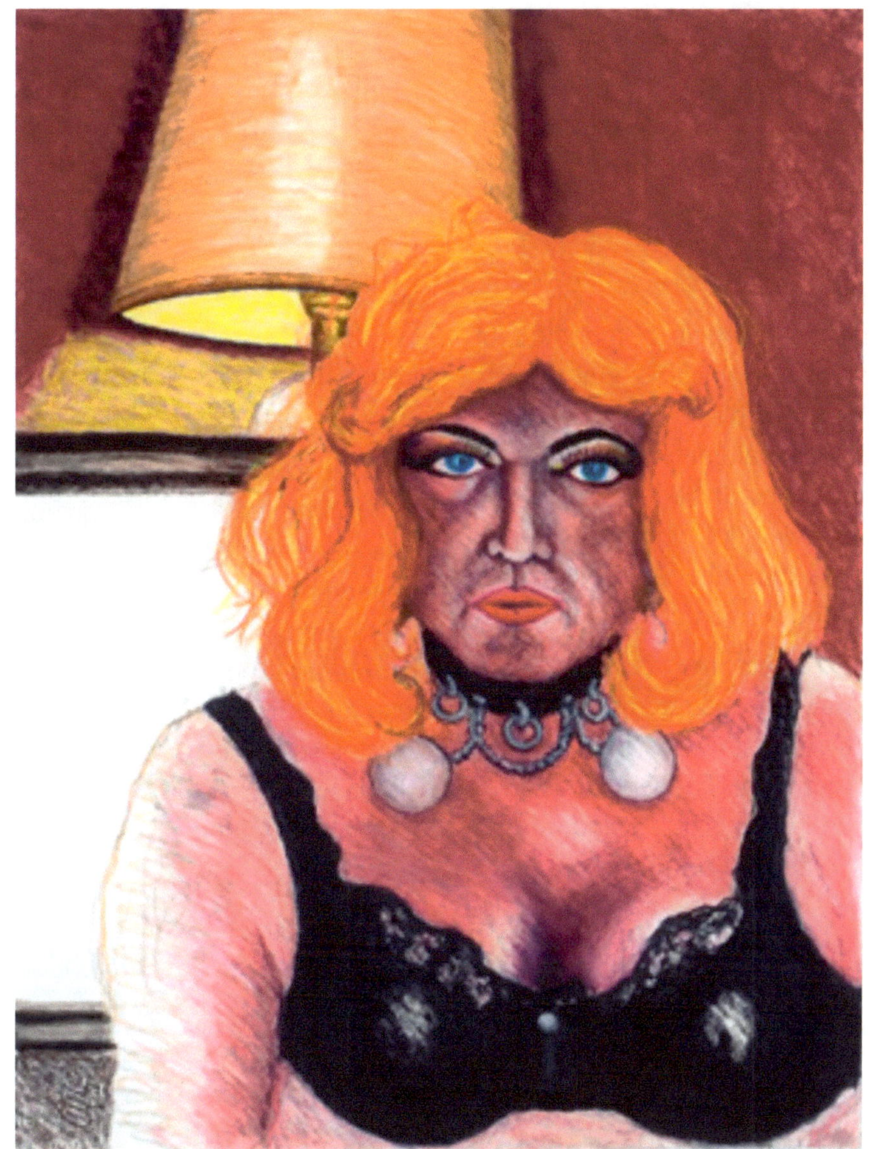

Self-portrait as Carlotta, 1995, Carlton Davis, colored pencil on paper, 30" × 22" (66.2 cm × 55.8 cm)

CHAPTER 14

1995
CRACKED UP

Lying in his garret
Without a bloody cent
Gnawing on a carrot
Inspiration spent
Reading Henry Miller
On how to beat the rent
Bohemia's a killer
For this creative gent
(Once a sturdy pillar
Now more than slightly bent)
His hand is on the tiller

But his boat is on a reef
Happiness is filler
Reality is grief
Let's watch Phyllis Diller
And smoke a lot of kif
The artist's life is the only life
Where suffering is cool
The artist's life is different
From what they teach in
school

Live fast, die young, be
famous
Ignore the Golden Rule
The artist's life–the pain, the
strife
The artist's life with passions
rife
The artist's life, his art, his
wife
For me!
—Poem by Peter Lownds

started to smoke crack in 1994 at the age of 50. Cannabis was fine, but I wanted the quickest, most destructive path to Hell. My throat and chest constricted with the first hit. My windpipe, lungs, and stomach filled with phlegm. I hawked and spat, smoked more, spat more, ran to the toilet, and retched. I retched in restaurants, bars, and gas stations and by the side of the road. My hands sweated, my joints ached, and I lost all manual dexterity and had trouble locking and unlocking doors. I lost 40 pounds in a couple of months, but I was still a big fat white man. In 1955, when I was eleven, Tennessee Ernie Ford's version of Merle Haggard's song about a coal mining John Henry type captured my imagination. It began, "If you see me comin', better step aside/a lot of men didn't and a lot of men died." I was the only person who was dying in my crack-smoking version of the legend.

Once, my sister showed me our Grandma Nonnie's closet. It was an anteroom to the attic, and you had to climb a hidden staircase in the Davis house in Rochester to get there. The room was lined with pine paneling and had a single window that overlooked a narrow porch roof and the front lawn. As she opened the door, she put her finger to her lip and spoke in a whisper. I was almost five years old, and she was six. There were two big boxes there she said were "steamer trunks" and I thought of them as "dreamer skunks" because dozens of malodorous moth balls were dispersed among the treasures. There were velvety cloche hats in rainbow colors, silky scarves and dozens of dresses, high-heeled shoes, feather boas, piles of costume jewelry, brocade shirtwaists, beaded tiaras, and a long white gown she wouldn't let me touch because it was sacred. When it was time to eat, the grownups shouted our names, my sister would yell down the staircase, "We're coming!" at the top of her voice. I can hear it in my mind as an adult as clearly as if it were yesterday.

For most of our time up there, we tried on clothes and shoes and laughed at how silly we looked or sat together on the window seat with imaginary cups of tea. My sister taught me that play had a serious side, especially when playing with what she called "real things." We could spill our make-believe tea and break imaginary cups and saucers, but real things had the power of place and you had to treat them with care. She was very conscious of who she was. It's a skill some children acquire early. My sister kept track of, unfolded, and refolded the clothes with care. There was no full-length mirror, so we posed and strutted our finery in front of the window and, when it got dark, lit the incandescent light bulb that dangled from a cord attached to the roof beam.

My grandparents legally adopted my sister when she was a baby. She had her own room with adjoining bathroom. The grownups smiled when they saw her. She got lots of hugs and kisses, while I was yelled at and spanked. I had to suppress my girly side with everyone but her, especially at a foster care facility known as 'The Farm,' where Nonnie delivered me later after my mother left. I was six years old. A couple of adolescent boys there had their way with me sexually, leaving profound, invisible wounds from which I am still recovering.

Carlotta prepared to sit for her first official portrait. She loved the way her legs looked in stockings, so she wore two pairs: a fishnet body stocking that stretched from toes to mid-chest, with black nylons on top. Because she recognized this as an important occasion, she took a 24-hour break from smoking crack so her hands were nimble enough to put on the pair of thigh-high stockings secured by a garter belt.

Marcel Duchamp mystified and enchanted the American art world for more than half a century. He was a master of nonchalance and an accomplished jokester. He turned a urinal upside down and exhibited it as a piece of sculpture, or drew a mustache and goatee on a copy of Da Vinci's *Mona Lisa*. He saw the power of 'ready-made art.' Carlotta's ready-made was a luxuriant pair of black silk panties.

She wore them to celebrate her emergence. As Carl, I was into S&M and B&D. I pressed my hirsute breasts together and bound them with a sharp metal chain. Carlotta unbound them and shielded them with copious falsies and a frilly black bra. As she admired her splendor, I reappeared as Carl with a piece of drawing paper and a fistful of colored pencils and sat down to work. Carlotta modeled for

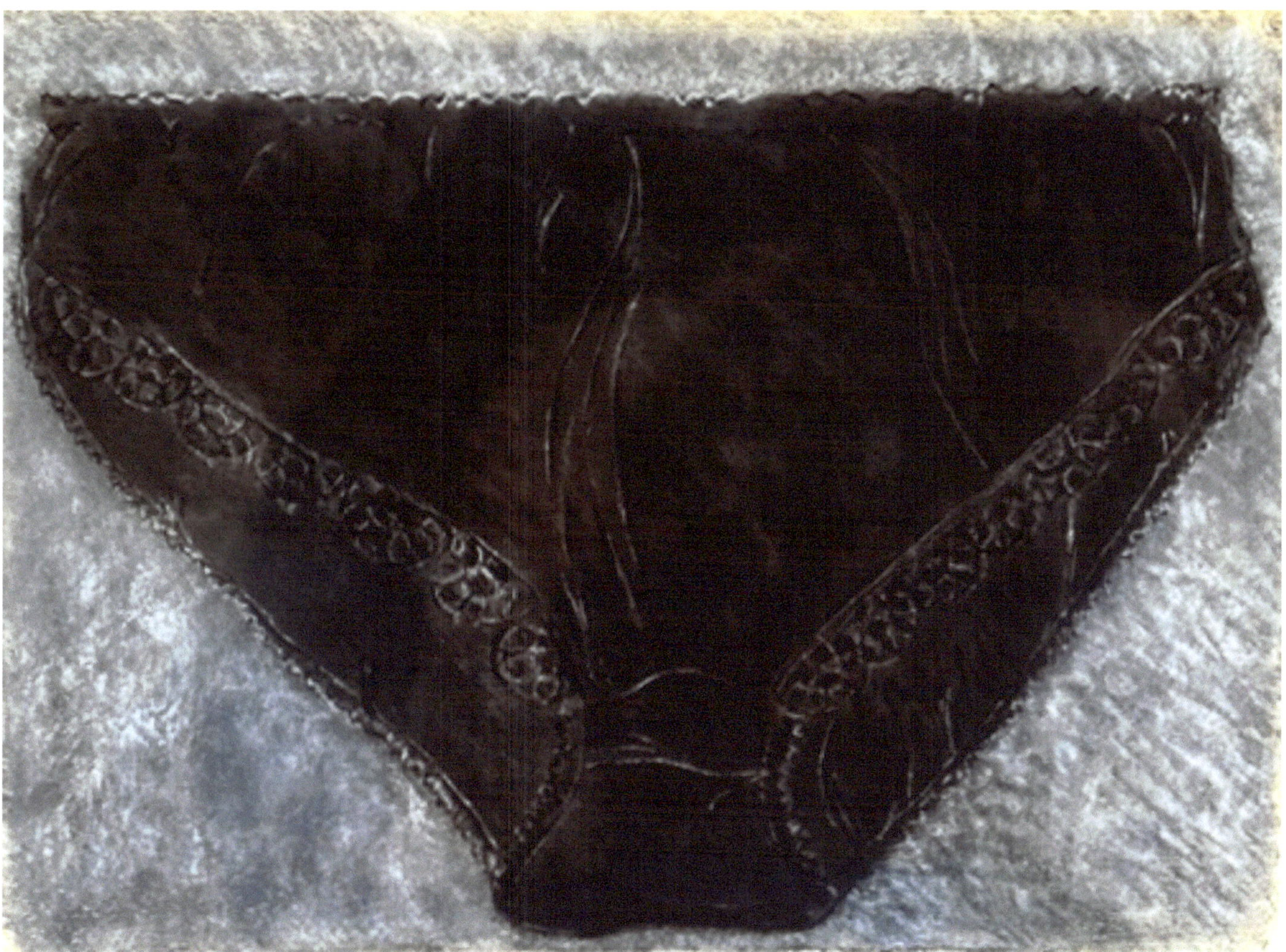

Black silk panties, 1974, Carlton Davis, pastel on paper, 22" × 30" (55.9 cm × 76.2 cm)

me but had trouble sitting still, and she got up often to look over my shoulder.

Carlotta: "You're like one of those TV wrestlers, Carl. You grunt and groan as you draw. Didn't you tell me the French guy whose photo you showed me was always pleasant and calm?

Carl: Marcel Duchamp talked about art with humor and insight, the same way he made it. His audiences were museum curators, wealthy collectors, and the most influential gallery owners. He lived and exhibited in New York for decades. He was an excellent chess player and a preeminent Dadaist, one of an international group of painters, composers, and poets who satirized and offended conventional taste. Duchamp delighted in blending art and technology, sex and abstraction, and images and languages. He called his graffitied Mona Lisa 'L.H.O.O.Q.,' which, if you pronounce each letter as the French do, translates as *Elle a chaud au cul* = she has a hot butt). He did something similar with the name he gave his cross-dressing self when she posed for his photographer friend, Man Ray—Rrose Selavy = *Eros c'est la vie* = Eros is life.

Carlotta: Stop, Carl! You're making me look like I'm ready to snarl. You seem to be in a hurry. That's probably because you want to smoke crack, take me to West Hollywood, and use me as bait for a john. Don't you realize I'm your savior? I had to fight like a tiger to get your stomach pumped when you washed down a bottle of aspirin with a bottle of hooch at Yale.

Carl: Please find something positive to say about me, Carlotta. Your recollections pierce me. You have been my saner self for years. Now that Ginger has assumed that role, I welcome you as my badder self.

Carlotta: I'm happy for all the attention.

Carl: I'm happy you're here to support me.

Carlotta: Imagine what it would be like to live another 30 or 40 years.

Carl: I love taking you to West Hollywood and watching the sex addict johns drool.

Carlotta: You make me bend down and peer into their cars, show them my bracelets and silver purse with an icepick inside I'll never use. Then you want me to say, "What's your best offer?" That's auctioneer talk. I'm not going to turn tricks, I'm here to see you through your crack addiction.

Exhausted by the effort to draw Carlotta while she was on her soapbox, I slept at the studio and remembered a dream. My tiger and I are camping in a national forest. My tiger is a hunter. She reclines by the campfire and stretches out with her head resting on her forepaws. A man and a woman I don't recognize approach me. They see my tiger and are fearful. My tiger stirs, raises her head, and growls, showing her terrifying teeth. "Quiet, girl," I say. She stops growling. I scratch her head. The campers come a step closer. "It's okay," I say, "she obeys me." I put my hand on her jaw. The tiger opens her mouth. I place both hands in her mouth and stroke her gleaming incisors. The campers come closer to the fire. The tiger rises and circles around the camp-fire and the campers before returning to my side. The campers watch in silence as my tiger rolls over. I ruffle and scratch her beautiful belly as she purrs and drops her paws to one side. "You're my pussy cat, aren't you?" I kiss her black velvet nose. The campers look at each other. The woman asks, "Are you allowed to have such an animal in the park?" I shrug my shoulders, "Who's going to stop me?" "But wild animals are dangerous," the man says. "Not for me," I respond. "Well, I don't like it," says the woman. "You shouldn't bring a terrifying beast, unleashed, to a public park." "Enough," I say. The man and woman stand up. My tiger rolls over and growls at them. "Cool it, girl!" She sits on her haunches. The couple scurries away. My tiger stretches and spots a family of deer. She rushes in the campers' direction. They

freeze in their tracks. The deer scatter in terror. My tiger isolates the eight-point buck, runs him down, and kills him. She drags him back to our campsite. I shout to the fleeing campers, "What can I do? She has a mind of her own."

I smiled as I recalled my dream. Joy had fled, a victim of crack abuse. When someone approached Carlotta and things turned transactional, she found an excuse not to go through with it, ran back to the truck, and we split. Fear of contracting a sexually transmitted disease dampens desire. I identified with Andy Warhol after he was shot in his Union Square studio and left for dead by Valerie Solanas in 1968. Warhol's art is very different from Duchamp's, but they were both masters of illusion and very conscious of the nature of the New York art world, which they studied assiduously and, in Andy's case, despised. Duchamp died the same year Warhol was shot.

They shared what Duchamp called an "anti-retinal bias." Both understood that the history of painting was a series of manipulations between art and reality. By producing hard-edged likenesses of Campbell's

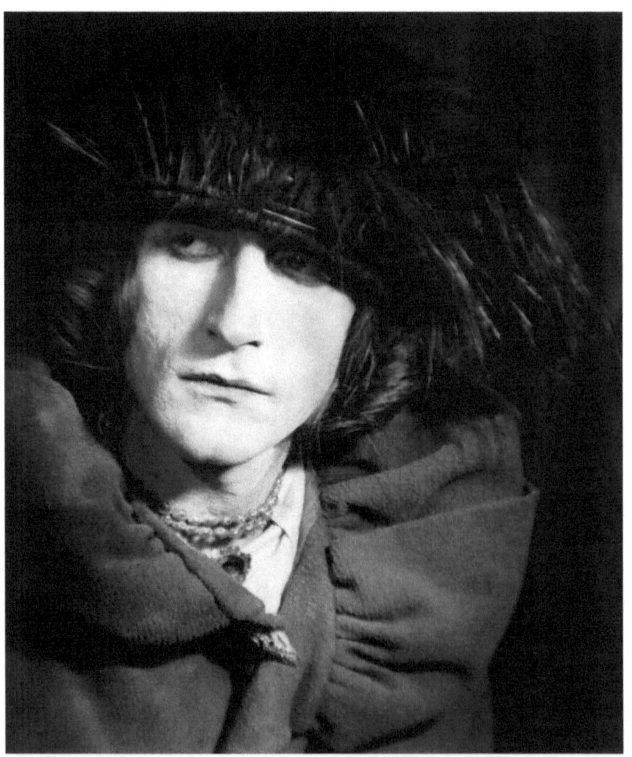

Rrose Selavy (Marcel Duchamp), 1923,
Photograph by Man Ray, private collection

soup cans on canvas and realistic sculptures of Brillo boxes, Warhol showed that the only difference between a sculpture that looks like a grocery carton and an actual carton is that the former is considered art and the latter is not. In 1962, Campbell's soup cost 33 cents a can and Andy's paintings of cans sold for $200 each in Irving Blum's Ferus Gallery in Los Angeles where he had his first public show. Blum exhibited the 32 identical canvases side by side. They are what Duchamp would have called *objets trompe l'oeil* – lifelike illusions, not of something natural but of something man-made in which the element of imitation has been eliminated. In other words, they don't depend on the viewer's ability to separate illusion from reality. What you see is what you get and, if you bought a Warhol Tomato Soup Can painting in the early 1960s and kept it, you are a rich person today.

In 2024, today 62 years from when Andy Warhol exhibited his Campbell's soup cans paintings, the soup cost of a real can of Campbell's Tomato soup is 92 cents a can at Walmart. This is a 280% rise in cost. Inflation is a real thing. Today Warhol's Soup Cans fetch a much higher price. At auction the series of 34 cans cost $11.8 million or $368,750 for a single can of Warhol's painting, which is a 1,844% rise in value. Who can say art is a career that doesn't pay well? Warhol died a millionaire. For most artists, even those who engage in anti-retinal art, it is not exactly a very profitable professional endeavor. I have been in search of a late-in-life role as an artist. Do I expect to make the money Warhol did? Not at all. I have been engaged in retinal art realism for 22 years. Finding a new path for life, like illusion, is unlikely. Nor have I found a new way to express anti-retinal art, which Warhol and other Pop artists like Oldenburg did. Their work was a deadpan allusion on everyday real objects. In Warhol's case the work is an anti-emotional yet powerful vision of culture in its stripping bare art from ordinary realities. It is soup without soup. You can't slurp it. You can only look at it. The emotional result is the conflation of art and anti-art. The art I have been seeking is not realism per se. Each drawing has emotional content,

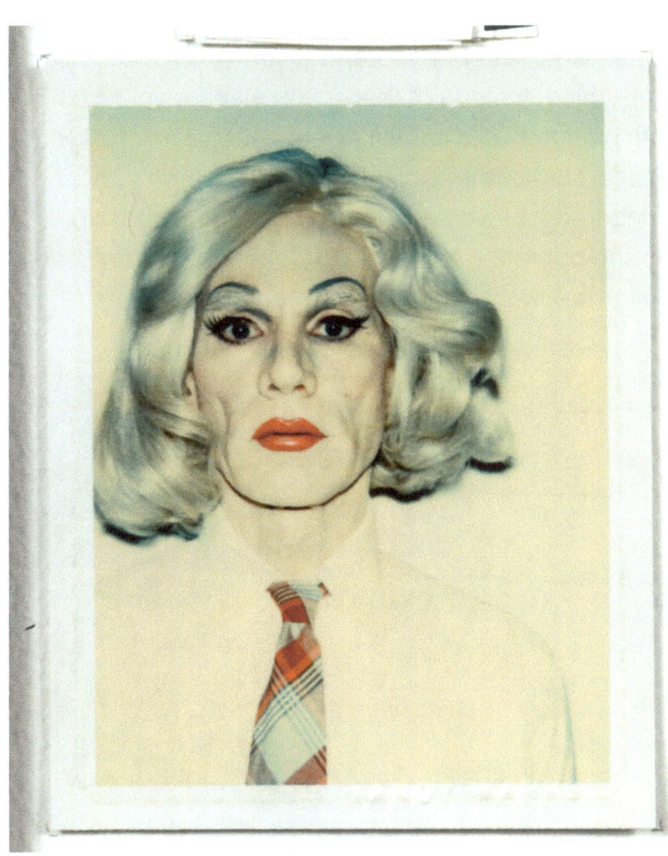

Self-portrait in drag, 1981, Andy Warhol, polaroid photograph, 4.25" × 3.35" (10.8 cm × 8.5 cm)

and it can be looked at as a singular event, which makes it part of a worn-out path, but what I have been searching for is a new path, which can only be seen when the viewer takes in the totality of all the drawings. I have made 14 individual images that have emotional content. In this way they are retinal but seen as a group they reveal the person, not his singular feel on a certain day or year. Without the totality they provide, they don't provide a different path to retinal art. Without this totality they are just one soup can of art. The real value remains here. While it probably won't ever have a value increase of 1844% over the price paid at the beginning of my venture, since now their value is 92 cents. But we can always dream.

Duchamp, the acknowledged genius of the avant-garde for more than half a century, is quoted in an ad-lib interview as saying, "The danger is to please an immediate public that comes around you and takes you in and accepts you and gives you success and everything. Instead of that, if you wait for your public, that public should come 50 years, 100 years after your death. That's the public I want." Conversely, Warhol hungered for love and fame in his lifetime and expired on the operating table at 59. Cardiac arrhythmia, for which he was being treated, is not ordinarily fatal.

Perhaps he died of psychological wounds sustained 18 years earlier in his confrontation with a homicidal feminist agitator. Marcel Duchamp enjoyed what appears to have been a charmed life and died at 81. Both were instrumental in changing the public's concept of the nature of art.

Salut les artistes!

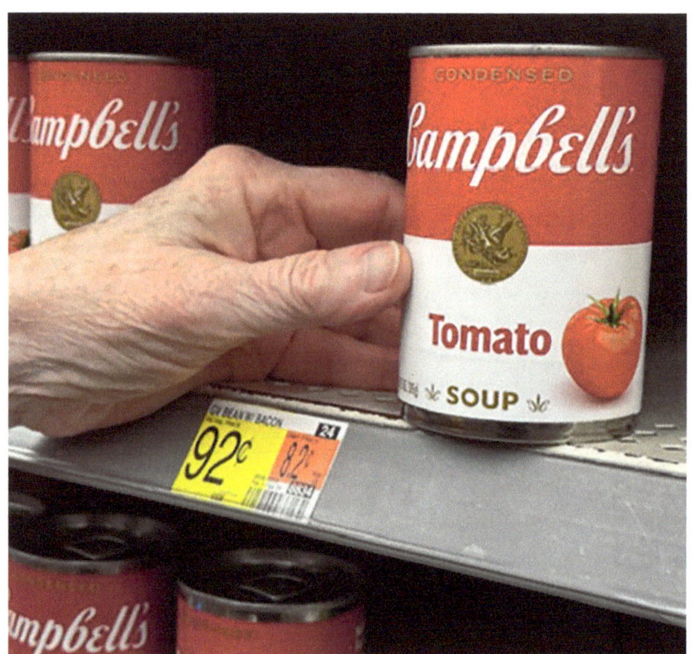

Campbell soup cans at Walmart, October 24th, 2024, photograph by Carlton Davis

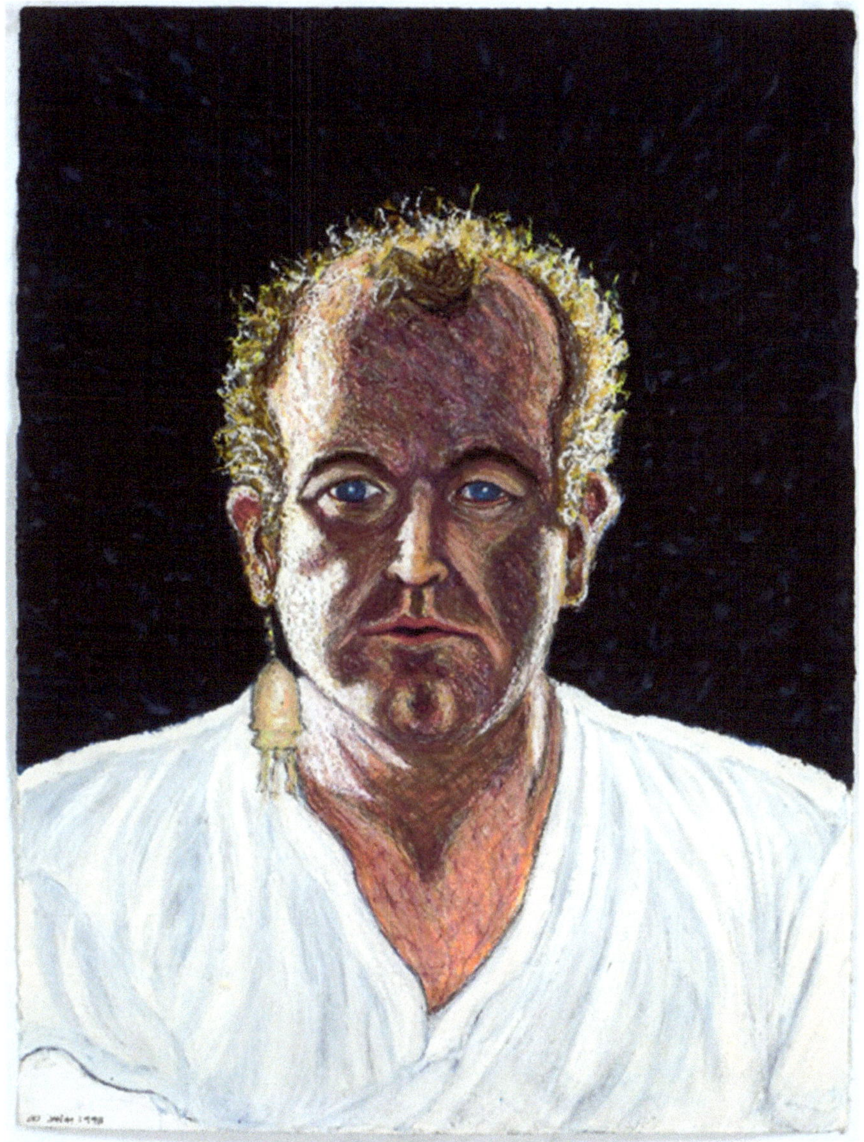

Self-portrait, 1998, Carlton Davis, oil stick on paper, 30" × 22" (76.2 cm × 55.8 cm)

CHAPTER 15

1998–1999
TRANCE AND TRANSFORMATION

"Midway through the journey of my life
I found myself in a dark and tangled place
The narrow path I was on had vanished
I have no idea how I got here because
I had been asleep for most of the way."

—*Inferno*, Dante Alighieri, Canto I

"When the Intellectual is cut off from the world of physical production and the social organization of labor, the divorce between physical and mental labor is complete. The individual worker and the Intellectual are no more than the sport of vast forces over which they have no control (…) The resentments, the passions of frustrated social existence take revenge in the wildest of individual aberrations (…) Before such forces, psychoanalysis is powerless."

—C.L.R. James, *Beyond a Boundary*, 1984

started to make art again, beginning with a new self-portrait, which revealed my continued connection with my female alter ego. The earring dangling from one ear indicated that Carlton and Carlotta were still one and the same. Carlotta smiled her wickedest smile. "You are not done with me yet," she whispered in my ear as I pretended to make a serious work of art. "I will take my revenge in the wildest deviations."

Daily Diary Pages, November 20 &21,1997, Carlton Davis, colored pen and ink on Paper, 8.25' x 5.5", (26 cm x 20.3 cm)

After my work on the North Hollywood Metro Station was done, everything fell apart. Most days, I went to the studio to smoke crack cocaine and dress up as Carlotta. At night, Carlotta and I went looking for trouble, cruising in the black pick-up truck she christened *le cygne noir*, the black swan. At 2 a.m. on one such occasion, I heard the whoop of a siren and saw flashing red and blue lights in the rear-view mirror. I pulled over. I was dressed and made up as Carlotta, and my crack pipe was lying in the tray next to the steering wheel and several packets of crack wrapped in plastic lay next to it. I grabbed everything and stashed it under the seat.

Two police officers approached the truck and ordered me to get out and stand on the sidewalk. I did as I was told, tottering on my high heels. One cop shone his light on me while the other questioned me.

"What are you doing driving around at two in the morning?"

"I'm on my way home after a costume party."

He looked dubious and turned to consult with his partner. I trembled with foreboding, imagining the humiliation of having to spend the remainder of the night in the slammer and Ginger's reaction to having to bail me out in the morning and bring me back home in full drag. A high-decibel voice came over the patrol car's two-way radio, "Shooter at Alameda and 30th!" The officers scurried back to their car. As they drove away, tires screeching, the cop riding shotgun shouted, "Nice outfit, girl!"

Although I thought of myself as a 'functioning addict,' I was decidedly not. My ability to work dissolved, and Ginger fired me. I had already lost my Center Street studio when the building was closed, and I thought I needed a studio. We made space behind the office and I went there to practice my addiction. Unemployment, drug use, sporadic

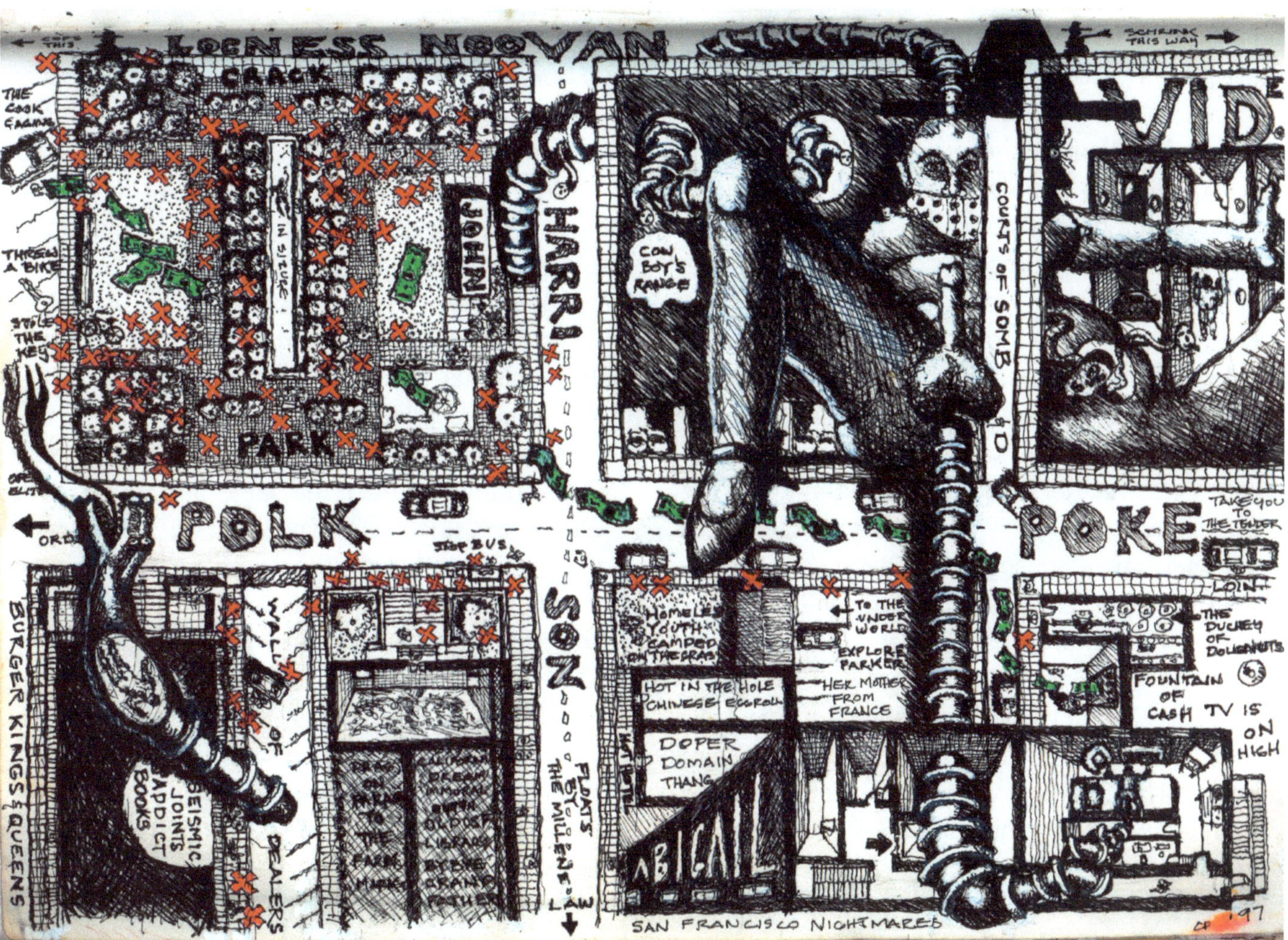

Polk-Poke, sketchbook page, buys on Polk Street, 1997, 8.5" × 11" (21.56 cm × 27.99 cm)

periods of internment in mental hospitals and halfway houses, a relapse, and resumption of employment, followed inevitably by another relapse with periods of sobriety in between. Ginger persuaded me to get help. At Las Encinas Hospital on my nine-day detox hold, a voluptuous psychologist in a scarlet dress that Carlotta coveted insisted on using the term 'alcoholic' and not 'addict'. I rarely drank great quantities of alcohol and refused to accept alcoholism as an umbrella term for substance addiction. On day three, when I tried to leave, the medical director would not allow it, explaining that I needed to cooperate with their treatment program. Reminding myself of Ginger's generosity and belief in me, I relented and spent the remaining days of the hold as part of a group of resident substance abusers working the AA Twelve Step program with the psychologist, whom I called the "Nazi Baroness" under my breath. At a time when Alcoholics Anonymous programs were the *sine qua non* of recovery, I was reluctant to surrender my addiction to 'a higher power' or identify myself as an alcoholic.

At Ginger's urging, I checked myself into a 28-day program at the Betty Ford Center near Palm Springs, where they assured us I would be treated as a drug addict. I was placed in a very nice room with a view of the duck pond. My roommate Jim arrived from Anacapa Psychiatric Hospital the same day I checked in.. He was worried that the Betty Ford Center had sheds like the ones at Anacapa where, he claimed, monkeys were chained to the walls. Jim explained that small vents hidden by smoke alarms regularly dispersed 'knockout gas' in the dormitories at Anacapa. After the patients passed out, men in white lab coats came into their rooms and extracted small pieces of their brains, which were swapped with similar fragments of the brains of the captive monkeys. A patient at Anacapa would wake one day in a monkey suit and chained to a wall, while the monkey with a patient's brain particles escaped and went shopping on Melrose Avenue. I kept my mouth shut listening to Jim's explanation. Telling him I was born in the year of the monkey would have confused him. He returned to Anacapa the next day.

The Betty Ford program was based on the Twelve Steps of AA, with lots of homework between sessions. When I wasn't attending meetings, I struggled to answer questions like, "What are the consequences of your substance abuse?" I took daily walks around the duck pond and the wall that separated the center from the rest of the Eisenhower Medical Center and enjoyed playing water volleyball in the swimming pool. About a week before my 28-day program ended, I accidentally hit Jerry Garcia of the Grateful Dead in the head with a volleyball. He left the center the day after I beaned him and died the next week. My chums, four guys all named Bob, accused me of killing him. I relapsed right after my release.

After 28 days at The Betty Ford Center, I closed my studio, relapsed for a week, got sober for several days and then decided to follow my Betty Ford therapist's recommendation and go to Henry Ohlhoff House, a residential treatment center in San Francisco. I stayed clean and sober there for almost three months and spent days working on the San Francisco Airport enlargement project for the architectural firms of Skidmore, Owings, & Merrill, and Delcampo & Maru. One day, while riding the streetcar from work in downtown San Francisco to Alamo Square, I recalled being repeatedly raped in the foster home by two older boys. After debarking, I found a bench and sat weeping for more than an hour, reliving the trauma I had buried for nearly half a century and making myself late for dinner, which led to my being expelled from the house.

. . .

Civic Center Park, bounded by Van Ness Avenue and Polk and Harrison streets in downtown San Francisco, was a magnetic draw for people swimming in crack cocaine, dealers and buyers both. I was one of the buyers, and I unwittingly booked a room at the Abigail Hotel nearby and from there illustrated all the dysfunction I witnessed and imagined. It could have been the 'dark and tangled place' of Dante's *Inferno*. The Poisonous Pilgrim swimmer, recognizable by his/her distinctive high black-brimmed hat, had a snake coming out of his/her ass. The snake was seismic with mechanical joints that allowed it to expand and contract, the same principle used to protect multistoried buildings during earthquakes and which enabled the snake to wriggle through the drug-addicted underworld of what I called 'Polk-Poke,' seen on previous page.

The reptile expanded to its full length, went through the hotel wall, crossed Polk Street, penetrated the Pilgrim hermaphrodite, came out of him/her head first, slithered down Van Ness Avenue, found its way through two glory holes, surfaced, crossed Harrison Street, tunneled under the sidewalk in Civic Center Park, went underground again across Polk Street, and emerged by the dealers' wall. It flicked its reptilian tongue at the spot where a dealer threw his bicycle at me when we couldn't agree on the price of a crack purchase. The reptile had already swallowed one crack swimmer. Another backstroked in the bathhouse with multiple glory holes, while a baby reptile was born out of the belly button of the Poison Pilgrim, now seen in profile. The baby snake stuck its head through a glory hole and razzed the swimmer below. Holes were everywhere in the Duchy of Doughnuts right next to the Abigail Hotel, where Carlotta and I booked a room.

Right next door was the convenient cash machine hole where I gathered the green to support my $100-a-day habit, which is symbolized in the sketch by greenbacks floating above Polk-Poke. Red Xs mark the locations, over time, of these purchases that were carried out under the nose of the San Francisco Police Department. If you got hungry in the throes

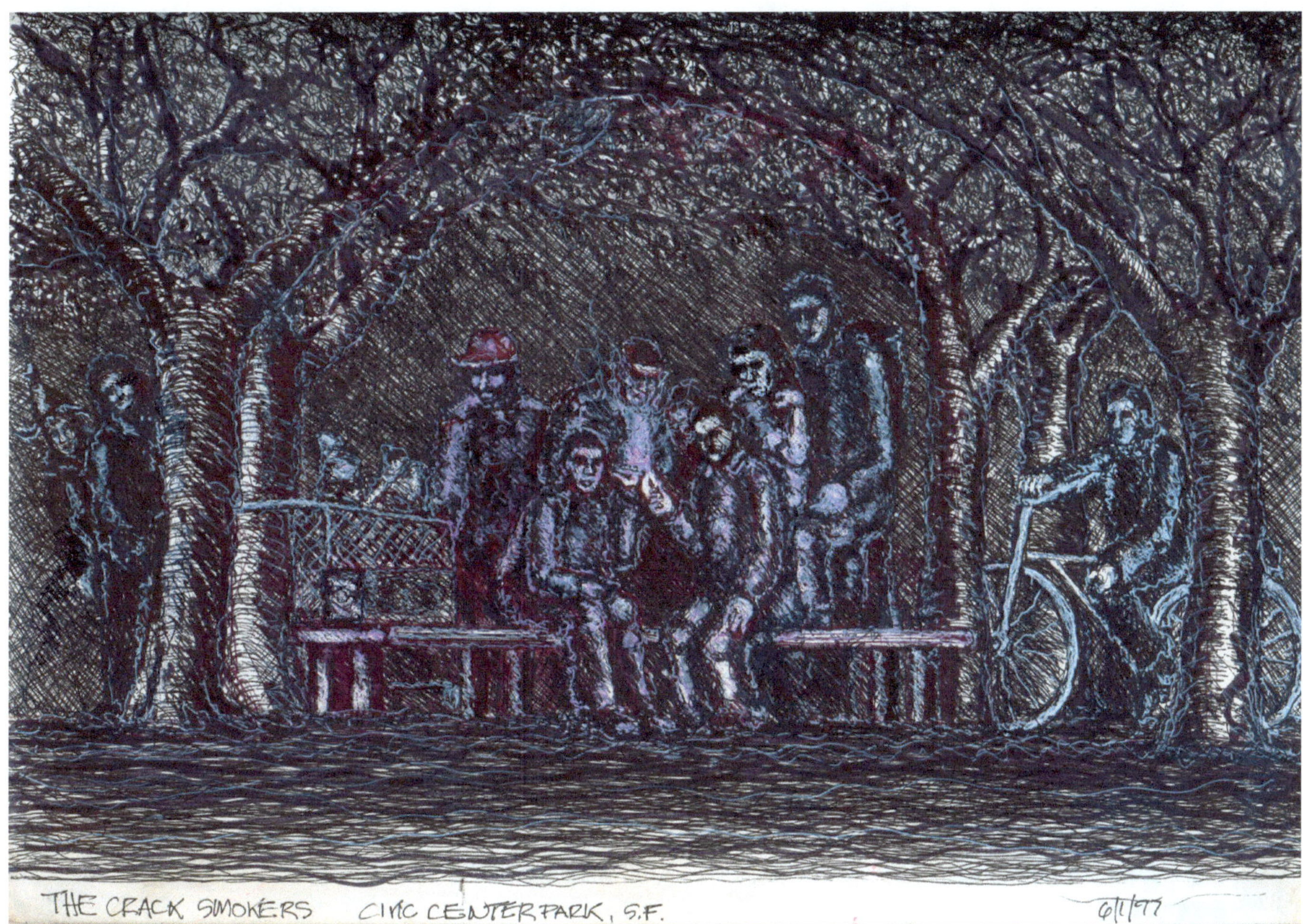

The Crack Smokers, June 1, 1997, Carlton Davis, ink and Wite-Out on paper, 8.5" × 11" (21.56 × 27.99 cm)

of crack delirium while navigating the Civic Center drug emporium, there were several all-night eateries nearby, populated by transvestites, Carl and Carlotta renamed the restaurant "Burger King and Queen". At A Roll in the Hole, you could stuff your churning gut with Chinese egg rolls. At the Duchy of Doughnuts, doughnut holes reigned supreme.

I returned to LA in 1997, hired as part of a team rebuilding 'back of house service facilities', all in preparation for the new Disney California Adventure attraction. Despite my drug addiction, I was still employable because I could hide my destructive habit. I was the on-site architectural engineer on a team to erect 27 prefabricated steel buildings all within a year. My design contribution was adapting the metal buildings to Disneyland's requirements. The buildings included a dog kennel, an aviary, a carriage house for Cinderella pumpkin shell coaches, a service station for the Disneyland tram, a power station, a big building to house Disneyland merchandise, and a storage facility for cast members' costumes.

While enforcing Disney contracts, I participated in what political activist, writer, and cricketer CLR James called "the sport of vast forces over which [we] have no control." Contractors love writing change orders that are the bane of architects' plans. When a contractor requested a change order, I could say, with the power vested in me by Uncle Walt Inc., "That situation is covered in the contract Disney signed with you." I experienced power by proxy each time I shook my head, looked a greedy contractor in the eye, and said, quietly but firmly, "No change. Check your contract."

The I-5, the major north-south traffic artery, was

being widened when I was commuting from Pasadena to The Magic Kingdom. One evening on my way home the five lanes of traffic in front of me lurched to a sudden stop. I slammed on my brakes with such force that my Ford Explorer executed a semicircle, and I was looking at the five lanes of traffic behind me that hadn't gotten the message yet. "I'm a dead man!" I thought as the car spun on two wheels and fell on its side. The rearview mirror punched out the driver's side window, cutting my arm. I was scrunched sideways between the front seat and the dashboard and couldn't reach up to open the door. Then, I heard a man say, "climb out the back." My savior was Latino. "Jesus must love you, man!" he said repeatedly in his heavy accent. He walked me to the side of the freeway and then, with three others, he righted my car and pushed it next to me. My rescuers disappeared, and I was left standing next to my car. Traffic resumed its intensity, and I stood there waiting for a highway patrol car. None came. When my head cleared, I climbed back into my car and started the engine. I drove home holding my bleeding arm out of the shattered window. Thank you, Jesus! My transformation had begun.

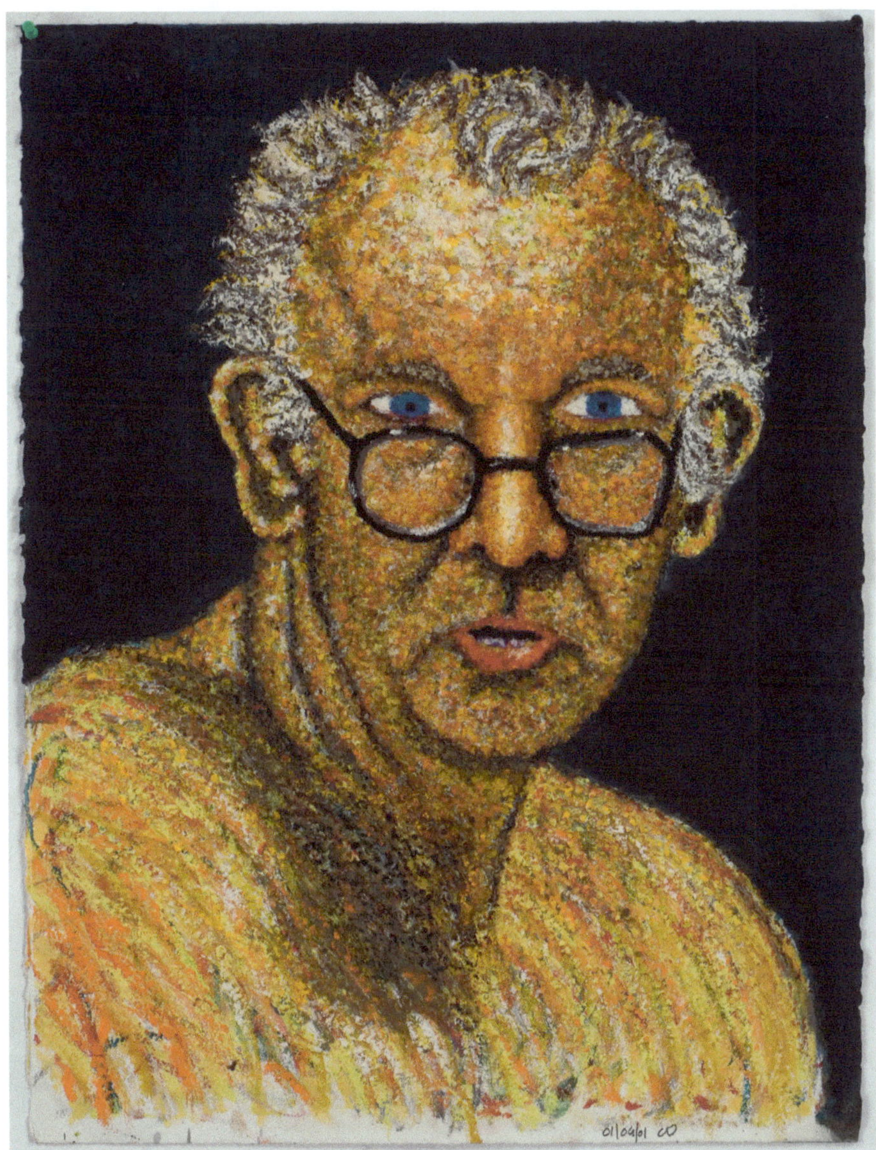

Self-portrait, 2001, Carlton Davis, oil stick on paper, 30" × 22", (76.2 cm × 58.47 cm)

CHAPTER 16

2001
BURNT BACON

On the 11th day of a September morning in the second year of the 21st century, the American dream ended. The sun had risen in Los Angeles, and I was preparing breakfast when Ginger yelled from upstairs, "Turn on the TV! A plane has crashed into the World Trade Center Towers in New York!" I watched fires explode from both 110-story structures, releasing a dense cloud of black smoke into the bright blue autumn sky. I had worked on the design of 'Windows on The World,' a restaurant with a panoramic view of Manhattan atop one of the towers, and I saw it pancake down and disappear from the skyline. I gasped as human bodies tumbled down the walls of the towers.

Incredulous commentators described the ensuing calamity. Remote airborne video cameras

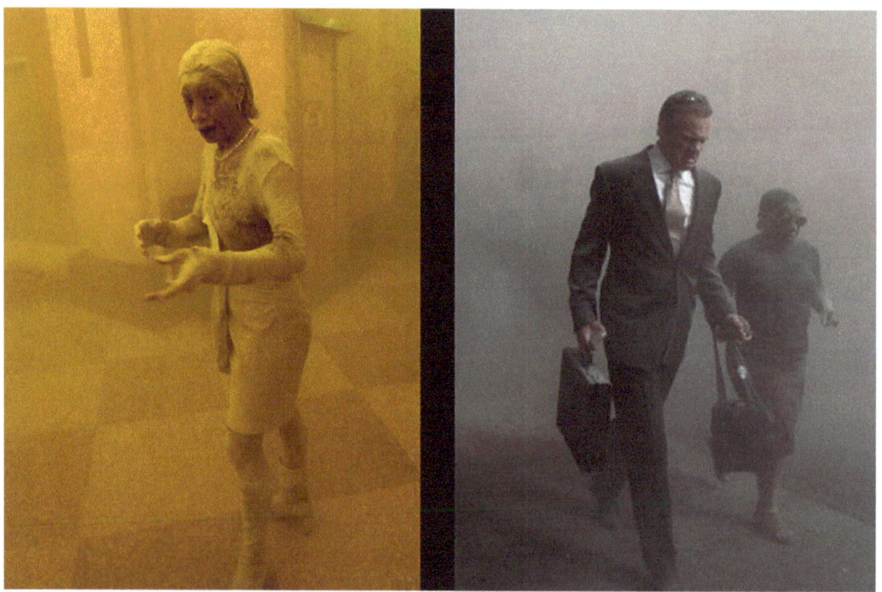

Dust people, 9/11/2001, New York City, photographers unknown

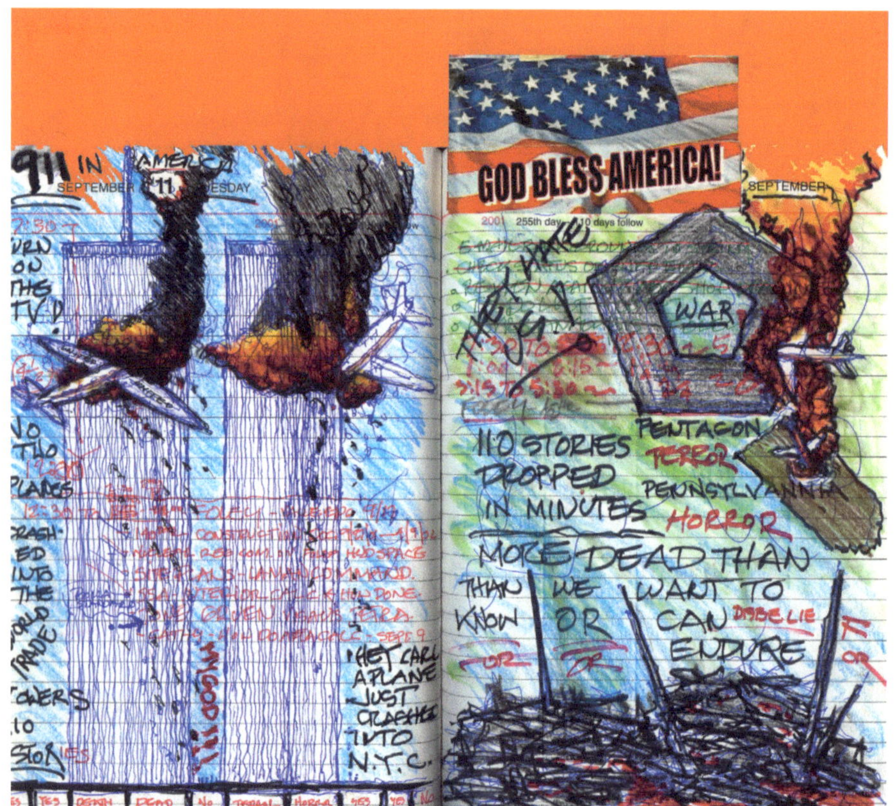

Daily diary pages, September 11 & 12, 2001, Carlton Davis,
colored pencil and pens on paper, 8.25" × 5.5" (26 cm × 20.3 cm)

showed the dark gray cloud rising and spreading across the city and captured the towers' floors dropping on top of each other and disappearing into the enormous cloud of debris engulfing the lower portion of the island of Manhattan, known as the Battery for a 17th Century fortress the English built there. Mobile cameras broadcast haunting images of men, women, bystanders, and witnesses to the tragedy making their way through the ground smog in their workday suits and dresses that had become dusted with gruesome gray flecks of falling particles. Their open mouths exposed their teeth as they gasped for air, fleeing from what must have seemed the wrath of God. I had left the bacon sizzling in the pan when Ginger had shouted news of the catastrophe, and now our kitchen was filled with acrid smoke.

We threw open the windows of our 19th-century house 3,000 miles from the scene of the tragedy and rushed back to the screen. We were two architects hypnotized by the destruction of the tallest buildings in the world, filled with ordinary humans doing business at the dawn of a new millennium. Little did we know we were witnessing a challenge to the way we lived and the role we played in the world.

My attention was riveted upon the people who jumped, were pushed, or fell from the upper floors of the towers when no other escape was possible and the smoke and fire were too much to bear. I had experienced 'suicidal ideation' since I was six years old and had attempted suicide with alcohol and aspirin when I was a junior in college. Launching yourself into the heavens 1,000 or more feet above the sidewalk when the only alternatives were suffocation and immolation seemed to me a liberating alternative, but I realize that many people observe religious and ethical strictures about taking one's life. Rather than share these moody thoughts with Ginger, I opened a volume of Francis Bacon's paintings. One of the highlights of my first trip to Europe was encountering his *Self-Portrait, 1971* at the Centre Georges Pompidou in Paris. I felt as if I had been drinking absinthe, "Or emptied some dull opiate to the drains one minute past, and Lethewards had sunk," as Keats phrased it in *Ode to a Nightingale*.

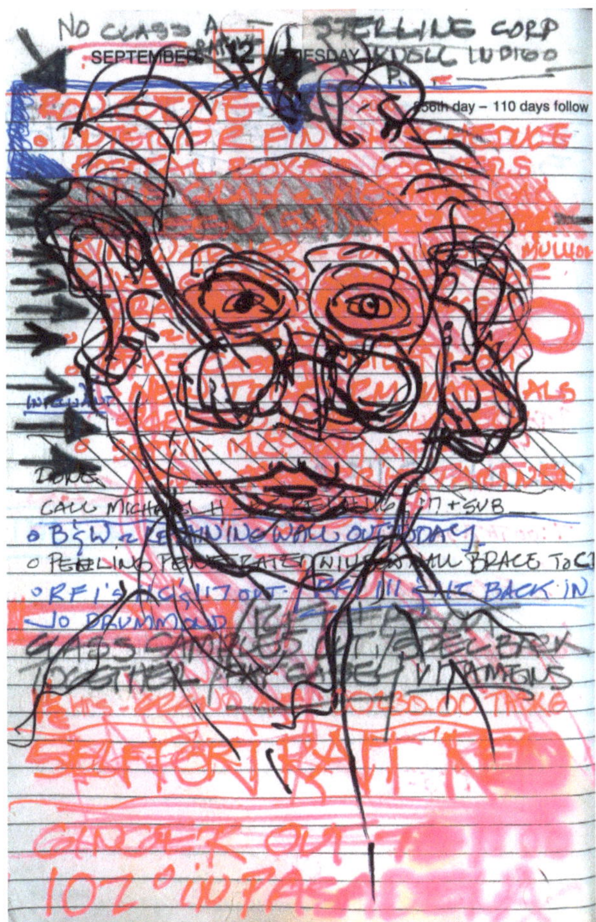

Daily diary page, Sept 12, 2000, Carlton Davis, 8.25" × 5.5", (20.95 cm × 13.97 cm)

I knew that I was moving toward self-inflicted oblivion when I drew over a rough sketch I made in my daily diary of September 12, 2000. The sketch was scribbled over notes from my humdrum career as an architect upon which I spilled water of Lethe, the river of forgetfulness, on the page. How symbolic! In the year preceding the Twin Towers' collapse, I witnessed my own disintegration. I was expiring in the addictive haze of crack cocaine. My body was falling apart, my breathing was labored, and my joints were painfully stiff. After a hit, I would gag and vomit gray bile. Yet I was still semi-functional. I did not perform as I would have if I were well, but I could hold down a job.

At the end of the day, I would puff on my glass pipe, which eventually disintegrated into curved shards too short to bear a wad of crack in a small wire nest at one end. I'd buy more pipes at a Skid Row liquor store. Each contained a tiny fabric rose with a wire stem inside a utilitarian glass tube. I put the paper roses in a box that was growing fuller each week. Then, I'd drop by my dealer's place. He cooked his crack in a small house in a gang neighborhood not far from my studio. I'd buy 8 to 12 irregularly shaped, pill-sized tablets and smoke them in my car until I was high enough to return to my studio. I promised myself that tomorrow, I'd stop this slow-motion suicide. What I didn't share with my psychologists and psychiatrists was that I believed that the more dissolute my behavior, the more creative energy accrued to me.

I spent a lot of time thinking about the mess I had made of my life. Trying to clean up in Alcoholics Anonymous wasn't working. I was hopelessly addicted to crack. Even though I drank, When I expressed in a meeting that I was a drug addict, the others in the room nevertheless termed me an alcoholic, which infuriated me. If I responded to this in a meeting, it made everybody angry. Residence at the Betty Ford Center kept me sober for only a month. The Henry Ohlhoff House in San Francisco didn't work. I was thrown out for flouting their rules and relapsed immediately. I went home empty-handed and imploring myself to stay sober. If I didn't kick the

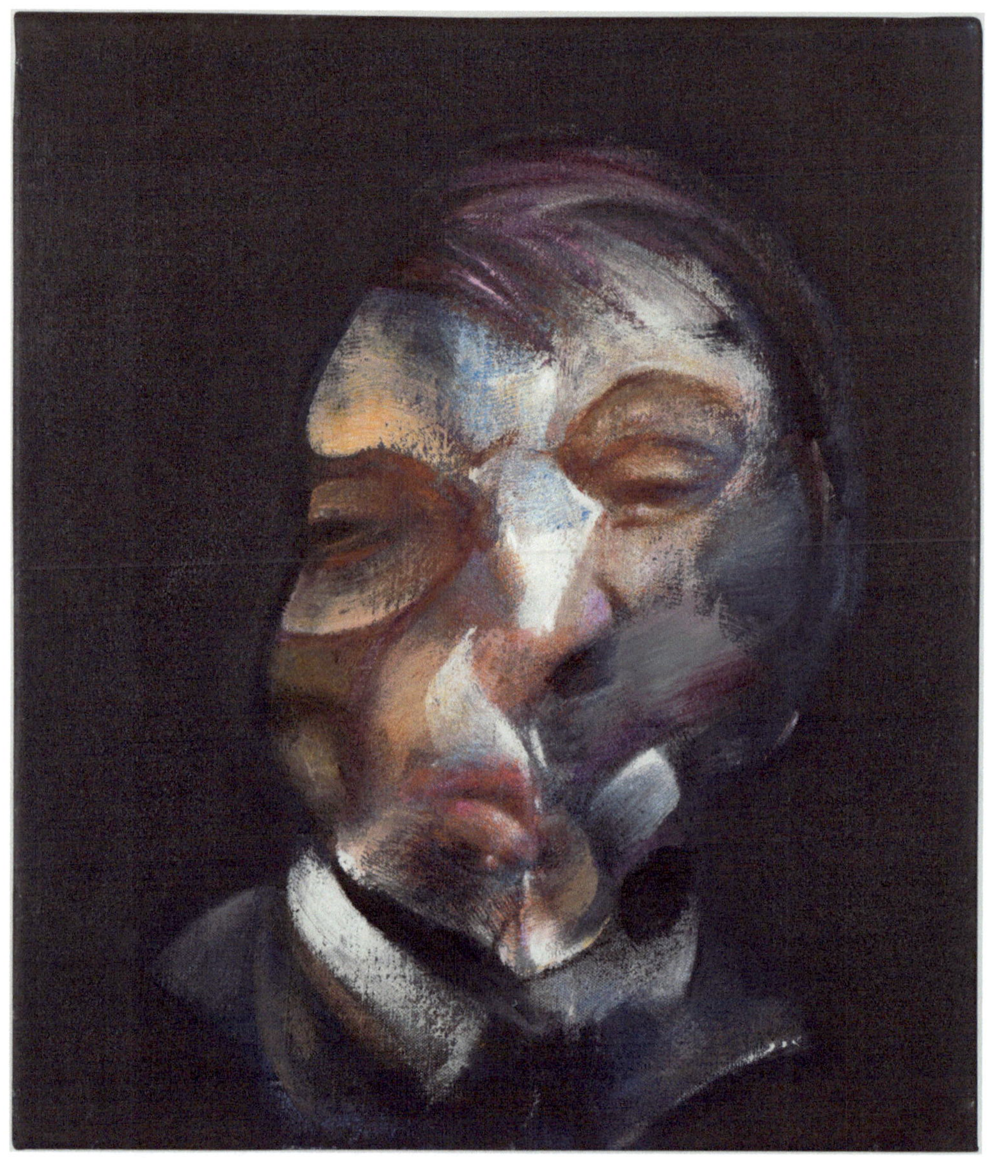

Portrait, 1971, Francis Bacon, oil on canvas, 14" × 12", (35.5 cm × 30.5 cm), Centre Georges Pompidou, Paris

habit, I'd die. Only two things gave me hope: my wife stood by me, and I kept trying to make art.

"You won't recover until you hit rock bottom," AA members warned. I felt I had descended into a chasm of despair. Suicide was what artists resorted to when pain supplanted inspiration. Even in despair, some part of me felt my art would soon bloom. I didn't want to emulate Francis Bacon, but I wanted to paint with his intensity. My 2001 self-portrait may appear troubled and doubtful, but I was alive. My ears had been primed by years of tinnitus to what Edgar Allen Poe called the "tintinnabulations" of the death knell. My millennial drawings scared friends, relatives, and acquaintances to whom I showed them because they saw that the person who made them was in agony. But they gave me hope.

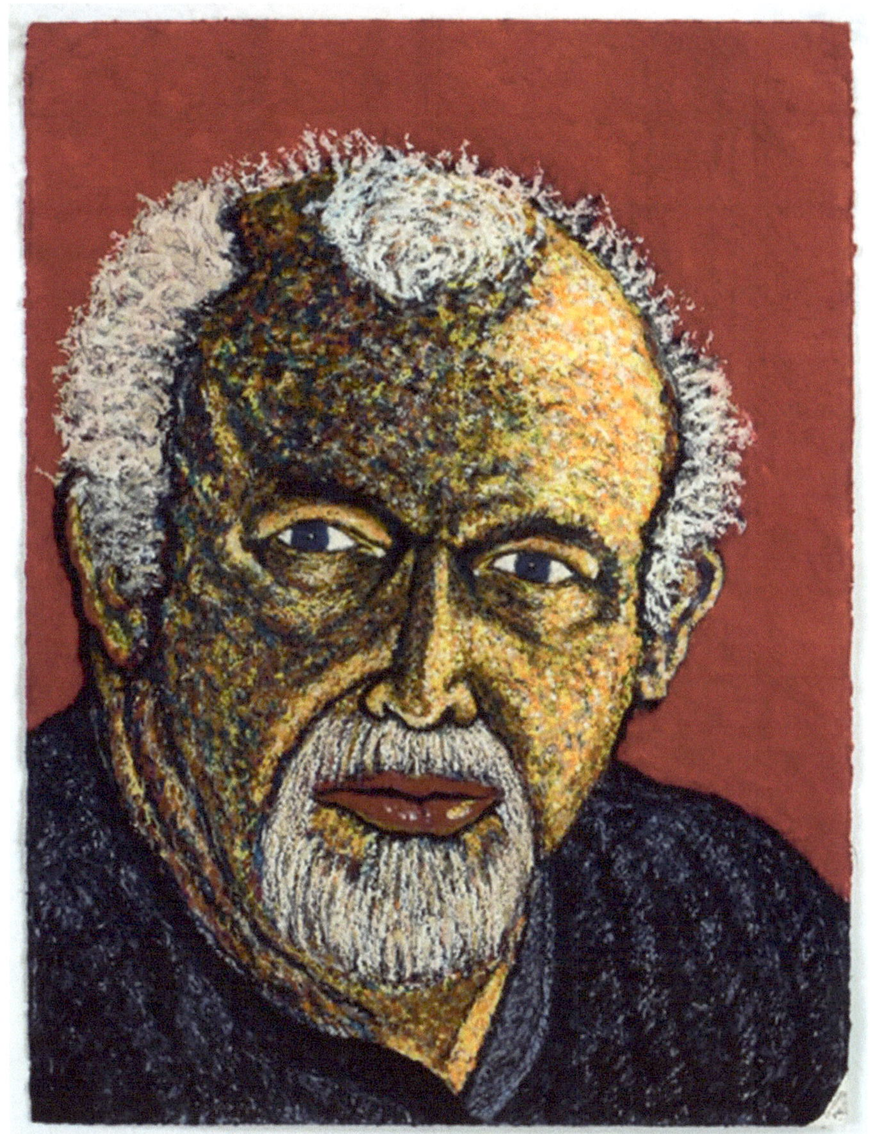

Self-portrait, 2004, Carlton Davis, oil stick on paper, 30" × 22" (76.2 cm × 58.47 cm)

CHAPTER 17

2003 – 2004
THE LUNATIC BABOON BLUES

All right, enough already! You don't want to know, but I'm going to tell you anyway. This is how low you can go when you're out of your mind and addicted to crack.

I had developed a blood clot and was hospitalized at Huntington Hospital in Pasadena for it. Next thing I knew, all hell broke loose, and I was screaming!

"I don't know what's happening, you motherfucking pigs!"

My bellowing bounced off the walls of a windowless cell. I tried with all my might to break free from the straps that bound me to the vinyl-coated slab I lay on. Four giant 'disorderlies' dragged me to what they called the 'Quiet Room' of the hospital's mental ward, and then strapped me down when I resisted their efforts to restrain me. I fantasized I was a soldier of the Jihad, a foiled suicide bomber who, instead of being served like a Pasha in a harem in paradise had, ended up in Abu Ghraib Prison in Baghdad. I'd been bitten by mangey hounds, sodomized with a patent leather dildo by a woman soldier in uniform, wired with electrodes, stripped naked, made to wear women's undergarments and an eyeless felt hood, paraded around for the troops' amusement, and strapped to an iron gate. I wanted to behead my captors with a gleaming scimitar. The nurses and doctors who ordered my confinement treated me no better than a caged baboon. Artists were the enemies of the corporate state. Sycophants and flunkies would beat me with clubs if I didn't cooperate or inject me with sodium pentothal until I squealed

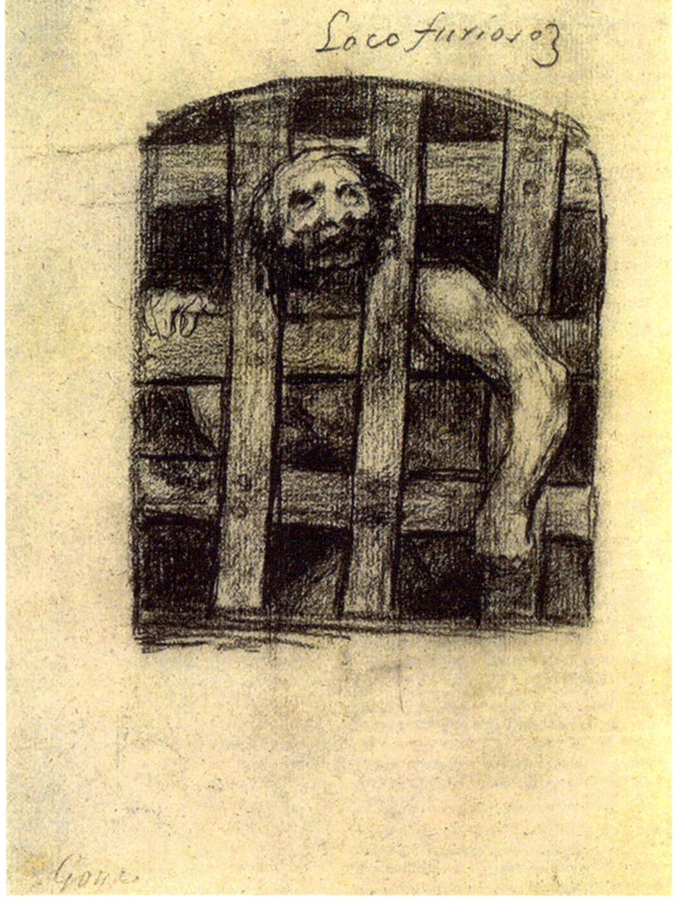

El Loco Furioso, Francisco Goya, 1824-1828, drawing black chalk on paper, Album G (60-page sketchbook), private collection, photograph, courtesy of the Frick collection.

like a pig. I was a threat to the fascist warmongers. I would not march and sing hymns like a Christian soldier. Like the besotted Welsh poet, I raged, raged against the dying of the light.

I was a 21st-century version of *El Loco Furioso*, the Furious Madman in Album G of Francisco Goya's astonishing sketchbooks, the great artist's version of the hooded man with outstretched arms and electrical wires dangling from his fingers in a photo from Abu Ghraib. Goya found an indelible image for the lunacy of war in his 1823 masterpiece *Saturno Devorando Su Hijo* which now hangs at the Museo del Prado in Madrid. Saturn, the Italian god of harvest and planting time, whom the ancient Romans identified with the Greek god Cronus, bug-eyed with madness, had already devoured his naked son's head and right arm and was jamming his outstretched left arm into his maw. *La Saturnalia*, a joyous weeklong celebration of life, the predecessor of Christmas, had gone terribly wrong. A hundred eighty years later, all that was missing in the Abu Ghraib photos was a colossal American Saturn devouring Islamic insurgents after electrocuting them. In this, my third potential incarceration in the nuthouse, exhausted from shouting and pointless struggles to free myself, I conked out.

I lay waiting in an open-assed hospital gown strapped to a slab in the windowless room for what seemed like hours. I heard the screams of a patient in the next room as he was being dunked into a tub full of ice. I knew this was what they would do with me if I refused to cooperate. The door opened and a man in a white lab coat entered saying he was the admitting psychiatrist.

"What did I do to end up in this nightmare? I came to the hospital because of a problem that has nothing to do with my sanity."

"You threatened to shoot a staff member," said the shrink.

"I did no such thing. You want to hear my side of the story?"

A disorderly unbolted the straps and I asked if I could sit upright on my vinyl-coated slab. The shrink nodded and sat in the cell's only chair with a pen in

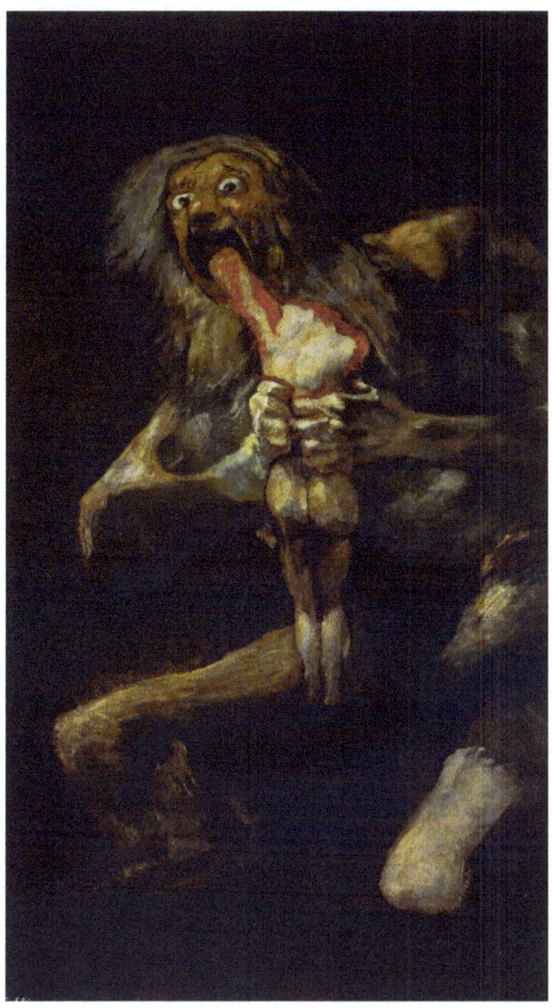

Saturn Devouring His Son, 1823, Francisco Goya
Museo del Prado, 48" x 28" (144.73 cm x 83.82 cm)

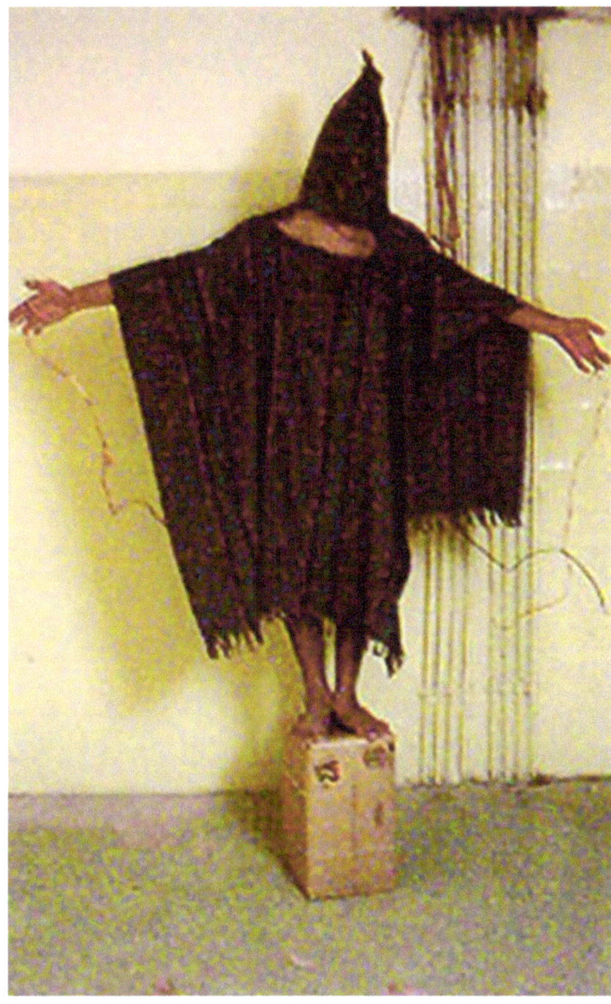

Abu Ghraib Prison, Iraq, 2003
Economist Magazine Photograph

his hand and a green laboratory notebook in his lap.

"Four uniformed men appeared in my hospital room as I was preparing to leave. The lead security guard demanded I follow him and the other three guards. I asked, 'Why?' 'Don't give us trouble,' he said and shoved me in the direction of the door. The four men marched me down several corridors, and then, we took a service elevator one floor up and went through a locked set of doors to the nurses' station. 'Is this the Gulag?' I asked. I was frightened and backed away from the men who had brought me there. The tone of my voice and the fact that I stepped back instead of proceeding to where they wanted me to go was a mistake. The guards pushed me against a wall near the nurse's station and forced me into a nearby room with no windows and a padded slab with straps. I was forced to lie down, and I raised my voice to protest. The guards secured me to the slab with the straps and left me there until you arrived."

"Why did you threaten a staff member?" the doctor asked.

"I have no recollection of doing that."

I told the psychiatrist I was going home when this unfortunate situation arose. My shoes and socks had disappeared. My cursing at the thievery in the hospital may have been why I ended up strapped to a slab. I must have convinced him I was sane, but I wasn't. My clothes were returned, and I went home in bare feet. It was a week later I went into Las Encinas for the second time.

I had agreed to go to this psychiatric hospital a second time because I was angry with life, my job, and the state of the world. I was smoking crack and engaging in other self-destructive acts. My wife had finally drawn the line. She and our doctor convinced me to seek medical help. I consented to go to Las Encinas, the famous mental health hospital in Southern California, where Marilyn Monroe and W.C. Fields had been hospitalized. I consented to go on two conditions — I wouldn't be strapped down, and I wouldn't be confined to a locked ward.

I went to Las Encinas full of confidence that my wishes would be met. The admitting nurse took me to a large room and commanded me to sit down. I took an immediate dislike to her. Assuming a wise ass tone I cynically answered her questions. She abruptly stood up and led me down a long pathway through the hospital's wood craftsman cottages to a lone one-story building at the far end of the hospital. She opened the entry door with a key and put me a room with a small wire glass window then closed the door behind me. I tried to open the door. It was locked. That's when I knew I had been betrayed. I was imprisoned in a locked ward.

After several days of incarceration, I was allowed to use communal areas inside and outside of what was called 'the isolation pavilion.' Sitting at a picnic table in the enclosed yard, I watched a fellow inmate pace back and forth as if he were caged. I fulminated against our imprisonment.

"Get off the cross! We need the wood."

The comment, coming from a fellow inmate, knocked me off my high horse. I laughed for the first time in a long time.

I asked not to be confined any longer, and the nurse explained to me that this would require a court hearing, to which I agreed. A week later, I met with two psychiatrists and a hospital administrator representing the court. I explained I needed to clear my mind and coddle my heart. If they insisted on confining me for another week, I would speak to my lawyer. They said I was free to leave, but I decided to stay. My mind was racing, and my nerves were shot. A French Canadian psychiatrist, Dr. Poliquin, became my doctor. We got along well. She said I

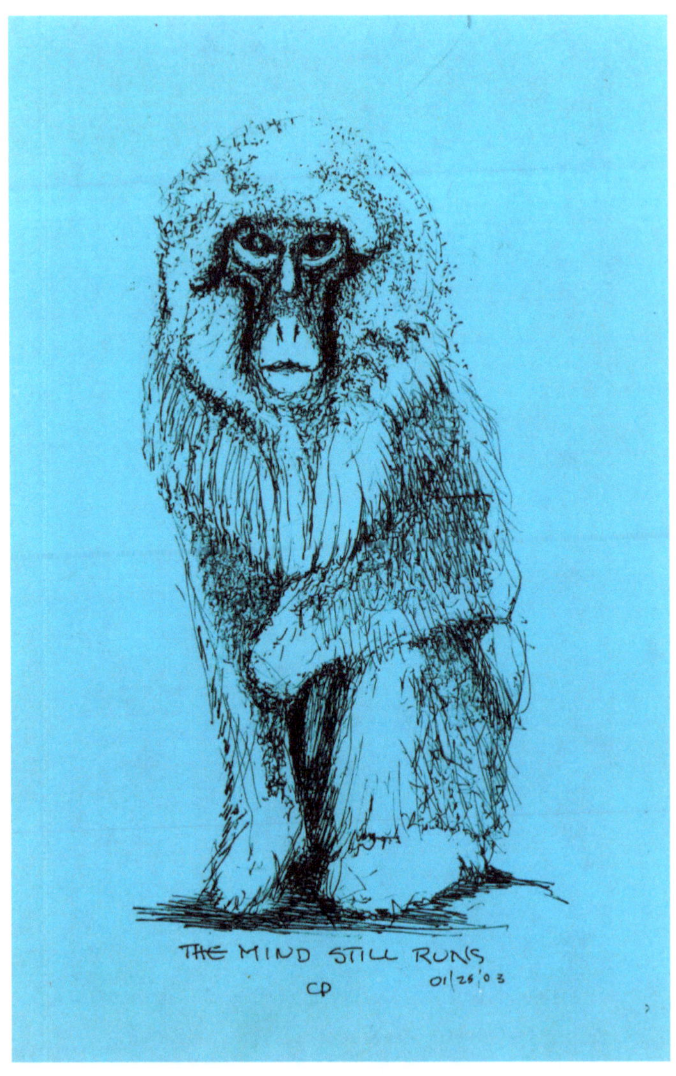

'Baboon' sketch, 2003, Carlton Davis, ink on blue paper, 10.5" × 6.25" (26.67 cm × 15.87 cm)

had bipolar 1 disorder, which was believed to be genetically transmitted. I was 59. Why was this the first time I had been diagnosed and given medicine to treat this condition?

With a single dose of the medicines she prescribed, and as if a light bulb had been switched on, I immediately stopped smoking crack. I stopped all self-destructive behaviors. I told my alter ego, Carlotta, that it was time for us to part. I began to draw again and felt I was on the path to recovery. Dr. Poliquin told me I could go home, and she recommended I go to outpatient therapy.

In early 2003, before my second hospitalization, I had made a drawing that captured my emotions. I drew a male baboon with a hairy mane and dark face looking directly at the viewer. In retrospect, I know I was prescient. Baboons travel in large groups led by a male who often displays aggressive behavior when other males attempt to usurp his leadership. My baboon radiated aggression. For me, he represented the attributes of bipolarity that Dr. Poliquin said I possessed. I was full of anger and often grandiose. When I wasn't manic, my mind was on a loop that ran endlessly until I strayed, sinking ever deeper into depression. Even when I experienced periods of abnormally elevated energy, they were marked by episodes of extreme irritation. Exhausted, I sought relief by acting irrationally, frequently putting myself and others at risk. Extreme ups would be followed by extreme downs, which, in my case, flip-flopped for years. Despite my flaws, impaired judgment, and attraction to risk, I could be a dignified, fun-loving baboon.

From what I can gather, Gustave Courbet and Francisco Goya were of the same ilk. Both painters, one French and the other Spanish, were energetic, vainglorious, irritable, and not at all risk-averse. They both sought and gathered admirers who proclaimed their skills and introduced them to influential patrons, and both were involved in radical politics. Courbet, known as one of the most talented mid-19th century 'realist' painters, had a narrower focus than Goya. He was, first and foremost, a romantic. As a young man, he was a handsome poseur. His dramatic 1845 self-portrait, *L'Homme Désespéré, The Desperate Man*, is one of 24 self-portraits he painted in the 1840s. In his celebrated 1855 painting, *L'Atelier du peintre, The Artist's Studio*, Courbet included himself, brush and palette in hand, seated at the easel surrounded by an adoring naked model, pets, children, and a room full of admirers from all walks of life. He supported the removal of Napoleon's Column from La Place Vendôme and was a leader of the artists allied with the short-lived 1871 insurrection of the Paris Commune. Napoleon's Column was restored after the insurrection was suppressed. Courbet was sentenced to prison and charged by the court to pay the cost of Place Vendôme's restoration. Instead, he fled to Switzerland where he taught Swiss painters to imitate his style and subject matter in images which he later sold as his own to finance his flamboyant life. This scoundrel was more interesting to me than his work.

Francisco de Goya y Lucientes was very different from Gustave Courbet. He was much more of a depressive, perhaps because he had been completely deaf from 1793 to his death in 1828 at the age of 82. I studied his many drawings of what were then called 'lunatics' because they were thought to be under the maleficent influence of the moon, as well as his series of etchings, *Los desastres de la guerra* (1810) depicting the horrors of the Spanish War of Independence from Napoleonic France. These were my favorites of his works. Many of his *manicomio* (lunatic asylum) sketches are bound in sketchbooks, which weren't exhibited during his lifetime. Drawn in black chalk on

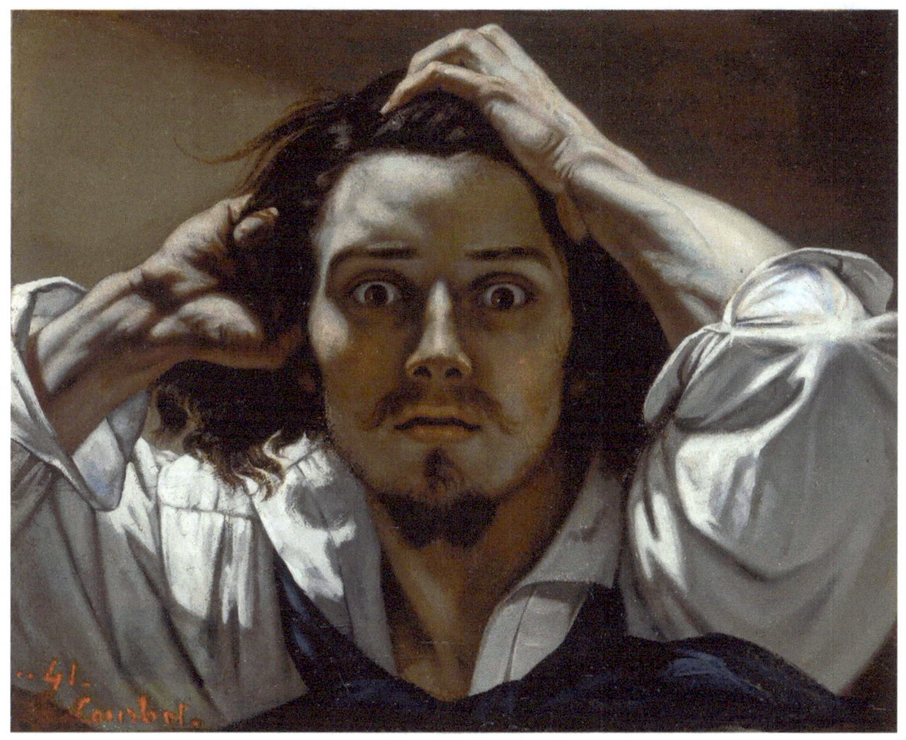

Desperate Man, 1845, Gustave Courbet, oil on canvas, private collection

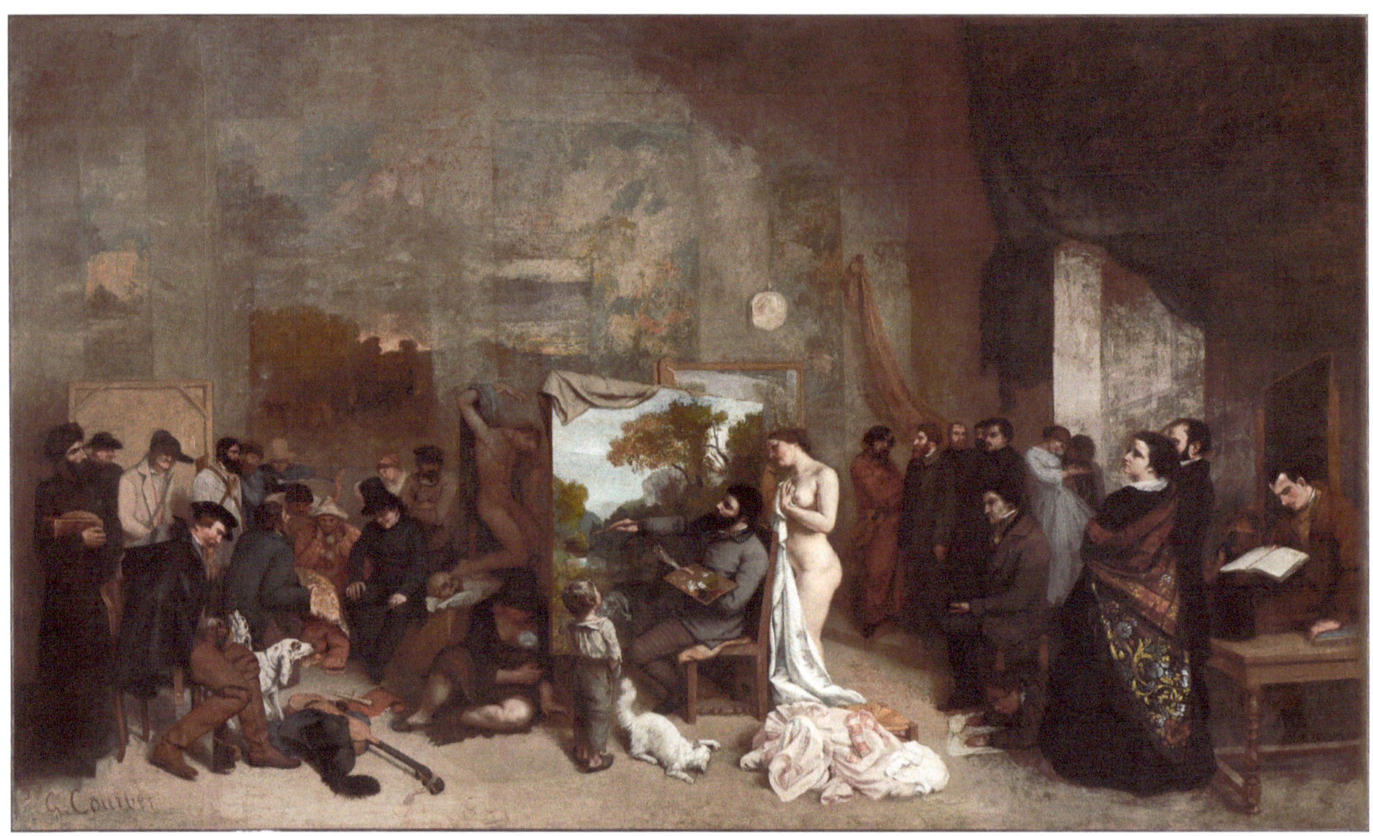

The Artist's Studio, 1855, Gustave Courbet, oil on canvas, 141" × 235" (359 cm × 598 cm), Musée d'Orsay, Paris

paper, his masterful sketches are studies in human pathology. The drawings are imbued with Goya's empathy for the distressed and revulsion for the asylums in which most were confined until they died. Ironically, Goya was interned in a home for the deaf in Bordeaux, France for the last four years of his life (1824-28). His *Pinturas Negras* (black paintings) were painted in oil on plaster walls between 1820 and 1823, just before he left for Bordeaux. These included *Old Men Eating Soup* and *Saturn Devouring His Son*. They captured Goya's rage and grief about the human condition.

When I returned to my studio after my third run-in with a psychiatrist where I had to talk my way out of that room with the strap-down table, I redrew my white-haired self-portrait against a deep red background. It was executed with a speedy drumming on the paper surface. I attacked the image, marking and remarking it. I worked spontaneously, self-judgment acceding to passion. Like the baboon sketch of the year before, the subject seems vigilant. For bipolar people, stability requires constant vigilance. Many artists struggle with madness. This drawing and its predecessor were breakthroughs. My aging monkey mind finally admitted the possibility of making art worth looking at and thinking about.

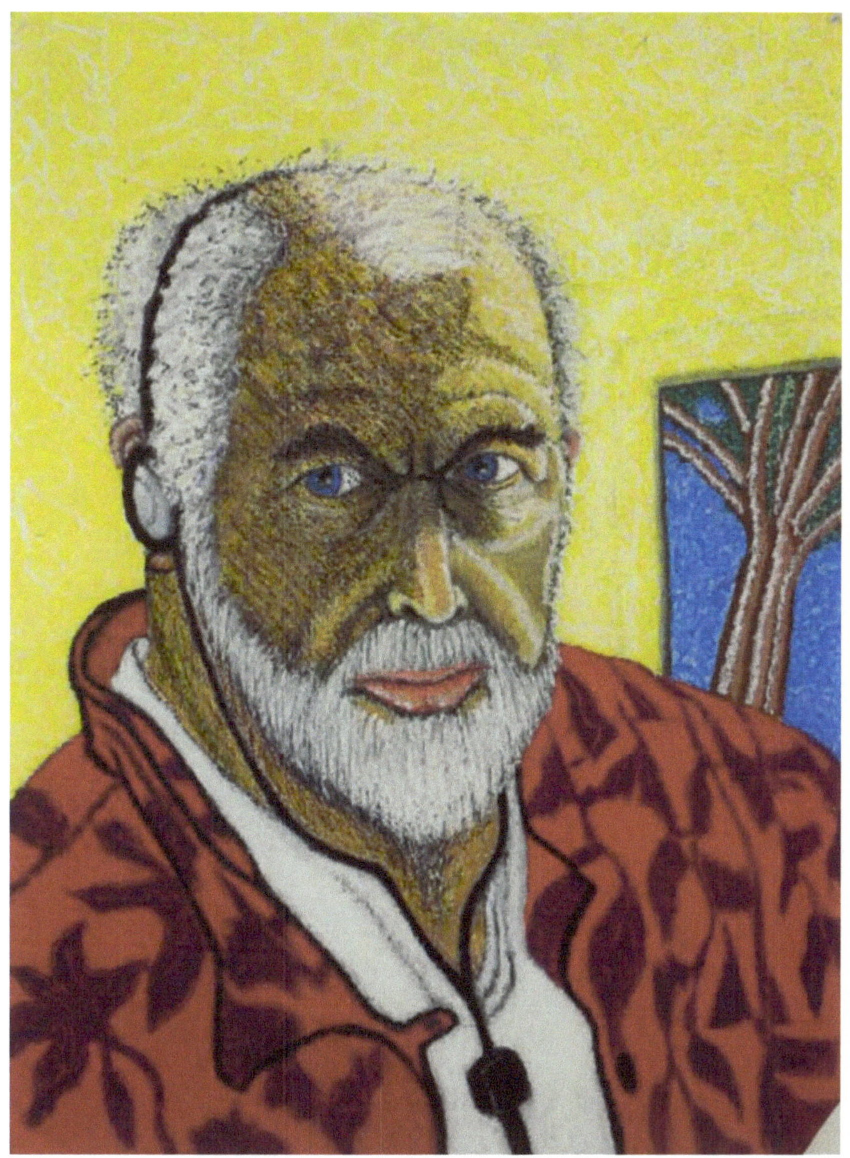

Self-portrait, 2009, Carlton Davis, oil stick on paper, 30" × 22" (76.27 cm × 58.97 cm)

CHAPTER 18

2008 – 2009
VIVA VAN GOGH!

Auvers-sur-Oise, July 27, 1890

Dear Theo,

Someday, I shall find a way to have an exhibition of my own in a café. Some canvases will one day find purchasers. I have a new study of some old, thatched roofs, and two canvases representing vast stretches of corn after the rain. Since the thing that matters most is going well, why say more about things of less importance?

With a handshake in thought, Vincent[1]

---

1 *Dear Theo; The Autobiography of Vincent Van Gogh*, edited by Irving Stone (NYC: Doubleday & Co., 1950), p. 565

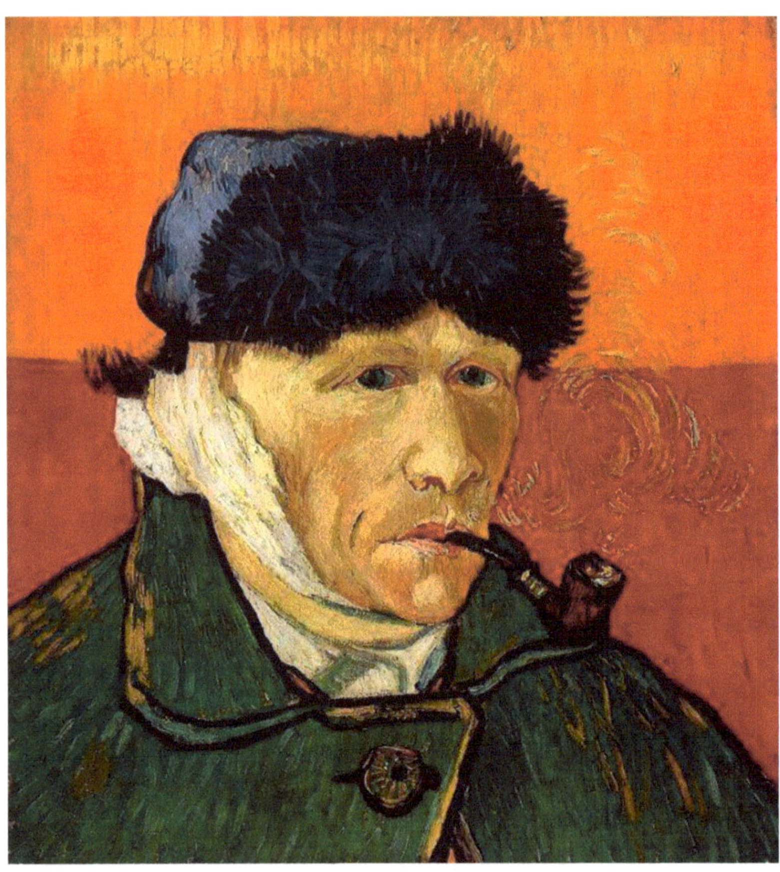

Self-Portrait with Bandaged Ear & Pipe, 1889, oil on canvas, 23.8" × 19.6" (60.5 cm × 50 cm), Kunsthaus, Zurich

Vincent van Gogh has always seemed like my brother. Theo, his younger brother, acted as his agent and provided financial support and unshakeable belief in the artist's work in the final, difficult years of their lives. Vincent wrote him detailed letters, which I read as if they were written to me. Vincent and I had a lot in common. We experienced sudden and inexplicable mood swings that we tried to assuage with alcohol, drugs, and sex. We attempted suicide and were confined in asylums. We believed 'the thing that matters most' is making art.

On the same Sunday he wrote Theo the letter of July 27, 1890, Vincent shot himself in the stomach on the way to a cornfield. He had his paints, palette, brushes, and easel slung over one shoulder and a pistol in his pocket he'd borrowed from another painter to scare off the crows, or so he said. He survived another 36 hours. Theo traveled 20 miles from Paris to Auvers when he got the news on Monday morning, and the two brothers talked for hours. At one o'clock on Tuesday morning, Vincent muttered, in Dutch, "I wish I could go home now," and died. He was 37 years old. Theo died less than a half year later at 33. The brothers' remains were laid to rest side by side not far from the scene of Vincent's agony.

Earlier in 1890, six Van Gogh paintings hung in a Brussels exhibition of twenty impressionist painters, including Cézanne, Pissarro, Redon, Renoir, and Toulouse-Lautrec. Van Gogh was praised in a long article by the art critic Albert Aurier to whom Theo had shown dozens of his brother's canvases, framed and unframed, that he had stored in his Paris apartment. Aurier wrote about Vincent's "ebullient brain which irresistibly pours its lava into all the ravines of art," called him "a terrible and maddened genius, often sublime, sometimes grotesque, almost always pathological," and claimed he was "the only painter who perceives the color of things with such intensity." [2]

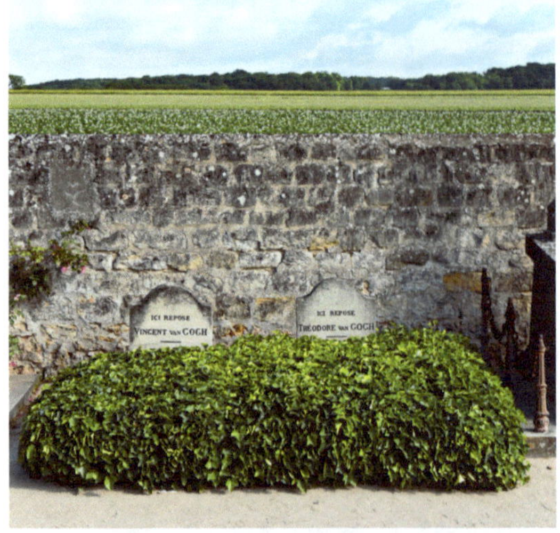

Graves of Vincent van Gogh and Theo van Gogh, Auvers-sur-Oise, France

---

2 *The World of Van Gogh,* by Robert Wallace & Editors (Alexandria, VA: Time-Life Books, 1969), p. 161.

"Please ask Monsieur Aurier not to write any more articles about my paintings. It pains me more than he knows," was Vincent's response to Theo who sent him the article. Nothing, including internment in a madhouse, obstructed his desire or ability to make art. In *Self-Portrait with Bandaged Ear & Pipe,* his gift and agonized mentality collide. Aurier's revelation of the painter's "terrible and maddened genius" was painful because it was true.

Sheet from letter, June 19, 1888, Vincent van Gogh to Emile Bernard

Van Gogh included several sketches in a letter to Émile Bernard in 1888. The ink from the sketch and the script are commingled in the June 19th letter. This happens in my journals, too. Over two days in May 2013, I sketched ideas for a drawing I was working on in the countryside of Pennsylvania near where my wife grew up. We bought a former church there and my studio consists of a platform, a balustrade, and two church windows where the altar once was. The drawing is called *Reuben Drumgold and His Wife in the Orchard.* It may be more surreal than impressionistic; I'll let the reader decide. What mattered most, as Vincent reminds us, was that my work was going well.

In 2009, I turned 65 and survived a pulmonary crisis. I found it impossible to keep up with Ginger and my daughter Sarah when we visited her in London. Back in Pasadena, I went to Huntington Hospital and was prescribed antibiotics for what they thought was pneumonia. However, an X-ray revealed a large blood clot in one of my lungs. Forty percent of my left lung was necrotic and had to be excised. I remembered something Shinzen Young, my Vipassana teacher, had said about "dying into life." I left the hospital a month later, filed for disability insurance, and retired from the practice of architecture.

I am no longer angry with myself, my parents, other people, or the country in which I was born and have lived most of my life. I identified with my roiling resentments, and I could not believe they would ever be lifted. Now, it seems, a good-natured, compassionate person has arisen from the wreckage of my past. I am growing fond of this newcomer. He rolls with the punches. He takes in his stride the things that used to bother him. And he writes books and makes art.

When and where are the past buried and the future born? In 2006, I had interred the ashes of my father close to his parents' graves in the family plot of a cemetery in Elizabeth, New Jersey. A small square hole had been dug in the earth and I placed a white sack containing a box of his ashes there. Several years later, I traveled to New York State to visit another cemetery in Buffalo where my mother, Lynn Quinn, had been buried at the turn of the millennium. On my way, I stopped in Rochester where my grand-

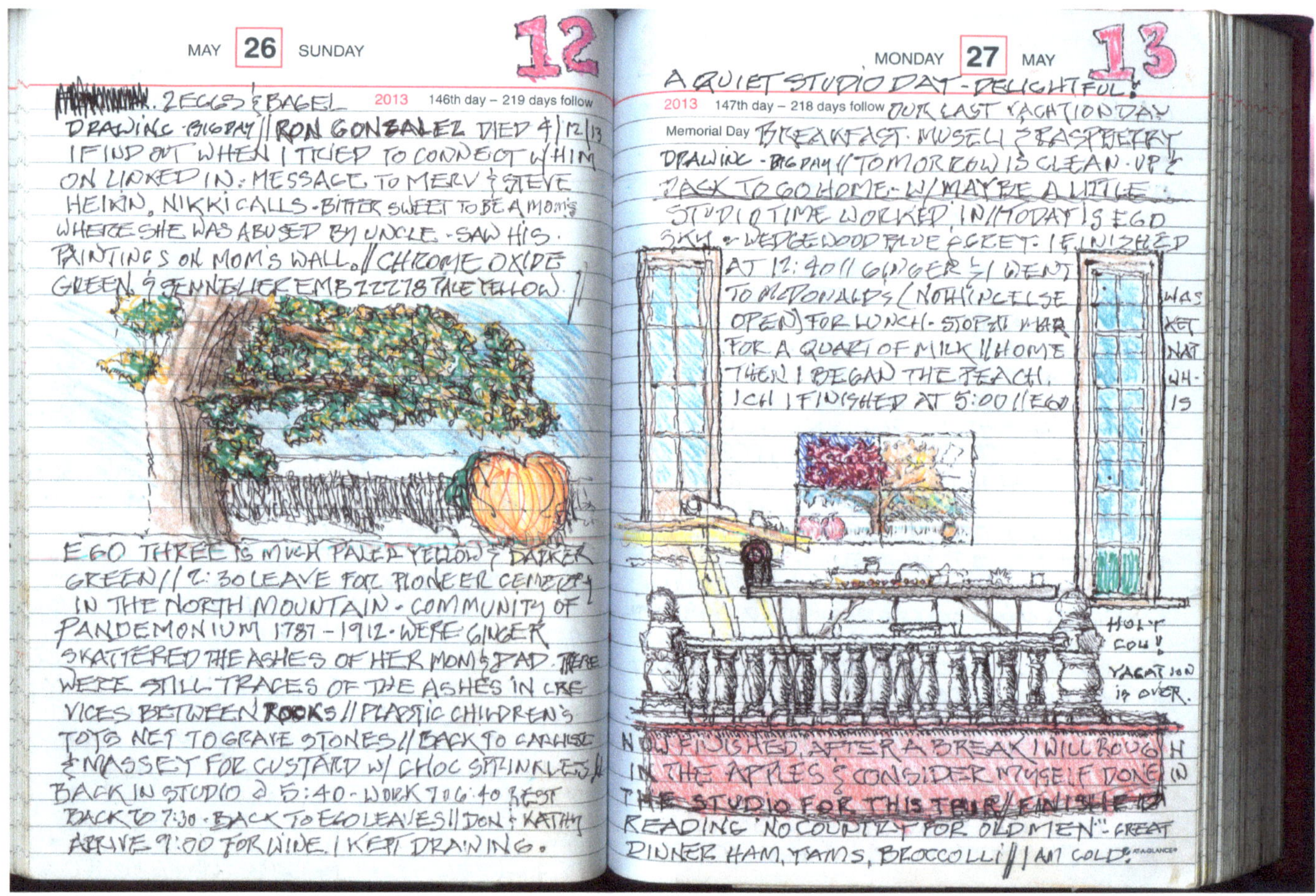

Daily diary pages, May 26 & May 27, 2013

mother had held court in the 1950s, and in Corning, New York, where I lived from ages five to fifteen.

In a rundown area of Rust Belt Buffalo, I first met my half- brother in his plating shop in an area of tenement houses and small workshops and next to an expressway obscured by scrawny trees. When I had called ahead, he directed me to his workshop and agreed to take me to the nearby cemetery where our mother was buried. I entered an office strewn with papers and walls covered with pinup girl calendars and asked a man sitting behind a desk, "Are you Arnold?" "He's in the shop," he replied and directed me outside and around the corner to where the plating was done. I found Arnold there among several open bays where metal parts were being dunked in chrome-filled vats. Arnold was a large, stubble-cheeked workman in a baseball cap, soiled sweatshirt, and overalls. We climbed into his big black truck, and he drove me to a cemetery nearby.

"Mom's over there, just behind the hedge."

I walked down a path lined with brass markers. There, side by side were plaques for Lynn Quinn Collier, my mom, her third and final husband, and Helen Carloni, her sister, from whose New Haven home my father had snatched me 60 years before. In my mind's eye, Helen's profile was clearer than my mother's, but what was she doing here in Buffalo? I had no idea, but I did have a dim memory of Helen and her husband Frank yelling at the cop and my father for taking me into their custody when my mother went away to sing in a night club. Lynn had also left me with them when she had to go to court to contest my custody. This was the last time I saw my mother for 30 years.

She and I were reunited at a Las Vegas hotel she and her husband frequented on New Year's Eve,

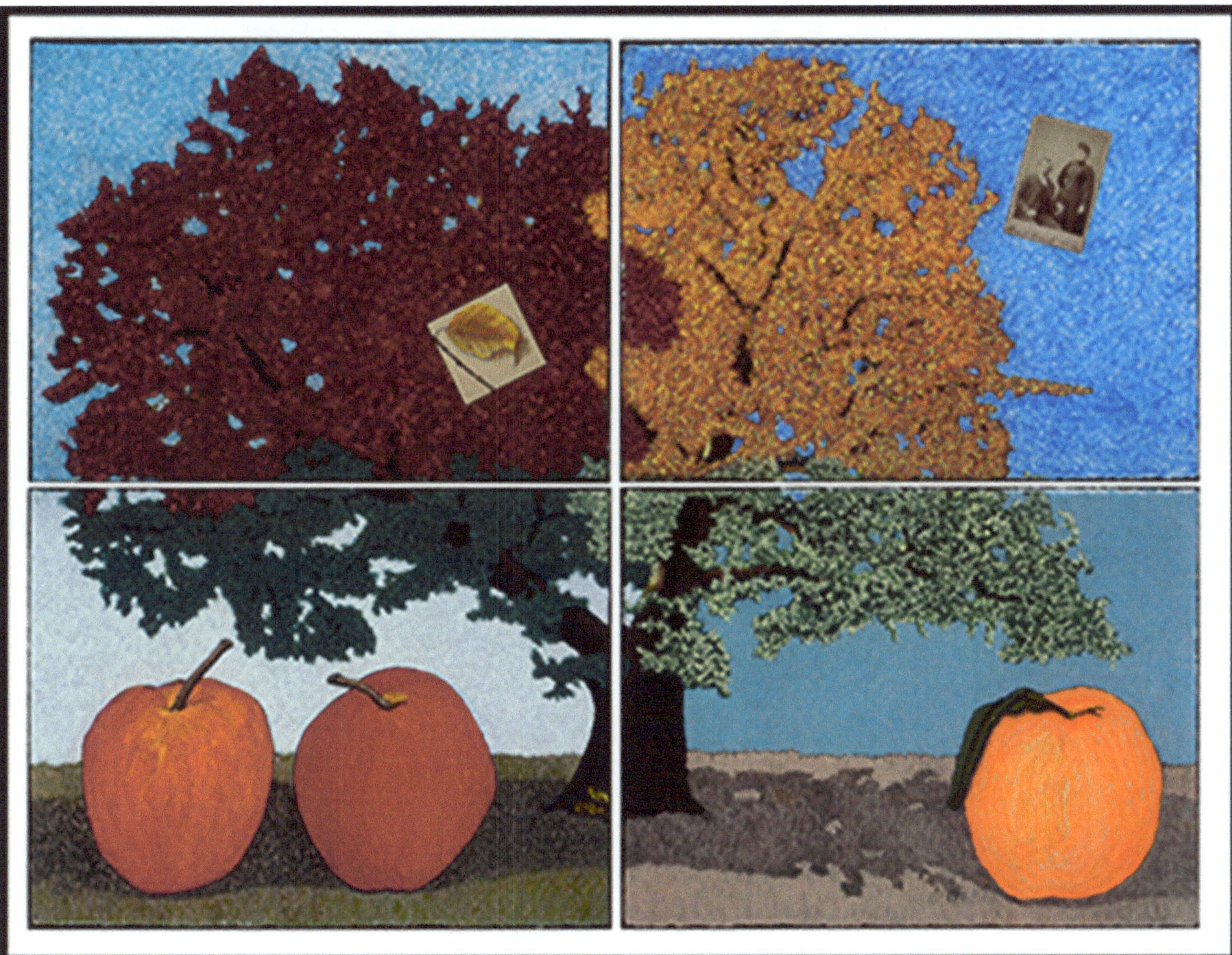

Reuben Drumgold and His Wife in the Orchard, drawing, 2013, Carlton Davis,
oil stick and collage, four drawings, 22" × 30" (55.88 cm × 76.2 cm)

1981. She was dressed for a night of dining, drinking, dancing, and gambling. Her elegant, aquiline face reminded me of my grandmother, her nemesis. My middle-aged half-sisters were drunk and disorderly. I found their company disheartening, and I excused myself before dessert, went out, and smoked a joint. I saw my mother only once more before she died.

Now, looking down at her grave, I found myself humming a song she sang to put me to sleep when Helen and Frank couldn't babysit and she'd have to take me with her to the nightclubs where she sang.

"No one here can love or understand me
Oh, what hard luck stories they all hand me

Pack up all my cares and woe
Here I go, winging low
Bye, bye, blackbird."
—A song published in 1926 by Jerome H. Remick and written
by composer Ray Henderson and lyricist Mort Dixon

From Buffalo, I drove to Rochester and located what was once my grandparents' house on Council Rock Avenue. I was surprised at how small it seemed. I rang the bell. A woman answered the door. She said she and her husband were both doctors. I heard children playing. I asked her if I could have a quick look around. "Sure," she said. I walked down the hallway to the fancy staircase leading up to the second floor. Everything seemed smaller and more cramped than I remembered. Instead of a bronze dog and an eagle on the hallway table, there were toys. I climbed to the second story and turned to ask the lady of the house whether she would mind if I peeked into the attic. She smiled. The attic stairway was narrower than I remembered, and the ante-room was even smaller. I felt a twinge of emotion, recalling the hours my sister and I had spent there. The woman said she wanted to show me something and opened the door to the room where I used to sleep. She took a skeleton key off a hook on the wall behind the door.

"Do you recognize this key? It was here when we moved in."

I said I didn't, but I did. It was the key they used to lock me in every night when I was five and couldn't be trusted. The sound of children playing on the ground floor of a residence that used to be stuffed with antiques and where the only place a child could play was in an anteroom to the attic made my unan-nounced visit to the house on Council Rock Avenue worthwhile.

I went from Rochester to Corning, New York. When I lived there with my father and stepmother, the town had been dominated by the Corning Glass Works. I was here to see what had happened to the town dump, which was directly across the street from where we lived. As a boy, I was warned not to go there, but my friends and I found it irresistible. There were Steuben glass globules as big as pumpkins, old tires, and discarded copies of lurid men's magazines with titillating covers.

The dump had vanished. In its place was a chain link fence affixed with "No Trespassing" signs surrounding an abandoned elementary school. I went to a convenience store in the neighborhood and asked the guy behind the counter why the school had been condemned. He said it was because many shards of glass had risen from the ground beneath the playground.

Painful memories and unresolved family issues can protrude like shards of glass and wound us as we age. Exploring them and sharing them with others may help us put them into perspective. You may wonder how I have the temerity to juxtapose my *Self-Portrait with Earphones* with Vincent's *Self-Portrait With Bandaged Ear & Pipe*. My response is that my self-portrait is inspired by the artistic ferment and positive energy that contemplating Van Gogh's life and work has always released in me.

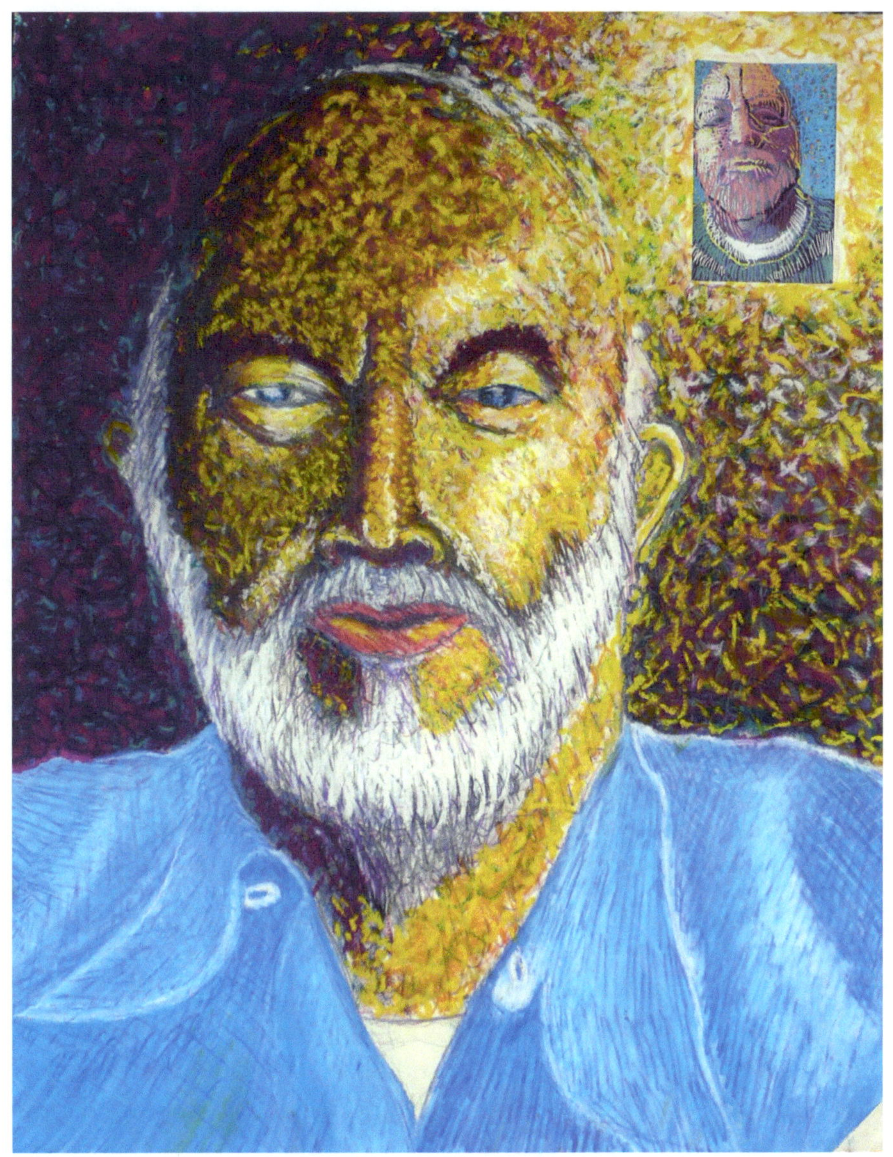

Self-portrait, 2010, Carlton Davis, oil stick on paper with altered computer image,
30" × 22" (76.27 cm × 58.97 cm)

CHAPTER 19

2010 - 2011
YALE-CHINA SCHOOL

When I was a student at Yale Art & Architecture School, my favorite professor was Charles Moore, a highly regarded architect and scholar. I was impressed by the relaxed and personable way in which he imparted information and the enthusiasm with which his students received it.

I never enjoyed teaching until it was almost too late. Over 30 years, I taught architecture courses at the University of Wyoming, UCLA, and Woodbury University. At Woodbury, most of my students were people of color, including Asians, African Americans, and Latin Americans, who took my courses to learn to read and render architectural plans. I was there to make sure they acquired critical skills that would help them find jobs in a lucrative field that had been closed, at its most remunerative level, to their hard-working parents.

I retired when I was 66, resenting that I had spent my most productive years struggling with mental illness, drug addiction, gluttonous excess, and a desultory career. When I read a blurb that year in the Yale Alumni Magazine that a group of volunteers was headed to Xiuning, China and that teachers with professional experience were being sought, I signed up.

One hundred eighty Yale-China Project volunteers gathered in Shanghai. We were bussed several hours southwest to Xiuning County in Anhui Province, a rural agricultural district with 250,000 inhabitants challenged by poverty, illiteracy, and lack of medical care. I was to teach high school students drawing, English as a Second Language (ESL), and art history. The high school where I would teach was 70 stone steps above street level. I weighed 320 pounds, and 40% of my left lung had been removed after a pulmonary embolism. At first glance, the climb seemed insurmountable.

Our group was housed in the relative luxury of the Smoky Willow Resort. Yale and China had enjoyed a 125-year-long relationship, and ours was the largest and last group of volunteers that would be invited to visit, although we didn't know it then. On the first morning, we were greeted with a marvelous breakfast, comprising bacon, sausage, boiled eggs and omelets, hash browns, steamed vegetables, and familiar and unfamiliar local fruit. At the orientation, our leaders advised us, above all, to be flexible. I had prepared nothing in the way of an art history or ESL curriculum, so I was asked to assist the instructors of those subjects in any way they saw fit.

Soon after we arrived, I went on a walk with several other Yale-China volunteers. I bought 25 ping guos (apples) from a greengrocer. The shopkeeper refused the yuans I had bought in Shanghai. I gave her a couple of dollars, and the deal was sealed. We got back to the Smoky Willow in time for another feast. Later on that endless first day, we were taken on a bus tour of Xiuning, saw the middle and high schools we would teach in, and asked questions about Chinese public education.

Kathy, the Yale group leader, invited local junior high and high school English teachers to speak to us. From them, we learned that, beginning at age six, 'promising' children from peasant families in the countryside surrounding Xiuning were located, interviewed, and invited to attend city schools and live in dormitories on their campuses. Their parents and guardians brought them to town a week before classes began for vaccinations and health checks. If they showed any evidence of communicable diseases, they were sent back home.

The children saw their parents and grandparents during school holidays. They had a three-hour evening study hall every day but Saturday. Most had no siblings as their parents and grandparents were subject to Mao's revolutionary restrictions on family size. They became Communist Party 'pioneers' by second or third grade, and were responsible for dressing, bathing, and grooming themselves and helping to keep their communal bathrooms and dining areas clean. The children selected to study in first grade were joined by other promising candidates from middle and high school, watched closely, and frequently exhorted by their teachers to study nonstop for the GaoKao college entrance exams in their high school senior year.

There were 25 students in my drawing class. I handed out the pencils I had brought, which ranged from hard to soft. I had them draw lines and curves with pencils of various weights; rudimentary stuff. Chinese high schools have no art classes. In 2010, computers were not yet affordable, so most students were accustomed to taking notes by hand. My students, mostly young women, were proficient in English and eager to converse with a native speaker. A couple of boys who goofed off tested my patience, but I used Vipassana breathing to restore my equanimity.

As I had to deal at least twice a day with the 70 steps and two flights of interior stairs, teaching my drawing class and aiding two other teachers in unairconditioned classrooms became a workout, too. Returning to the Smoky Willow for lunch, I would go to my room, shower, and change my clothes before I ate as slowly and carefully as I could under the circumstances. I began working on a plan to turn a historic, empty house on campus into a museum. A fellow volunteer and six young Chinese women would work with me. Kana, the student leader, was tall and slender with beautiful eyes and a determined mouth. Her English was excellent. All the students had to choose their anglophone names in elementary school. In the afternoon, we gathered to brainstorm ideas for the museum project. At 5:00 p.m., we volunteers were bussed back to the Smoky Willow Resort for dinner. After dinner, I created a plan view drawing of the future museum's ground floor.

The next morning, I would struggle up the steps again. The first class was art history. My fellow volunteer was ambitious; she expected to cover 2,000 years in four days. She made it clear that she did not appreciate my chiming in. In my drawing class, I wanted the students to work on shading and perspective. I immediately recognized the big personalities: Kobe, Sally, and Shiveley. Kobe loved basketball and had adopted his idol's name in homage. When I told the class I lived in Los Angeles, he asked if I had ever seen 'the real Kobe' play.

"Yes, many times, mostly on television," I replied.

He stood, threw both hands in the air, and executed a jump shot with an imaginary ball. He pumped a victorious fist. His classmates laughed and applauded. There was a palpable release of tension. Art class is supposed to be fun! Sally and Shively could really draw. They started by designing miniature hats that were perfect for a stylish mouse. If China and the US are to remain on amicable terms, a few days of hand and heart dialogue with energetic young *pong yos* (friends) cannot hurt.

I took photos of the six girls in the old house and together, we drew up plans for the second-story alterations. Someone told me she had complained

to their English teacher about being bored by the project. The other, Yale volunteer Cece, was concerned that the influencer was Kana. "What can we do?" she asked. In the Smoky Willow VIP room, we discovered a trove of art 'bling,' comprising T-shirts, Play-Doh, wrapping paper, paints, brushes, balls of twine, and rubber gloves. What a joy it was finding the excess kindergarten supplies and putting them to good use in the young adults' museum project.

In my drawing class, I had handed out the 25

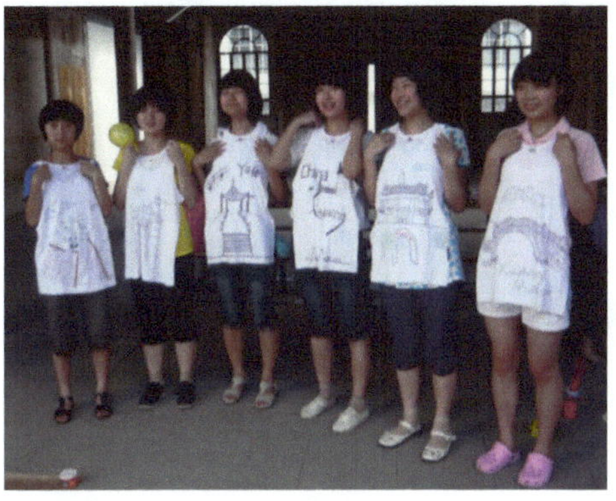

The design team with their tee shirts. Photograph by Carlton Davis

apples I bought on the first day along with colored pencils I had brought with me. "*Hua da ping gao!*" ('draw big apples!') was the assignment. I noticed that the students seemed not to know what to do after drawing a circle and a stem. I showed them how to create a volumetric form using stippling. I drew a big circle on the classroom blackboard and start to stipple by tapping my piece of chalk on the board. My strenuous tapping disintegrated several lovely long pieces of chalk. I turned from the board, lowered my head, and puffed out my cheeks in exasperation. The whole class laughed.

As the sound of my tapping became measured and rhythmic, I started to bounce on the balls of my feet. When I looked over my shoulder, I saw that some of the girls had covered their mouths to keep from giggling or perhaps to hide their shock. Kobe said something in Mandarin, and the entire class laughed again. I turned back to the board. I kept my stipples close together at the outer edge of the apple and farther apart as I moved toward the middle. The three-dimensional form was taking shape. I danced around the room, helping them stipple and responding to the

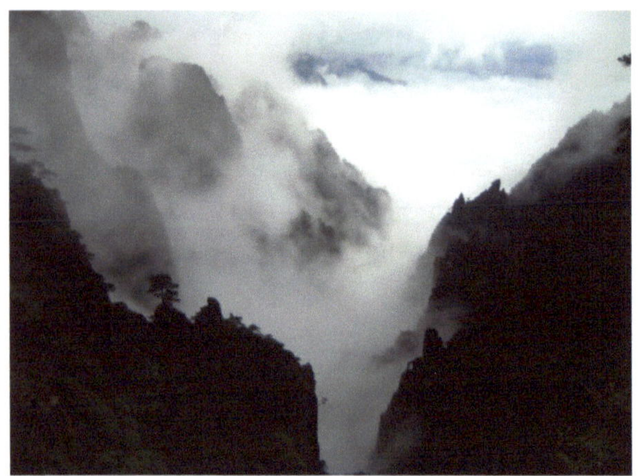

Huangshan (the Yellow Mountains) Photo by Carlton Davis

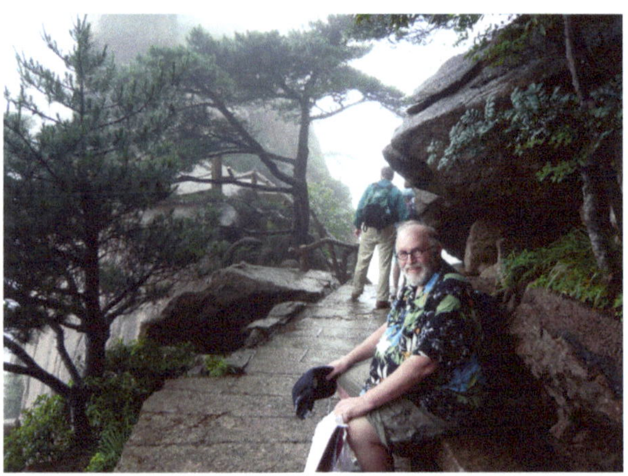

Carlton Davis at Huangshan, Photo by Nancy Yao

rhythm of 25 students tapping in unison. I picked up and showed several students' efforts to the rest of the room. Their apples were turning three-dimensional amid excited chatter and laughter. After lunch, the museum design team appeared. They enjoyed the new supplies and at once, began to custom-design their tee shirts. I was relieved to see that Kana seemed to be enjoying herself.

On Thursday, we volunteers took a bus to *Huangshan*, which is Mandarin Chinese for Yellow Mountains. It was raining and the mist was thick. I found myself climbing winding stone stairs in a fog. I couldn't see the craggy peaks, but I felt their proximity. The air was moist and heavy. I ended up walking the trail with Nancy, the director of the Yale-China Association. She shared my trepidation. We stopped to enjoy our Smoky Willow box lunches while sitting on a bench along the trail.

Huangshan is like China's Grand Canyon. I had seen the image of hovering mist with rocky pinnacles peeking through on silken wall hangings. The mist dispersed, and it was thrilling to watch the view unfold before my eyes.

We then went on the bus to Huangshan City, which used to be called Tunxi, where a glorious, multi-course lunch awaited us. After lunch, I bought ten sheets of calligraphy paper, brushes, ink, an ink well, a Chinese scroll illustration of Huangshan that I intended to use as the background for a drawing, and a lovely Chinese scarf with matching beads for Ginger.

The next day, I handed out prints of drawings by well-known artists and asked the students to make freehand copies. One of the boys put his drawing up to the window to trace the view. Kobe, the class clown, did three quick drawings, including stippling with a handful of pencils. I showed them to the class and praised his effort as free and interesting. Shiveley drew Albrecht Dürer's lion beautifully. Everyone seemed to be having fun. "There are no rules!" I told them. "I love to draw. It has nothing to do with official knowledge. There's no right or wrong way to do it. It improves with practice, keenness of observation, and sureness of hand. I have learned from Chinese master draftsmen that what you don't draw is as important as what you do. Empty space makes things stronger."

I invited Kana to interpret what I said in Mandarin. She must have done a great job because my 25 students nodded and smiled. On the final day of class, each student handed me an origami crane inscribed with their name and best wishes. Several used the word 'love.' It made me wish I had taught more when I was younger. On my last day in Xiuning, I climbed up and down all the steps and stairs without hesitation.

On returning to Beijing, our group visited Tiananmen Square. There were at least 50,000 people snaking in a line across the 40 acres of Tiananmen to view Mao's body in his mausoleum. Our group gathered around Frank, our blunt

Chinese tour leader carrying a small Yale flag, and we watched a large group of Chinese soldiers practicing Qigong in unison. We entered the Forbidden City through a huge portal hung with the image of Mao Zedong above an immense red wall. Passing through the deep shade of the entry, we came into another vast plaza surrounded by lower pavilions with curved up eaves capped with brilliant blue tiles.

Frank told us the story of the last emperor, Puyi, who collaborated with the Japanese, abdicated, was impotent, and ended up a gardener. The plaza was filled with other groups, each flying the little flags on poles carried by their group leaders. We joined the crowds ascending a long shallow ramp into a second part of the palace and filed past the emperor's throne. After a quick camera stop, with blinking cell phones held high, we were out of the palace and into a garden marked by oddly shaped rocks with holes in them standing in planters filled with vegetation. Soon we were back in the immensity of Tiananmen Square where hawkers sold souvenirs. I bought a wristwatch faced with Mao. The watch never worked.

In the late afternoon, after a rest and a bath in the Grand Millennium hotel, where, while luxuriating in the tub, I had a view out my window and could see the burgeoning building going on in the city of Beijing, I looked out upon a skyscraper under construction where a very large crane was positioned over an excavation and long sheds that I was

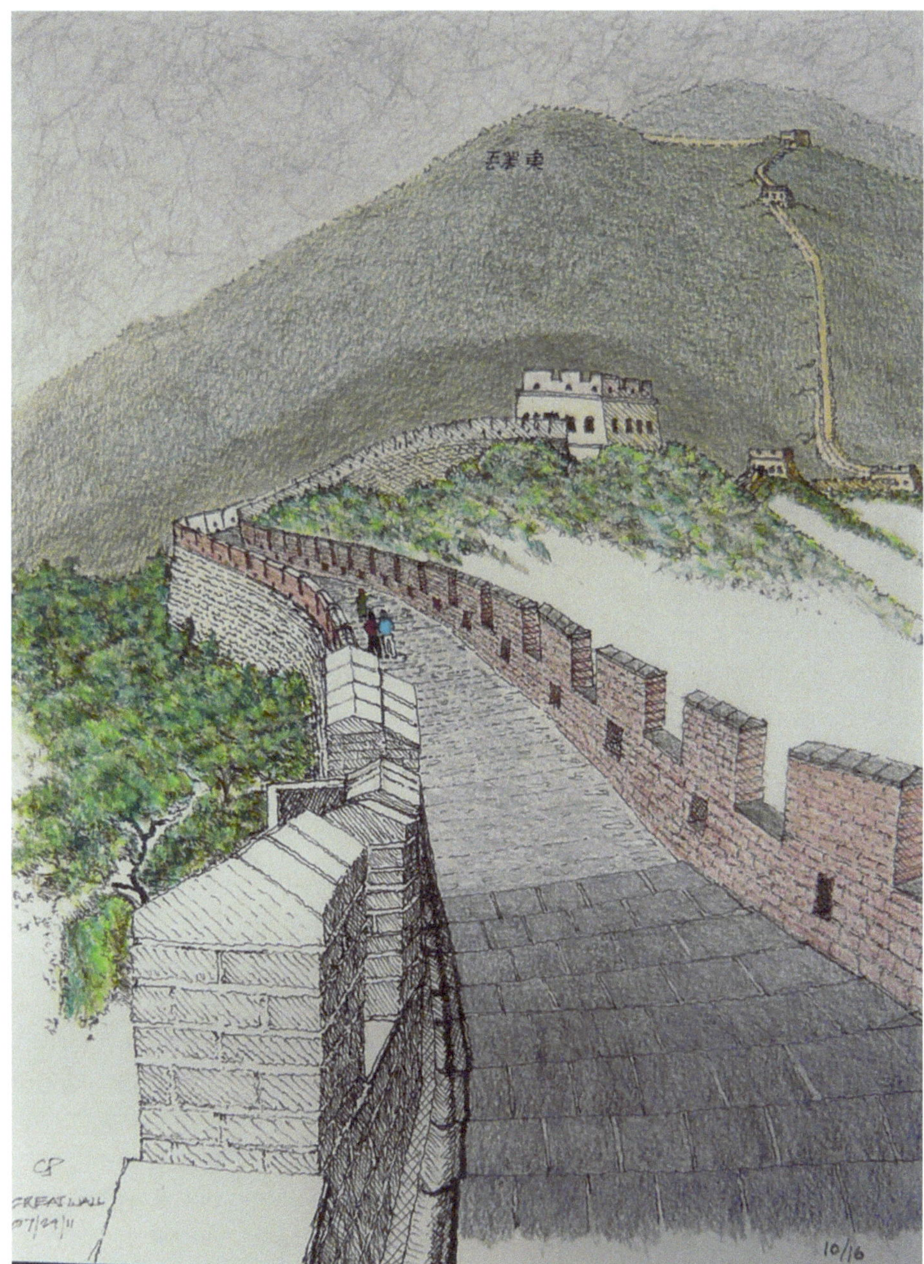

Great Wall of China, 2023, sketch, Carlton Davis, pen and colored pencil on paper, 11.29" × 8.5" (28.67 cm × 21.59 cm)

told housed the construction workers. After a fine dinner at a Peking duck (or is it now called Beijing duck) restaurant, I went for a walk that took me around the two angles and connected towers of the Chinese Media Center designed by Dutch architect Rem Koolhaas. I couldn't see much of the building as construction fencing obscured the base of the still-unfinished structure, so I continued walking. I was surprised at how few pedestrians there were.

This center of the new city wasn't much different from the empty corporate and banking zones of American cities.

My wandering led me to a Chinese foot massage parlor, where even though my knowledge of Chinese was so limited, I managed to get myself a foot massage. I had been studying Chinese with a tutor for over a year for two days a week, but language is not my forte. The parlor was up several floors in a high-rise building off a dimly lit street. The parlor must have had some western patrons since they waved me in and gladly took my yuan. I had no idea if they swindled me, but the massage was a fun experience. I returned to the hotel on relaxed feet.

The following morning, Cece, who collaborated with me on the museum project in the Xiuning school, and I visited a hutong, one of the old city neighborhoods that are being replaced with residential towers. This turned out to be a Tibetan hutong, where we explored alleyways off a main drag too narrow for cars. The alleyways were circuitous and empty; we were soon lost. A woman appeared from nowhere in the alley and waved us to enter a low doorway covered by heavy green canvas and flanked by a wheelbarrow. Inside, the woman motioned us to enter a room where a man appeared and with his hand indicated to me to sit down in a chair in front of a table. He gestured again for me to give him my hand. I placed it over the table, and the man began to examine my hand, all while carrying on a dialogue with me where my only response was "yes. His fingers moved across the creases in my hand. Then he drew out a sheet of white paper drawing lines between Chinese characters, while he continued speaking. I shrugged to Cece that I had no idea what the man was saying or marking on the piece of paper. He then seemed to grow very excited. His voice grew into a mild crescendo. He thrust the paper to me then he was gone. The woman showed ten fingers to me, and I gave her a 20 yuan note, laughing as I did so.

From the emptiness of the morning, the afternoon found the Comeau family of four, Rick and Else, and I were trying to board a subway train in which the crowds crammed behind a platform edge door in front of the train. We towered over the Chinese crowd, but they didn't give us an inch. We were pushed forward by the crowd and finally got onto the train, and fortunately it was going in the direction we wanted. We spent the afternoon in a multi-storied silk emporium. I purchased 100-yuan worth of fabric for Ginger and a buddha mask. The shop proprietor quoted me 2800 yuan for the mask. I offered 40. He scoffed. I walked from his shop. He pulled me back in. With his calculator, he invited me to write what I was willing to pay. I was willing to pay 100 yuan (20 bucks). He frowned. I walked away again. He grabbed me again and accepted my offer. I didn't have a 100 yuan note and had to find my friends to borrow 100 yuan to pay the vendor.

On our last day in China, Frank took our group to visit the Great Wall. My impression of the wall is that it is a typical tourist attraction. Access to the wall is by gondola, not unlike the aerial trams that take visitors to high mountains or skiers to the upper slopes. I rode a gondola up through the mist through a path cleared of trees to the exit platform that provides entry to the wall. I didn't walk the wall. I found a convenient spot where I could see a lot of the wall disappearing into the distance and the place where, on a less foggy day, you can see Mao's Zedong's name marked with stones on a hillside beyond. Frank pointed it out to me, and I included it in my drawing I was reminded of all the towns I have seen in the American west where town names are spelled out in rock on hillsides. After I made my sole drawing of the trip, I took the sky cab down to a street of souvenir shops lining the one road up to the entry of the sky lift. I bought a red hat and a yellow t-shirt that says in Chinese and English "I climbed the Great Wall."

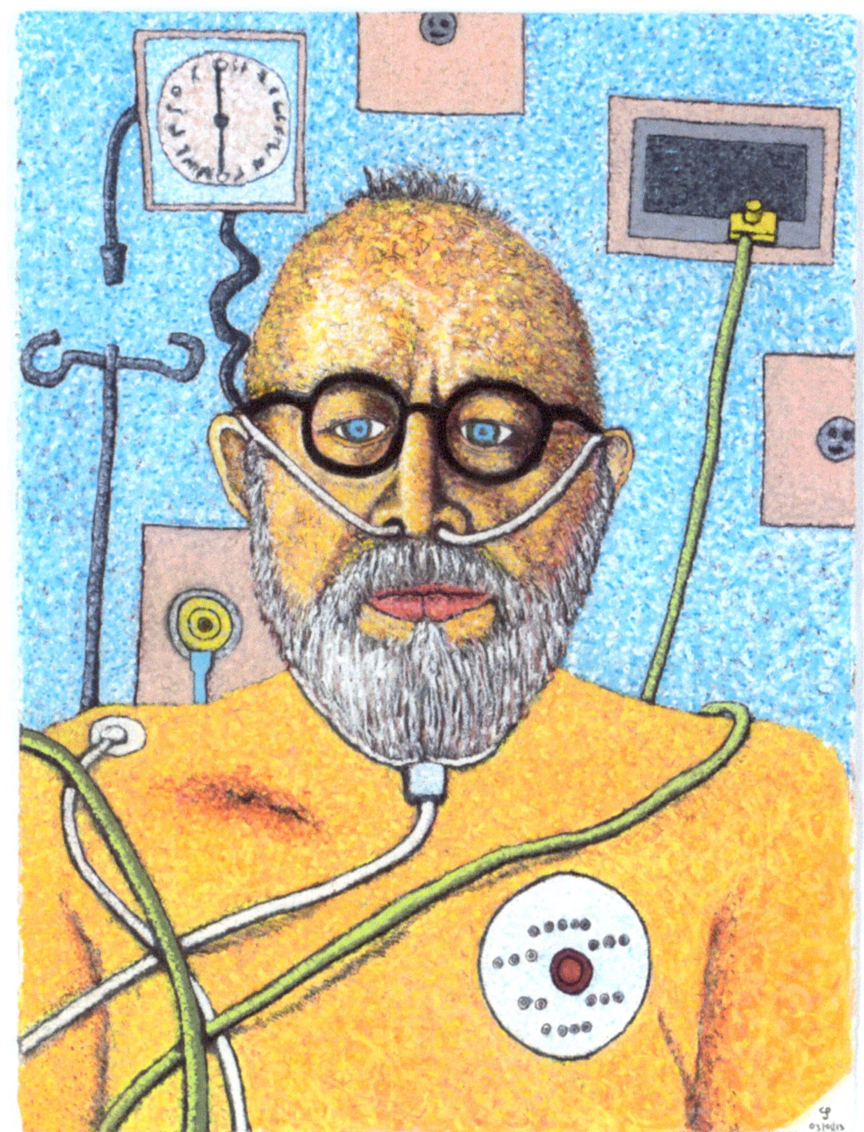

Self-portrait, 2013, Carlton Davis, oil stick on paper, 30" × 22" (76.27 cm × 58.97 cm)

CHAPTER 20

2013
HUNGRY GHOST STORY

n 2013, I was 69 years old and weighed 320 pounds. The burden on my pelvis, knees, and ankles made walking laborious. Meanwhile, I had written and self-published my first book, *Bipolar Bare*, and was doing my best to promote it. I was on my way to speak at the University of Wyoming at the invitation of Sharon, an assistant professor of psychology for whom I had signed a copy at a mental health conference in Washington D.C. In a letter I received weeks later, she wrote, "It's the first book-length, day-in-day-out account of what it's like to live with the disease that I've ever read" and informed me she had put it on her course reading list. It took her months to arrange my visit to Laramie, but she persevered. It was my first indication that the book would find an audience. When Johanna and I lived there in the late 1970s, Laramie's population was 24,000, of whom 3,000 were employees or students at UW. In the four decades since, Laramie had become a small city, and fast-food chains proliferated. I celebrated my homecoming with a couple of chicken sandwich specials at Jack in the Box. The next day, I spoke to Sharon's class, to the Arts and Sciences faculty, and, that evening, to the public at large.

At my evening presentation, I had read a passage about Carlotta, and several Wild West types in the audience began to hoot and jeer. I paused, hoping my alter ego would provide me with a sassy rejoinder, but what I heard was "time to split!" Laramie is 7,000 feet above sea level. After a celebratory dinner at a steakhouse, my lungs refused to function. I had to stop and gasp every few steps. Sharon and her husband offered to take me to the ER, but I didn't want to die with my boots on in some hick hospital where my daughter had been born. So I convinced them that three lectures after a poor night's sleep had done me in. After several hours of shuteye at the Dew Drop Inn, I drove my rental car back to Denver and jetted home.

Pasadena is only 863 feet above sea level, but my shortness of breath persisted. I was winded walking from my car to the house, and I had to rest after climbing the stairs. I tried several crash diet programs but found their prepacked food overpriced and indigestible. I submitted to 20-minute sessions of respiratory rehab, pedaling a stationary bike and walking on a treadmill, with no discernible improvement. Swimming slow laps in a pool seemed to help. Encouraged, I resumed my public speaking and was invited to speak at a mental health conference at a hotel in Duluth, Minnesota, where they served an 'English breakfast' of baked beans, breaded pork sausage 'bangers,' broiled tomatoes, and fried eggs. In Manchester, England, my next stop, I enjoyed a similar meal in the company of Dr. Thomas Szasz, author of *The Myth of Mental Illness* which came out in 1960, the same year as R.D. Laing's *The Divided Self.* Had someone put either book in my hands when I was young, lost, and suicidal, I might not have wasted so much time.

UCLA's weight loss clinic was my last half-hearted attempt to deal with my 'hungry ghost.' Buddhists know us by our Sanskrit name, *preta*, as pitiable creatures with huge, empty stomachs, pinhole mouths, and necks so thin they cannot swallow. The UCLA program required me to record everything I put into my pinhole. Although I had obsessively kept a journal for years, I refused. The dietitian to whom I was assigned advised me to eat 'watery foods.' I thought she meant soup. She explained that the aqueous category included a variety of fruits and vegetables. My favorite non-alcoholic beverage, root beer floats, didn't qualify. Nor did *horchata*, a blended rice pudding I often ordered in Mexican eateries along with *burritos de carnitas*, giant flour tortillas wrapped around heroic

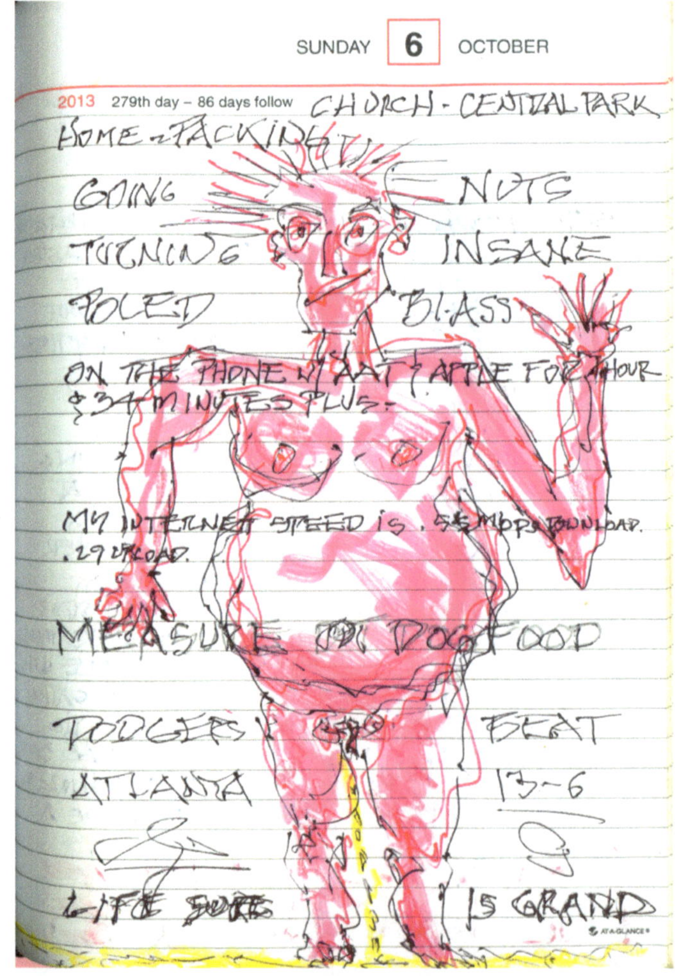

Daily diary page, October 6, 2013, Carlton Davis

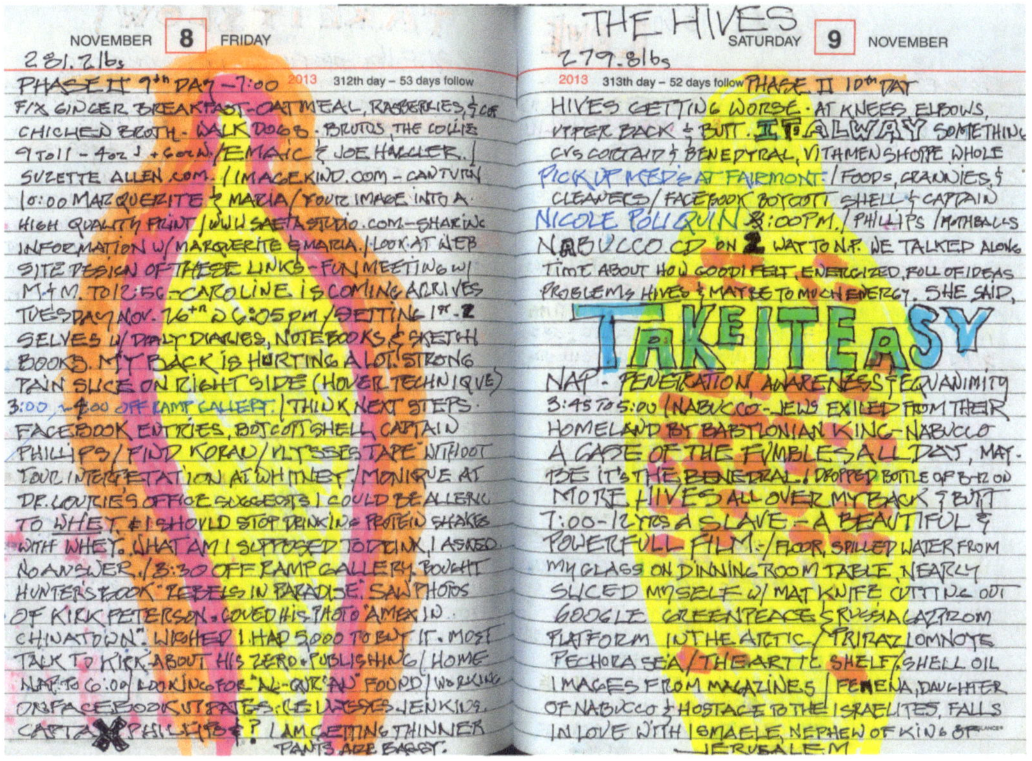

Daily diary pages, November 8 & 9, 2013

portions of slow-cooked pork, rice, and refried beans. My internal response to nagging nurses, know-it-all dietitians, and the supplication of my wife and daughter was "Fork you!" Shame is the turgid mush in which hungry ghosts wallow. I was ashamed of weighing more than 300 pounds and not being able to restrain my murderous appetite. Ginger saying more than once that she "didn't marry me to be a widow" led me back to Huntington Hospital, where I agreed to undergo laparoscopic bariatric surgery. The goal was to reduce the stomach's storage capacity by surgically removing its large bottom portion (or *fundus*) and reshaping and stapling shut what was left into a slender, banana-shaped 'gastric sleeve.' Two days after the surgery, on a strict liquid diet, I was already 10 pounds lighter.

Six days after the operation, I joined a bariatric support group in Pasadena. Several people assured me that the procedure had added twenty years to my life. Maybe this was the first glimmer of my connecting overeating to mental illness.

We discussed the stigma against fat people. I mentioned that it's like the stigma against the mentally ill. One morning in November I woke up itching all over. I called the surgeon's office to report it. The receptionist said I was probably allergic to whey, a key ingredient in the protein shakes on which I subsisted. I had what looked like hives on my back, knees, and elbows. I called Dr. Poliquin to inform her I'd never felt better, except for these pesky hives.

I was writing an essay *'Love and Isolation'* for my Bipolar Bare website, going to art gallery openings, attending Toastmasters and a writers' group in Altadena, and squeezing in some Vipassana meditation. Dr. Poliquin told me about drinks that substitute pea protein for whey and recommended I cut back on all my socio-literary activities and follow my diet to the letter.

On Thanksgiving Day, the first day I was permitted solid food, after a small amount of turkey, stuffing, mashed potatoes, gravy, and applesauce, I felt awful. My support group buddies told me to drink 16 ounces of water four or five times a day. I found that unimaginable. Why had I submitted to an irrevocable surgery? I projected my impatience and anger on Ginger, and I knew that was wrong. I had lost 40 pounds since the gastrectomy. Lesson learned.

After a routine visit to start the New Year, my doctor told me I was seriously dehydrated and that I should go to the hospital urgently for some tests. When I did, the first thing they checked was my blood sugar. "Why?" "Because you are diabetic." They injected me with insulin. My breathing was irregular, so they gave me albuterol, to which I'm allergic, because the hospital pharmacy didn't stock any alternatives. Then, they took an ultrasound of my heart. What did my heart have to do with my stomach?

By January 4th, I was back on the fifth floor. I walked seven times around the perimeter, cursing American healthcare under my breath. My sugar level was 6.3. Diabetics register 6.5 plus. The dietitian dropped by. She told me to stop eating cookies. I told her I was sticking to the recommended diet, but that was a lie. The next day, Dr. Poliquin called. I told her about the diabetes and heart exams and the albuterol prescription. She said it was possible that I had a urinary tract infection and asked about my mood. I told her that, now, life didn't seem worth living. I always get depressed in January.

In the years leading up to 2013 I spent a lot of time around hospitals, either in weight loss groups or as a hospital patient. On my way to an art opening, I fainted on the platform of the light rail train and was rushed to Huntington Hospital. I already had two pacemakers in my chest to regulate the beat of my heart. The first one had failed, and a second one was installed without digging out the original one. The second pacemaker wasn't working very well, and my cardiologist suggested I be seen by the LA expert on pacemakers.

The nurse overheard me on the phone with Ginger proposing to come home for a couple of days and that she could drive me to the hospital after the weekend. The nurse went ballistic, and in a flash, I was in an ambulance on a very fast ride to a hospital in Burbank. This doctor said my pacemaker was working fine, I didn't need either pacemaker; the reason I had passed out was that the pacemaker leads to my heart were infected. He recommended surgery to remove the infected wires. This would not be an easy surgery; it could fail, and I could die.

With no alternative I agreed to the surgery, and the risk it would entail. To my shock, the esteemed Dr Raymond Schaerf, said the operation would require a new procedure never done before. He explained that the leads from the pacemakers were tangled around my heart, and the only way to get them out was to draw them out through my groin. I survived the operation and woke up in my hospital room with more wounds and all kinds of wires covering my body. There were several patches on my chest, a tube that delivered medicine in my arm, two tubes that hooked up to mysterious connections in the bedwall, and a tube that supplied oxygen through my nose. The chest wound had a dual purpose, with a tube inserted to deliver medication to my heart and a pacemaker inserted to provide electrical stimulation.

After four days in recovery, I learned that I was even thinner after eating their special post-op diet. Just before my release, I was the subject of a television segment about the doctor and his new procedure removing wires from my chest. I told the world over the evening news that Dr. Schaerf had saved my life. I said the doctor had provided the chance that I could have an art show in New York. Only later did I learn that Dr. Schaerf's reputation is worldwide. I am just grateful that he saved my life. In the self-portrait my skin — stippled, discolored, and wounded — is the only visible surface evidencing my survival.

Over the years, my passion for drawing became increasingly challenging. I could no longer always rely on making clean lines and making strong strokes, and my hand developed a slight shake. As the years passed, my shaking became increasingly severe. I was diagnosed with Essential Tremor, which caused me to have DBS surgery and generators placed in my chest. The pacemakers' wounds were replaced by the two generator wounds. In my drawing studio I made a drawing about my hospitalizations, and I added a new technique to my repertoire by hammering the surface like stippling, only harder. I like the effect.

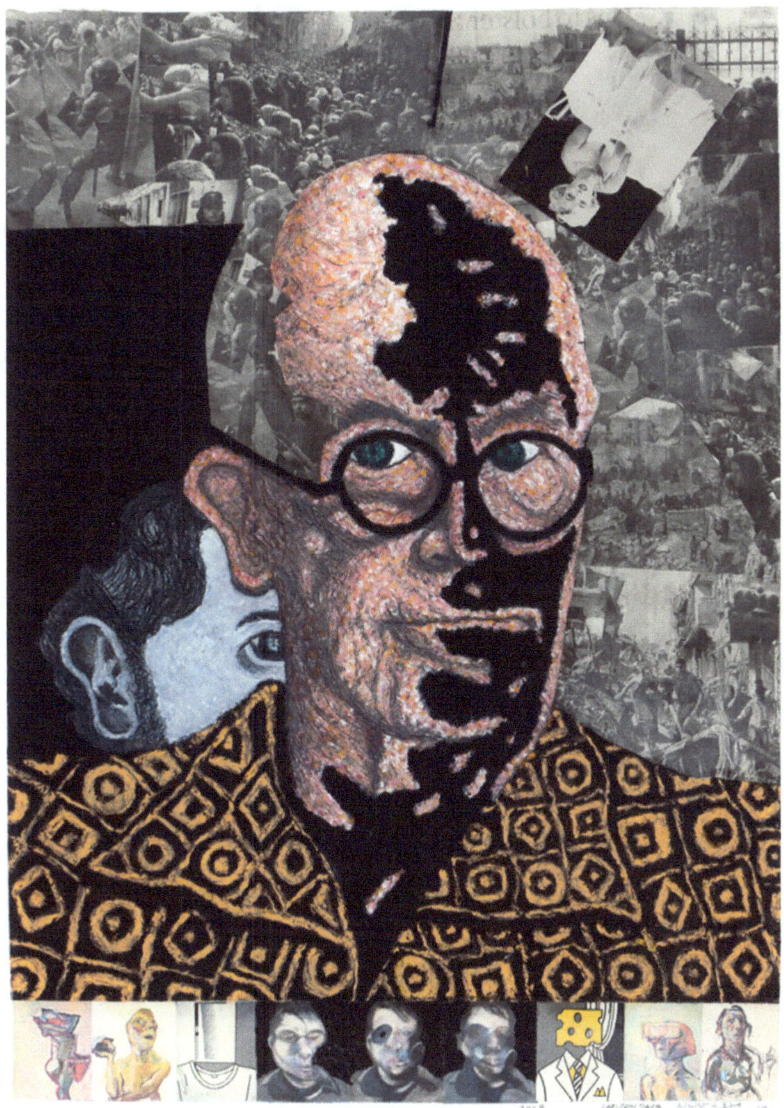

Self-portrait, Carlton Davis, 2014, oil stick, collage and postcard on paper,
30" × 22" (76.27 cm × 58.97 cm)

CHAPTER 21

2014–2015
CARLTON'S COMEBACK

I turned 70 in August 2014. I was healthier than I had been in years, and I no longer fantasized about suicide. Bariatric surgery had enabled me to shed 140 pounds, and the cessation of ravenous consumption allowed me to keep it off. I had abstained from crack cocaine and marijuana for more than a decade. The biggest breakthrough, as far as I was concerned, was that I finally felt like an artist. Seeds I planted when I was 30 and a frustrated architect with artistic ambitions had begun to bloom. My annual self-portraits allowed me to express things I had previously kept hidden. My 2014 self-portrait depicts a fractured, eggshell face with a pitch-black interior and an archipelago of buoyant shell specks in place of a brain. The eye, ear, and head full of hair behind my right shoulder belong to a much younger self. The photo collage refers to ongoing barbarities, including Hamas vs. Israel, Russia's annexation of the Crimea Peninsula, and civil war in Syria. The upside-down photo of Marilyn Monroe recalls my female alter ego, Carlotta, whom I had used and abused. The baseline strip of miniature portraits is comprised of inspirational self-portraitists like Bacon, Lichtenstein, and Lassnig. I have not left one iota of space for the viewer to rest their overworked eyes. I would be banned from Japan for lack of shibui (restraint).

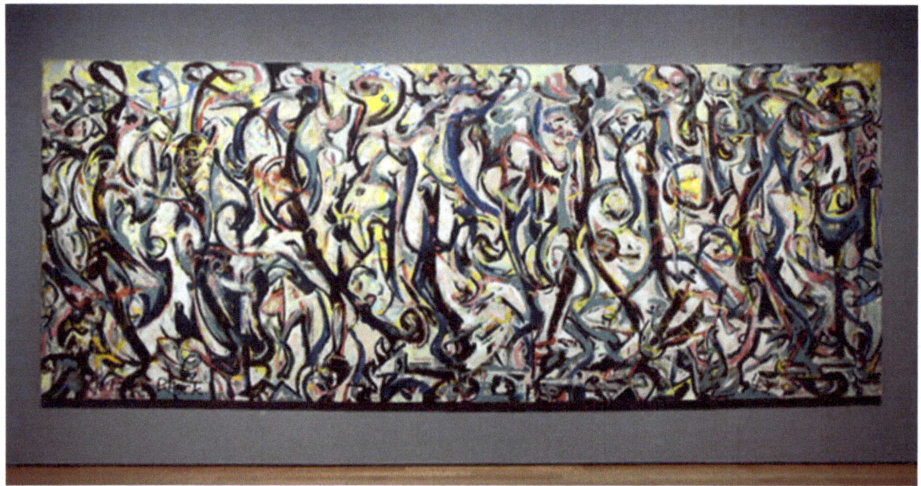

Jackson Pollock, Mural, 1943, oil & casein house paint on linen, 8'0" × 19'10", gift from Peggy Guggenheim to the Iowa Museum of Art, restored by and exhibited at the J. Paul Getty Museum, 2014, Photo by Carlton Davis

I had attended four memorable exhibitions in 2014: the public unveiling of Jackson Pollock's restored 1943 *Mural*, his first wall-sized work, at the J. Paul Getty Museum in Los Angeles, a panoramic Italian Futurism show at the Guggenheim, the last Upper East Side Whitney Biennial, and Maria Lassnig's post-mortem show at MoMA PS1 in Brooklyn. I stood as close as I could to peer at Pollock's cascading composition, his incredible shapes and colors, and his throbbing knots of paint. *Mural* is not a drip painting. It is, in many ways, a self-portrait of the artist as a young man. The power of his presence imbues every brush stroke, mark, dab, and dribble. This wild man from Wyoming was the heavyweight champ of the art world for a brief spasm. He died in a drunken car crash near his and his wife Lee Krasner's

home and studio on the eastern end of Long Island. His creative intensity was like Van Gogh's. They were both fiery comets, and that's hard to sustain. Jackson's flame was extinguished at 44 and Vincent's at 37. *Salut les artistes!*

I saw the Italian Futurism (1909-1944) retrospective at the Solomon R. Guggenheim Museum in Manhattan 'ass backward.' Because it is easier for me to descend than to climb, I started at the top of Frank Lloyd Wright's famous rotunda ramp. There, I was confronted with the collapse of the movement and of Benito Mussolini's fascist regime to which it had close ties. The movement began before World War I when founding futurists like Luigi Russolo, Carlo Carrà, Filippo Tommaso Marinetti, Umberto Boccioni, and Gino Severini portrayed speeding cars, soaring airplanes, weapons of war, dynamic architecture, splintered words, warped typography, electric illumination, and colorful robotic figures as the embodiment of the increasing importance of mass-production. Futurism's collapse foreshadowed the death of other publicized 20th-century movements that lost their juice in iterations and reiterations, devolving into historical fodder for theory and debate.

The 2014 Whitney Biennial was the nadir of our museum tours. Polluted by fatuous intellectualism and watered down by dreary derivatives of the once vital avant-garde, what was shown seemed to have been selected at random, and most of it was meaningless. I recalled some of the great shows I had seen at Marcel Breuer's Brutalist Blockhouse, including Joseph Cornell, Willem de Kooning, Helen Frankenthaler, Robert Motherwell, Alice Neel, and Andy Warhol. I adored them for their imagination, dexterity, and visual power.

This, the last show at the Madison Avenue Whitney, was a fire sale, a bargain basement offering. There was a huge strip mall sign with the sole point of interest being that the advertisements were all for Vietnamese businesses. There was a mediocre fabric display that celebrated frumpy knitted creations on three life-size mannequins and a huge bunch of hanging multicolored fibers looking like regurgitated spaghetti attached to the ceiling.

I looked out of the museum's huge oculus window at the bustling traffic on Madison Avenue and thought how the Dutch master Piet Mondrian had come here in 1940 and died here just four years later. His famous last painting *Broadway Boogie Woogie* looked like a map of the grid of Manhattan or a musical score with multicolored notes and stops of various sizes inspired by the 'stride' piano style of Fats Waller, Meade Lux Lewis, and Shirley Scott. In the 'stride' style, the pianist's left hand strides up and down the keyboard providing a repetitive rhythmic burden for right hand interpretations and improvisations at various tempos. Mondrian was astonished that this sophisticated Black music based on the blues mimicked the energy of tens of thousands of pedestrians stopping at intervals for red and green lights or threading their way through streets full of taxis, double-decker buses, and mounted policemen.

When I first saw Maria Lassnig's self-portraits, I was stunned by the vitality and vision of her work. Her images were powerful, loose, and semi-abstract. Lassnig stated that her self-portraits had developed over the years from "a reality within myself that was the realest and clearest reality." She exaggerated the body parts she felt as she worked, depicting them in bizarre colors and grotesque forms. Her brain emerged from her head like a growth in one painting. Lassnig was aggressive in her handling of paint, utilizing a gestural style she evolved from abstract expressionist roots. In *Transparent Self-Portrait*, broad strokes of color define the edge of limbs and sit like a transparent block in front of

her forehead, eyes, ears, and nose. Her cheeks are puffed, her mouth is open, and her hands hang limp. She has been caught unaware, her feelings stirred by the act of creation. Viewpoint and meaning float across the surface. She manifests herself as a veil covering the unseen and ephemeral, yet she is clear and present. Maria Lassnig was full of life when she painted these self-portraits and remained an active artist until her death at 94, just a few days before

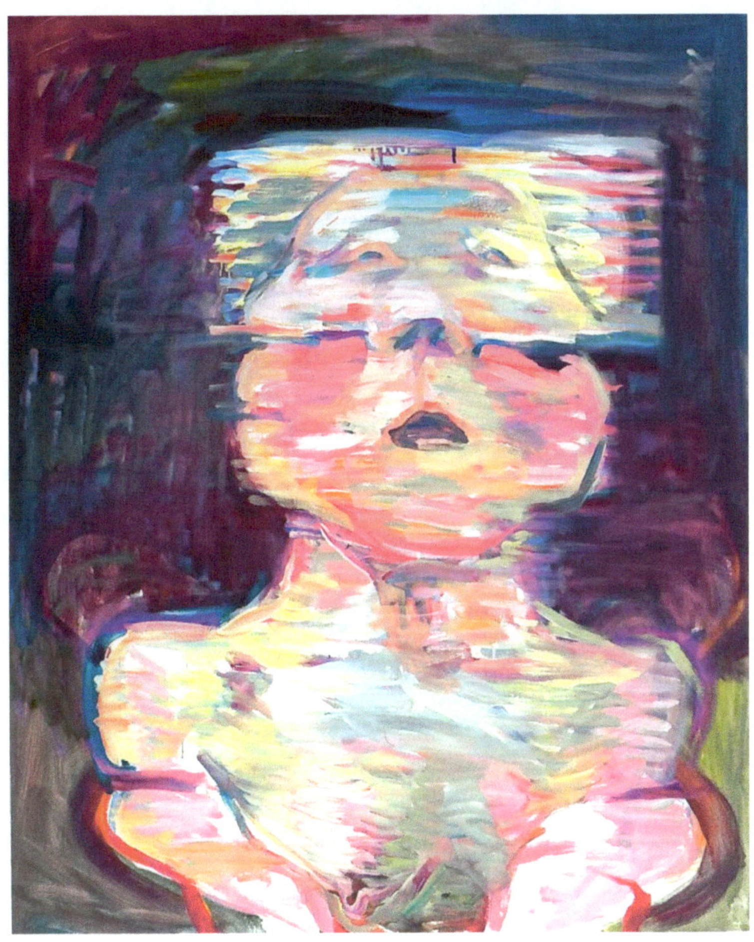

Maria Lassnig, Transparent Self-Portrait, 1987, oil on canvas, 49.25" × 39.5", MoMA, NYC, **pledged** gift from Marie-Josée and Henry R. Kravis

our visit to the museum. The paintings in her loose pictorial style bear the tint of impending death as if the smears of paint may soon disappear, as she did.

I had another feminine force in my life, my wife Ginger, who listened to my monologues and graced them with insight. She visited my studio after we returned from our museum hopping in NYC to see

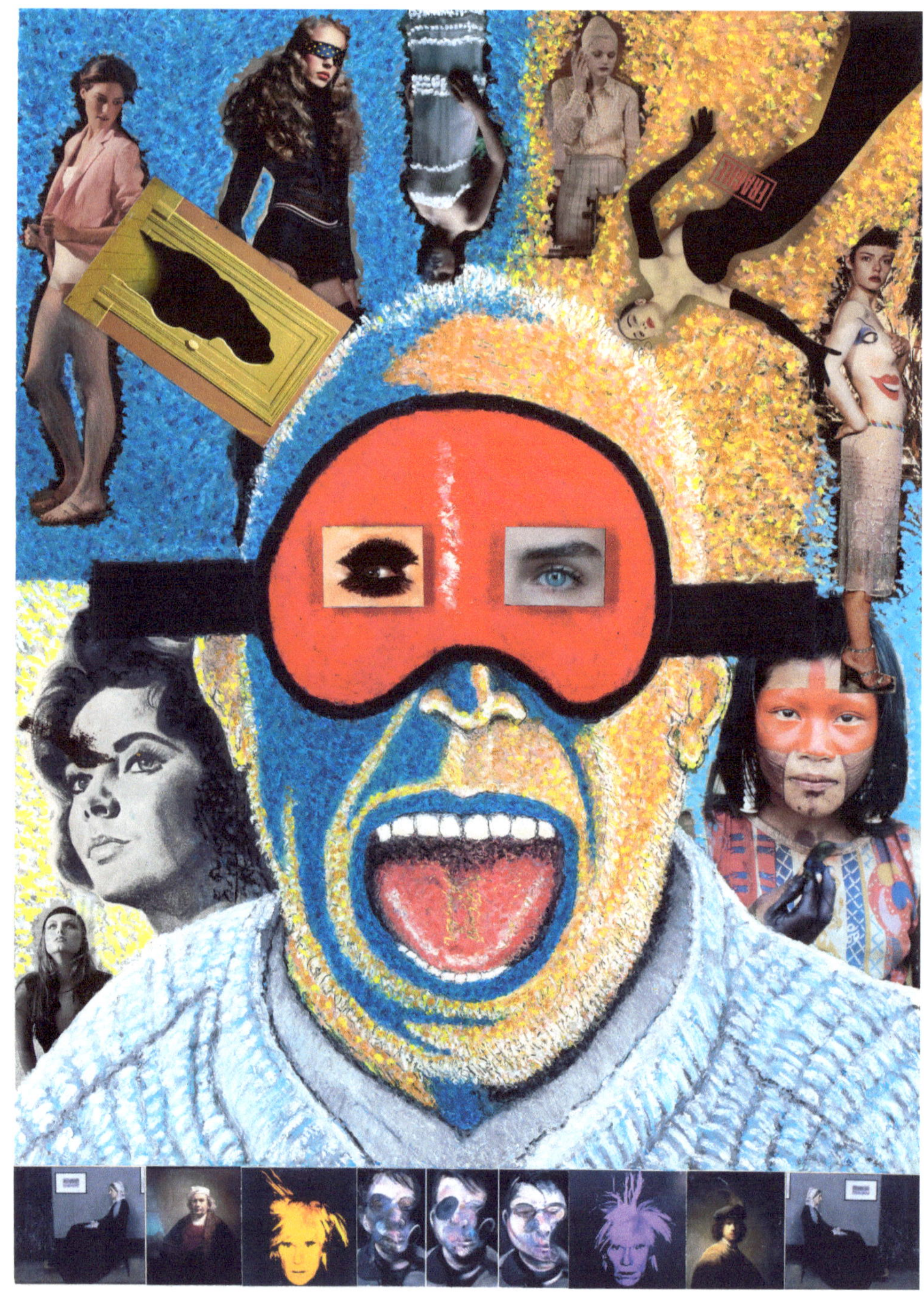

Self-portrait, 2015, Carlton Davis, oil stick and collage on paper, 30" × 22" (76.2 cm × 56.5 cm)

my latest self-portrait. I told her how impressed I was by Maria Lassnig's work and that, for the remainder of my time on earth, I wanted to inject her clarity and spontaneity into my drawings. She asked about the bas-relief of other artists' images. I told her they were all self-portraits that inspired me.

Ginger asked me about the 2015 self-portrait. I said it was inspired by Maria Lassnig's loose expressionistic style. It is my surreal nightmare drawing, which is revealed by the Magritte doorway. It could have multiple meanings, though this one obviously has something to do about women. The male in me awakens screaming. I am surrounded by women, from the movie star Elizabeth Taylor,

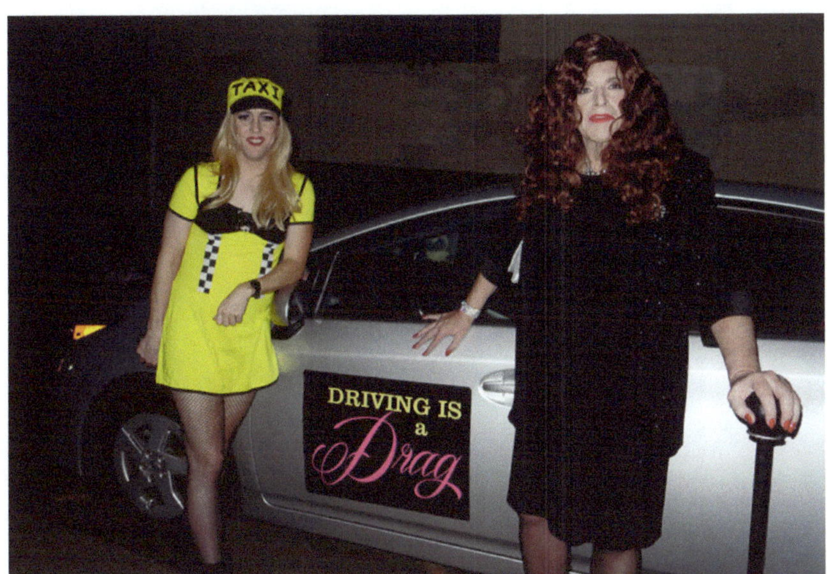

Carlotta arrives at Carlton Davis' exhibition, photograph by Ed Glendinning

My friends, artist Pamela Burgess and lay minister Rich Redman, giving up three days of their time to help me, installed the exhibition, which featured new artwork based on the hangings I had purchased in China, new work based on work done in the past, and old work like the self-portrait on window screen from 1992. The crowd that attended the opening and the people who stopped by over the next two months were worth all the exertion and expense. If they let me know in advance when they were coming, I offered personal tours. Artists Gary Lloyd and Jackie Dreager, and architect Anne Zimmerman were among the many to whom I gave personal tours explaining the artwork and the influences on my work by artists like Ai Wei Wei, Marcel Duchamp, Andy Warhol, Joseph Cornell, and Alfred Bierstadt.

through images of women in advertisements, and an Indigenous Amazon face-painted woman, all swirling around my head. I see through open eyes surrounded by red paint, while I am blinded by my red mask, in front of which female eyes float. This might have something to do with feminine forces that have driven my life, Carlotta would conjecture. This visual dream is the nightmare from which the male in me has awoken. It is a slice of the meaning in my life that I exposed in my first individual show."

2015 was a year of exciting events, in which I staged my first one-person exhibition and went to India to paint a collaborative mural inspired by Pollock. The show, held at the District Gallery in the Arts District in Downtown LA, close to where I had lived, was called *The Past Retooled; The Present Rebooted.* There was a big crowd at the opening, and I made an appearance as Carlotta, who had been absent for 14 years.

To create Carlotta, I hired Jodie Lynn of Le Boudoir, Hollywood's drag makeover place, to do Carlotta's' makeup Jodie gave her a complete makeover, including a wig, heeled shoes, bracelets, and an elegant black dress. I hired a crossdressing driver, whose business was called Driving is a Drag, to chauffeuse Carlotta to the opening. I made a YouTube video to commemorate the occasion.

After the exhibition closed, Ginger and I traveled to India with the Yale Alumni Service Corps where I taught a drawing class and Ginger taught geography in Kakelao village in the state of Rajasthan. The most exciting event for me was the collaborative work on a mural I designed, which was painted in an Anganwadi (women's building) where women go for health care, adult education, and child-rearing classes. My team of nine, which included four Yale Alumni women and five Rajasthani local high school

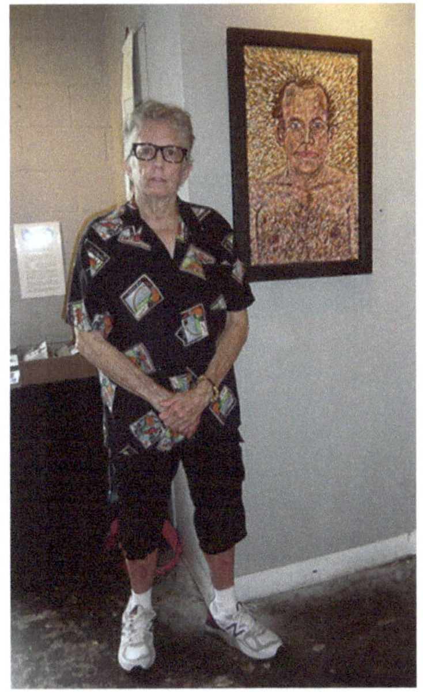

Artist Jackie Dreager, with "Self-Portrait, 1992" at the District Gallery, May 2015, photograph by Carlton Davis

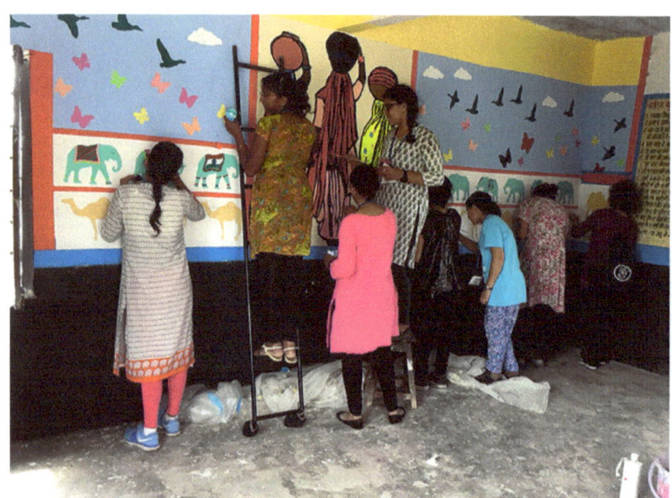 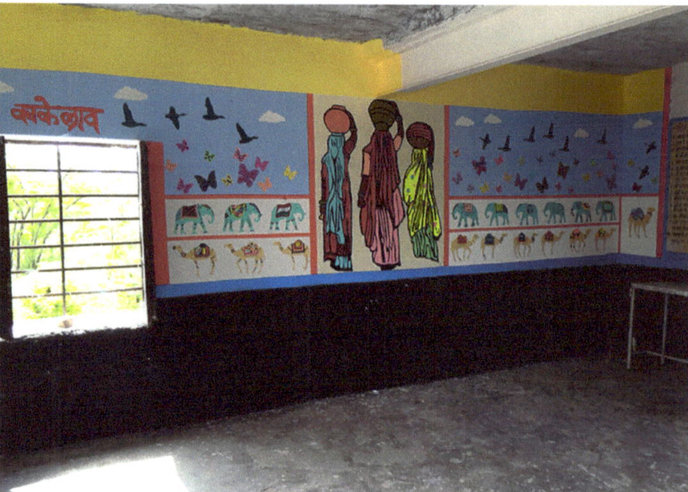

Women volunteers painting the mural and the finished *Three Women of Kakalao* mural, photographs by Carlton Davis, July 2015

students, painted the mural, *Three Women of Kakelao*. I prepared for the event several months in advance by making a large stencil from a photograph of three walking women carrying jars on their heads. The mural was approximately 30 feet long and seven feet high and included a three-foot high chalkboard surface which the children of the Anganwadi mothers could use to draw on. The whole thing took five days to complete.

My team of nine women had never painted a mural. I had no experience in either mural painting or designing a mural. The women were in charge. I sat on a tall stool on the far side of the room and directed the work. "Move those ducks up on the left side! Add two more ducks under the clouds! Stencil more butterflies on the right!" At that moment I felt like another Matisse as he was doing his late life work, in which he would direct his assistants to place his paper cutouts. I was honored to be treated this way and as if I were the wise old artist. I had made special stencils for the three water-bearing women on my bathroom door in Pasadena and was impressed by the collaborative spirit of the Rajasthani high school students and American volunteers. Each member of the team chose to create a decorative saddle for the elephants and camels. The women from Kakelao gathered daily to watch the mural grow with their husbands and children in tow. When it was finished, the villagers bowed in reverence to the artists. The mural was painted with inexpensive house paint and is not waterproof. It will need to be repainted often to survive the monsoons.

My self-portraits, my exhibition, and my involvement with the mural in Kakelao made me aware of the impermanence of life and the joy of creating art that honors it. When I returned to Pasadena, I photoshopped Gautama Buddha with a clown's nose. I laughed as I made it, imagining the squeak of a balloon being rubbed on Buddha's nose.

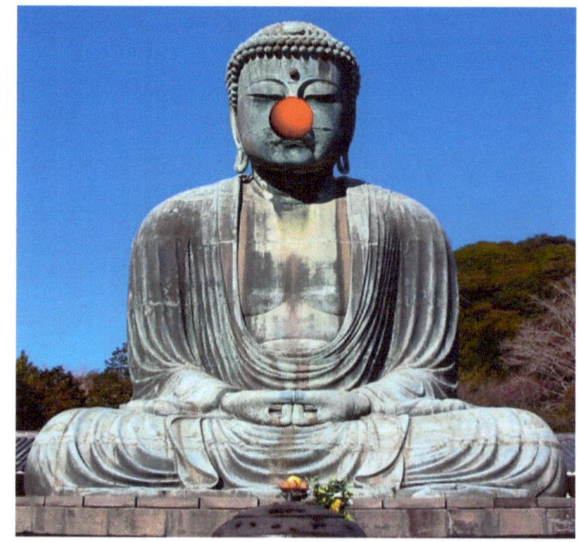

Buddha with a Clown Nose, 2015, Photoshopped by Carlton Davis

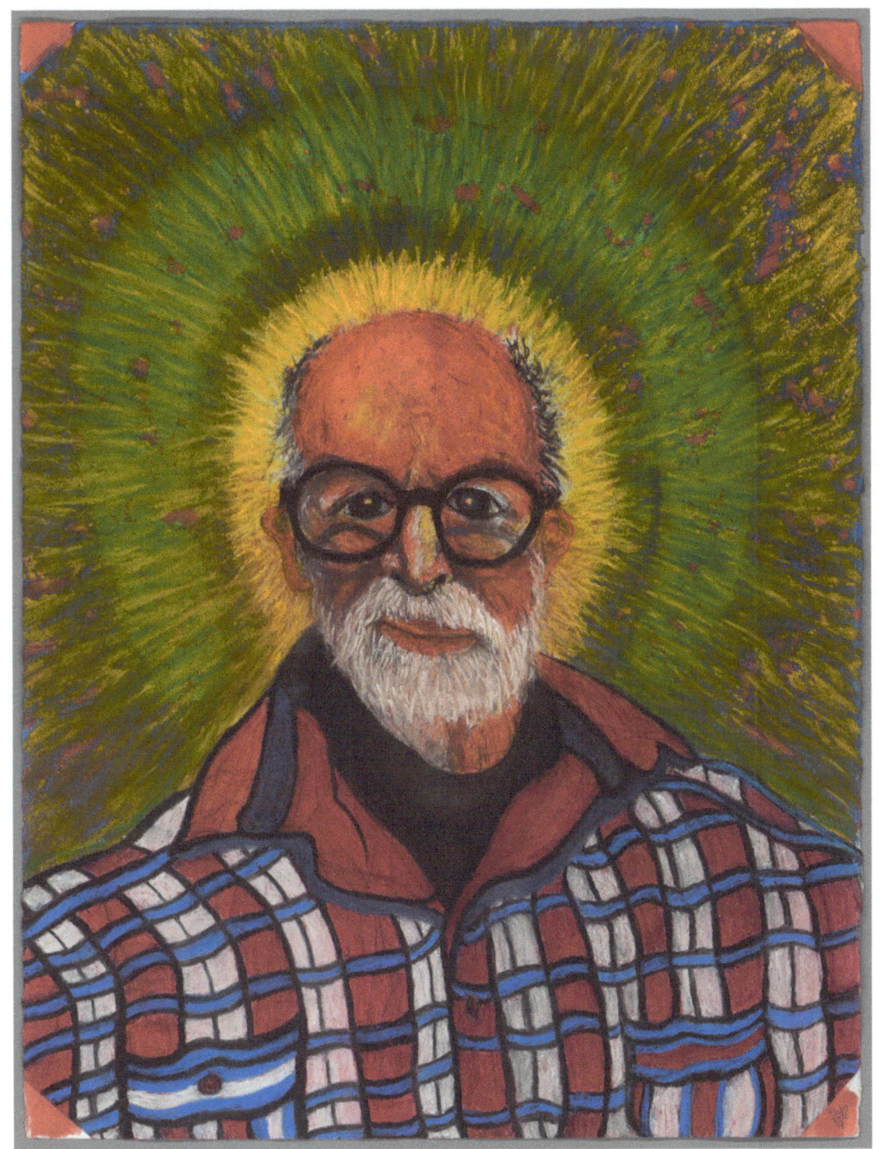

Self-portrait, 2022, Carlton Davis, oil stick, pastel, and watercolor on paper,
30" × 22" (76.2 cm × 55.88 cm)

2024

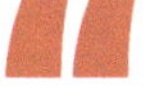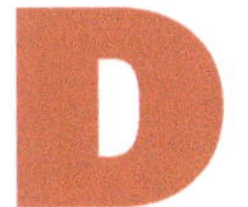"**D**rawing is the artist's most direct and spontaneous
expression. It reveals his personality better than
painting."

– Edgar Degas

"An aged man is but a paltry thing,
A tattered coat upon a stick, unless
Soul clap its hands and sing, and louder sing
For every tatter in its mortal dress,
Nor is there singing school but studying
Monuments of its own magnificence;
And therefore I have sailed the seas and come
To the holy city of Byzantium."

[Second verse of *Sailing to Byzantium*
by W.B. Yeats]

Self-portrait, 1900, Edgar Degas, pastel on tinted paper mounted on canvas, 18¾" × 12¾" (47.5 cm × 32.5 cm), Arp Museum Bahnhof Rolandseck, Remagen, Germany

Edgar Degas is another of my artist heroes. He was interested in process and experimentation, as am I. In 2016, I visited an exhibition of his monotypes, drawings, and prints at the Museum of Modern Art in New York. It was called 'A Strange New Beauty' and presented work from the mid-1870s until the year before his death in 1917. A monotype is a form of printmaking, made by adding ink, or in Degas' case, oil paint, to the surface of a metal plate. The plate is sandwiched with a piece of paper and run through a press. This process became Degas' obsession and liberated his anarchist spirit. I spent hours at the exhibition, imagining myself in his studio, looking over his shoulder. In his 1900 self-portrait, Degas *is* in his studio. He turns from a canvas he has been working on to face his observer. Sanguinary touches around his eyes and in his left nostril presage his encroaching mortality, yet he is steadfast in his goal to create while he can.

My final self-portrait is of an aged man of almost 80, only a few years younger than Degas. My red, white, and blue plaid shirt with double-breasted pockets is far from a 'tatter!' It's a remnant of a time when I was several sizes larger, every inch an American, who used to consume lots of fast food, sex, and drugs. The high-domed, ruddy greybeard who emerges from its patriotic expanse, clad in a black turtleneck and oversized oval glasses, is exuding yellow and green aureoles instead of 50 stars, one for every mood swing.

I began to create self-portraits because I wanted to be an artist. I didn't feel like one. I was an architect. Leonardo Da Vinci and Michelangelo Buonarotti were architects, engineers, poets, and artists. Most architects do not think of themselves as artists. Frank Gehry is an exception. Most are professionals who design buildings, create construction documents, and administer the construction process. Throughout my career,

I considered myself a professional who had inculcated the useful craft of making buildings. However, I aspired to be an artist and a writer. When I began this self-portrait project, I hadn't fully realized either desire and didn't feel particularly successful in either of these fields. So, what and why am I celebrating? I am celebrating my survival and my relinquishing the need to anesthetize physical and psychological pain by killing myself with barbiturates. The cessation of these behaviors and its unexpected and sometimes dubious reward is longevity. My marriage survived those worst of times, and I can now relax and enjoy life, no longer driven by those old needs.

The confidence to call myself an artist did not come from creating self-portraits. In 1981, I was required to purchase a license that allowed me to live in a loft building under the City of Los Angeles's Artist in Residence (AIR) ordinance. Ergo, I was an artist. Twice, I made public declarations to that effect. The first was when I was a brash man in my 60s practicing my nascent skill by drawing in the British Museum. A schoolgirl asked, "Are you an artist?" "Yes," I said, and she was gone. The same thing happened when I was sketching a Rembrandt in the Rijksmuseum in Amsterdam. "*Ben je een artiest*?" a woman asked, assuming I spoke Dutch. "*Ja,*" I replied with a smile.

Being an artist doesn't require a degree, a gallery, critical acceptance, or sales. It requires a passion for making things that may not have a specific use but that express the artist's take on life. The creation can have moral or spiritual significance as well, whether it is representational or abstract. Most children draw at some point or another and are often encouraged by their parents. The drawings I made by hand for architectural and exhibit projects, whether they were built or not, have a measure of art within them. My doodles are direct and spontaneous and often include writing and drawing. They incorporate a bit of what I like to think of as childlike enthusiasm. I often doodled in meetings. Here is one I made in 1997:

I consider my self-portraits 'fine art' drawings. I am not a painter. I prefer a hard substrate against which to scrape my pencil, streak my oil stick, or

dab my pastel. I need my left hand and, sometimes, my right to remain in close contact with whatever surface I am working on. My technique harkens back to the cartoons artists used to make before starting to paint. Collages and semi-abstractions have become part of my vocabulary. In the spirit of Degas and his monotypes, I declare myself free to do as I wish. After a lifetime spent wishing I were a well-known artist, I am content to create for creation's sake.

The monotypes and drawings exhibited in museums represent the distant past, like the hieroglyphics and mummies of Egypt, which inspire awe and stimulate my imagination.

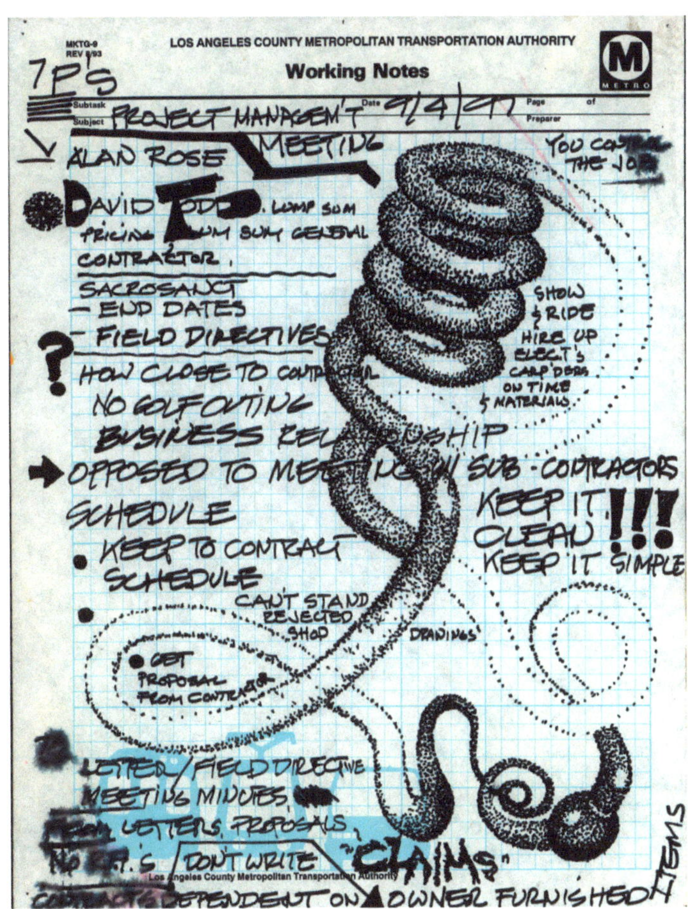

Doodle, 1997, Carlton Davis, pen on paper, 8 ½" x 11" (21.59 cm x 27.94 cm)

What will be the future of art in the next millennium? Who will dare use the precious commodities of paper or canvas for permanent images? Valuable digital images can now be transported easily and stored in protected files. The computer, while allowing the artist to make lines and colors of different widths, weights, and hues, cannot respond in the same fashion as a drawing on paper, wood, or canvas. Perhaps this will change one day, but even with artificial intelligence, a computer will always be a mechanical device. Meanwhile, I will continue to manifest my preference for a narrative aesthetic akin to those of our remote ancestors who recorded their perceptions on cave walls.

My self-portrait from 2023 is my most comical image, my scrawl upon the flimsy rock of my time. I am a green presence with blind blue eyes and eyes in the back of my head. Compared to the uneasy intensity of my 1973 self-portrait, I take myself much less seriously nowadays. After all, having eyes in the back of your head is a fantastic idea. As a child, I wished I could see with my back turned, the way a teacher does. Enough said. I have come to the end of my journey and am now what I always wished to be: an artist.

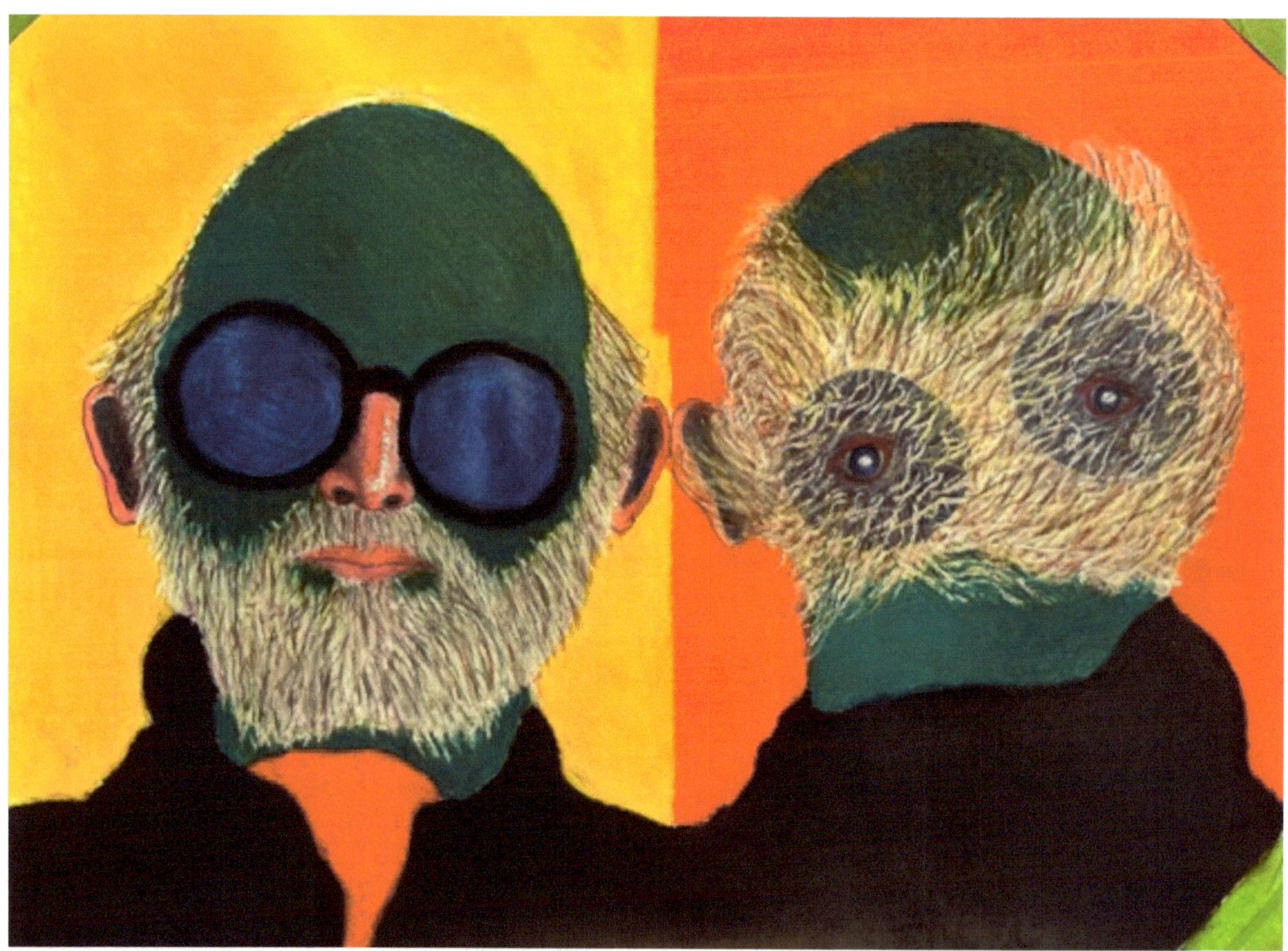

Self-portrait 2023, Carlton Davis, pastel on paper, 17¾" × 26¼" (45.09 cm × 66.675 cm)

CREDITS, COPYRIGHTS & SPECIAL NOTES

Preamble

Rembrandt Self-portrait 1665-1669
    Photo Credit- Historic Images Partnership
    © Historic England

Willem van de Velde the Elder,
The Battle of Scheveningen. 1657
    Photo Credit – unknown
    Rijksmuseum, Amsterdam
    Public Domain

Chapter 1

Picasso 1907 Self-portrait
    Photo Credit - Erich Lessing / Art Resource (AR), NY
    © 2024 Estate of Pablo Picasso / Artists Rights
    Society (ARS), NY

Picasso 1972 Self-portrait facing death
    Photo Credit - Album/ Art Resource (AR), NY
    © 2024 Estate of Pablo Picasso / Artists Rights
    Society (ARS), NY

Chapter 2

Claes Oldenburg, "Lipstick Ascending on Caterpillar
Tracks," 1969
    Harry Shunk and Shunk - Kender Photographs
    © Photograph: Shunk - Kender / J. Paul Getty Trust
    Getty Research Institute, Los Angeles (2014.R.20)
    Gift of Roy Lichtenstein Foundation in Memory of
    Harry Shunk and Janos Kender

Rodin, Salammbo Drawing
    Photo Credit – unknown
    Musée Rodin
    Public Domain

Chapter 3

Oldenburg and Coosje van Bruggen- Bat column
    Photograph by Jillian Cain
    © Shutterstock

Wolfy's
    Photo credit - unknown
    © Wolfy's Hot Dogs, Chicago Illinois

Thomas Hart Benton, Windmill 1926
    Photographer Sean Pathasema / Birmingham
    Museum of Art -rights and reproductions

© Artists Rights Society (ARS), NY / Birmingham
Museum of Art, Birmingham, Alabama

Chapter 4

William Fisk, Portrait of George Catlin, 1849
    National Portrait Gallery, Smithsonian Institution,
    Washington D.C.
    Photo by Mark Gulezian/NPG
    © National Portrait Gallery, Smithsonian
    Public Domain

Chapter 7

Frida Kahlo, Las Dos Fridas
    Museo de Arte Moderno, Mexico City, Mexico
    Photo Credit – Schalkwijk / Art Resource (AR), NY
    © 2024 Banco de México Diego Rivera Frida Kahlo
    Museums Trust, Mexico, D.F. / Artists Rights Society
    (ARS), NY

Chapter 8

Henri Matisse, Studio, Quai Saint Michel, Paris, 1916
    The Phillips Collection, Washington D.C.
    Photo Credit, The Phillips Collection
    © 2024 Succession H. Matisse / Artists Rights Society
    Any reproduction of this digitized image shall not be made
    without the written consent of The Phillips Collection,
    Washington, D.C. http://www.phillipscollection.org

Chapter 10

Frank Gehry, Fish Lamp Sculpture, Frank Gehry, 1984
    Fish Lamp (First Generation) produced by New City
    Editions, (Los Angeles, California, USA), 1984;
    Courtesy of Frank O. Gehry & Gehry Design, LLC

Chapter 11

Andres Serrano, "Piss Christ", 1987
    Cibachrome photograph, Public and Private Collection
    © Andres Serrano

Albrecht Durer, Self-portrait with sea-holly, 1493
    Musée du Louvre, Paris, France
    Photo Credit - Tony Querrec, / Art Resource (AR), NY
    © RMN-Grand Palais
    Public Domain

Credits, Copyrights, Special Notes, continued

Green Tara
> 8th century khondalite
> Photo Credit - Brooklyn Museum, NYC.
> © Brooklyn Museum, NYC.
> Carll H. de Silver Fund and Ella C. Woodward
> Memorial Fund

Chapter 14
Man Ray, Rrose Sélavy, (Marcel Duchamp), 1923
> Private Collection
> Photo Credit - Art Resource (AR), NY
> © Man Ray Trust/ ARS-ADAGP

Andy Warhol
Self-Portrait in Drag, 1981, Polaroid Photograph
> Photo Credit - Art Resource (AR), NY
> © 2024 The Andy Warhol Foundation for the Visual
> Arts, Inc. / Artists Rights Society (ARS), NY

Chapter 16
Francis Bacon, Self-Portrait, 1971
> Musée National d'Art Moderne, Centre Georges
> Pompidou, Paris
> Photo Credit - Audrey Laurans, CNAC/MNAM.Dist
> RMN-Grand Palais / Art Resource (AR), NY
> © The Estate of Francis Bacon All rights reserved. /
> DACS, London / Artist Rights Society (ARS), NY

Chapter 17
Francisco Goya, El Loco Furioso, 1824-1828
> Album G (60-page Sketch Book)
> Collection Andrea Woodner,
> Photograph Courtesy of the Frick Collection
Saturn Devouring His Son, 1823
> Photo Credit - Museo Nacional del Prado, Madrid,
> Spain /Art Resource, NY
> © Museo del Prado
Abu Ghraib Prison, Iraq
> Photograph, 2003
> © *The Economist* Magazine
Gustave Courbet, Desperate Man, 1845, Private Collection
> Photo Credit Historic Images Partnership (HIP) /Art
> Resource, NY
> © Historic England

The Artist's Studio, A Real Allegory, 1855
> Musée d'Orsay, Paris, France
> Photo Credit - Gérard/Hervé Lewandowski,
> Art Resource (AR), NY
> © RMN-Grand Palais

Chapter 18
Vincent van Gogh, Self-Portrait with Bandaged Ear &
Pipe
> 1889, Kunsthaus, Zurich
> Public Domain
> Sheet from Letter to Emile Bernard June 19, 1888
> © The Van Gogh Museum, Amsterdam, Netherlands/
> Huggins, The Hague
Graves of Vincent and Theo Van Gogh
> Photo Credit - unknown
> © Architectural Digest

Chapter 21
Jackson Pollock, Mural, 1943
> Gift of Peggy Guggenheim to the Iowa Museum of Art,
> restored by and exhibited at the J. Paul Getty Museum,
> 2014, Los Angeles, California
> Photo Credit - Carlton Davis
> © 2024 The Pollock-Krasner Foundation / Artists
> Rights Society (ARS), New York
Maria Lassnig, Transparent Self-Portrait, 1987
> MoMA, NYC, Pledged gift of Marie-Josée and Henry
> R. Kravis,
> Photo Credit - Art Resource (AR), NY
> © 2024 Bildrecht, Vienna 2024 / Artists Rights Society
> (ARS), NY

Epilogue
Edgar Degas, Self-portrait, 1900
> Remagen, Arp Museum, Bahnhof Rolandseck,
> Germany
> Photo Credit - Peter Schälchli, Zurich / Arp Museum
> © Remagen, Arp Museum Bahnhof Rolandseck,
> Germany / Collection Rau for UNICEF